The Stoic Mindset

Ancient Wisdom for Today's World

What Others Are Saying About The Stoic Mindset

A Masterpiece that Bridges the Ancient, the Modern, and the Practical

The wisdom contained in this book has the potential to be life-changing for everyone who reads it and applies it to his or her life. Dr. Sanders' way of taking ancient philosophy and applying it to today's world is nothing short of amazing. He understands how to take complicated issues and explain them so that everyone can understand them and apply them to their lives. His writings have inspired countless people around the world, winning awards for both their depth and their impact. This book is a true gem, a masterpiece that bridges the ancient and the modern, the philosophical and the practical, the timeless and the timely.

Sifu Al Dacascos
Founder of Wun Hop Kuen Do and Bestselling Author

Timely, Timeless, and Deeply Relevant...Destined to Become a Modern Classic

The Stoic Mindset is a masterful work that bridges the timeless wisdom of the ancient Stoics with the complexities of modern life. Dr. Bohdi Sanders distills centuries of philosophical insight into clear, practical guidance that anyone can apply. Each reflection is both profound and accessible, encouraging readers to cultivate inner strength, rational clarity, and unshakable peace in a chaotic world. This is more than a book; it's a daily companion for those seeking to live with honor, integrity, and resilience.

Dr. Sanders doesn't merely discuss Stoicism; he brings it to life on every page. Whether you are new to Stoic thought or a seasoned student of philosophy, this book will challenge, inspire, and transform the way you approach life's challenges. Timely, timeless, and deeply relevant—The Stoic Mindset is destined to become a modern classic of practical philosophy.

Grandmaster Phil Torres, Colonel of Marines, Retired
Hanshi—10th Dan American Karate and United States Martial Arts Hall of Fame

Perfect for Today's World...I Love It!

"Wisdom! Ancient teachings and quotes are made modern with Dr. Sanders' illuminating commentary. Practical and perfect for today's world. I love it!"
Dr. Joe Vitale
Author of Zero Limits and The Miracle

What Others Are Saying About *The Stoic Mindset*

Your Guide to Personal Freedom and Life-Changing Wisdom

The Stoic Mindset is the starting block as we propel our lives forward, and the stronger the block, the more advantage we have to go further faster. The Stoic Mindset is an exploration to take on a new race to new goals—self-control, wisdom, virtues, discipline, and inner peace. It is critical to have the Stoic mindset to resist falling into the trap of complacency and the hive mentality. I am not alone in this belief regarding its importance. Consider the following quotes.

"The individual has always had to struggle to keep from being overwhelmed by the tribe. If you try it, you will be lonely often, and sometimes frightened. But no price is too high to pay for the privilege of owning yourself." Rudyard Kipling

"Conformity is the jailer of freedom and the enemy of growth." J.F.K.

"In any free society, the conflict between social conformity and individual liberty is permanent, unresolvable, and necessary. Conformity is doing what everybody else is doing, regardless of what is right. Morality is doing what is right, regardless of what everybody else is doing." Evette Carter

The Stoic Mindset is a guide to your personal freedom, self-discipline, life-changing wisdom, rational thinking, a perpetually calm mind, and inner peace. Dr. Sanders provides you with all this and more in his timely new book, The Stoic Mindset.

Frank Dux
Martial Art Legend & Source Contributor US Navy SEAL CFC manual k-431-0097

Powerful and Timeless Words to Live By

The Stoic Mindset cuts through the noise of modern self-help and returns to what truly matters—character, discipline, wisdom, virtue, and peace of mind. Dr. Bohdi Sanders bridges ancient wisdom with real-world application in a way that feels timeless and urgently needed today. His insights are powerful and timeless words to live by for young and old.

Dr. Sanders writes not as an academic, but as a practitioner of Stoic philosophy. His message is that the Stoic mindset is about application, not debate—about living wisdom, virtue, and self-discipline, not memorizing a bunch of quotes. He hopes readers will use Stoicism to build inner strength, wisdom, a calm, rational mindset, virtue, and inner peace in a chaotic modern world.

Michael McCune
Martial Arts Master and Political Commentator

What Others Are Saying About *The Stoic Mindset*

This Book is a Gem—Timely, Timeless, and Transformative

The Stoic Mindset: Ancient Wisdom for Today's World by Dr. Bohdi Sanders is a powerful guide that takes timeless Stoic philosophy and brings it directly into the challenges of modern life. Rather than presenting philosophy as distant or academic, Sanders makes it practical, personal, and accessible to anyone seeking peace, resilience, and character in today's chaotic world. The book draws from the wisdom of ancient masters like Marcus Aurelius, Seneca, and Epictetus, but frames their teachings in a way that speaks to our daily struggles with anxiety, stress, division, and distraction.

Each section begins with a Stoic quote and is followed by Sanders' reflections, breaking down complex ideas into clear, relatable lessons. He shows how Stoicism can be used not only for life's profound difficulties—loss, grief, mortality—but also for everyday frustrations like harsh words, social media noise, and the pressures of work and family. The message is consistent and deeply encouraging—while we cannot control the world around us, we can always control our mindset, our values, and our responses.

Sanders makes it clear that Stoicism is not a quick fix, but a lifelong practice, a way of living that must be integrated into one's actions and choices every day. His writing challenges readers not to simply study philosophy, but to live it, and in doing so, to discover a sense of inner peace, strength, and freedom that cannot be shaken by external events. Part of what makes this book compelling is Sanders himself. Readers who know Dr. Sanders recognize him as a true teacher of life—one who blends philosophy with lived experience and a deep understanding of human nature.

The Stoic Mindset is more than a collection of quotes or reflections; it is a companion, a guide, and a call to live with courage and clarity. It reminds us that the wisdom of the ancients is just as relevant today as it was two thousand years ago, and that living well is less about controlling circumstances and more about cultivating the right mindset. For anyone searching for a path to resilience, peace, and honor in an unpredictable world, this book is a gem—timely, timeless, and transformative.

Master Ted Gambordella
10th Degree Black Belt and Bestselling Author

What Others Are Saying About *The Stoic Mindset*

Outstanding Philosophical Insight that will Improve Your Life

In his latest book, The Stoic Mindset, Ancient Wisdom for Today's World, Dr. Bohdi Sanders gives the reader a front-row seat to an ancient time when famous Greek and Roman philosophers such as Marcus Aurelius, Seneca, Epictetus, and others sat in the majestic shadows of marble-pillared temples discussing philosophy.

Dr. Sanders further expands on the ethics of Stoicism discussed by these brilliant thinkers in his down-to-earth, easy-to-understand style that he is famous for. His teachings clarify this largely misunderstood philosophy and provide the reader with a logical approach to living one's life in harmony with nature and understanding one's place within the natural order of the universe.

Each profound page of Dr. Sanders' book sheds light on living a life based on the philosophy of Stoicism, which sees the impermanence of life and embraces it with the same calm spirit as one would embrace inner peace and tranquility. Each reader will gain an understanding of how to live a meaningful life of purpose, virtue, and clarity, and how to transcend the everyday emotional rollercoaster of life. This amazing book will teach you to approach each day with a calm, clear Stoic mindset. The Stoic Mindset provides outstanding philosophical insight that will improve your life from an amazing author, martial artist, and modern-day warrior.

Grandmaster Robert Cutrell, Soke
10ᵗʰ Dan Black Belt and Founder of ChunJiDo and ChunJiDo International

A Tremendous Gift to Us All

Those of us on the path wish to attain the Stoic mindset; however, it can be misinterpreted and misunderstood because of how it has been presented in the modern world. The men in this book who were philosophers, rulers, and dreamers were just people like you trying to be better and understand how to live life in balance with their surroundings. They all had their trials and tribulations like we all do; we see them as more than they were, through the lens of history. They passed down the lessons of Stoicism to assist us with the chaos of life.

Being asked by Dr. Sanders to read the manuscript for this amazing book and endorse it is a privilege and an honour that I did not take lightly and will never forget. As with all of Bohdi's books, this one came to me when I needed it most. How Bohdi is able to put together a transformative explanation for some of the most profound wisdom ever written, and how he makes you think, is a tremendous gift to us all.

Triffon E. Peart
Host of the Unlocking the Code Podcast

The Stoic Mindset

Bohdi Sanders, Ph.D.

First Edition

Published by Kaizen Quest Publishing

The Stoic Mindset
ISBN – 978-1-937884-33-8
1. Stoicism. 2. Stoic Philosophy. 3. Philosophy. 4. Marcus Aurelius
5. Epictetus 6. Seneca 7. The Stoics 8. The Stoic Mindset 9. Title

WISDOM TEMPERANCE JUSTICE COURAGE

Table of Contents

VERY LITTLE IS NEEDED
TO MAKE A HAPPY LIFE;
IT IS ALL WITHIN
YOURSELF, IN YOUR
WAY OF THINKING.
MARCUS AURELIUS

Foreword

It is with great honor and deep respect that I write this foreword for my dear friend, Dr. Bohdi Sanders. When I first opened *The Stoic Mindset: Ancient Wisdom for Today's World*, I intended only to glance through its pages. Yet once I began, I could not put it down. The words of the ancient Stoic masters, written over two thousand years ago, resonated with me as if they had been spoken yesterday. Their wisdom, clear, sharp, and timelessness, speaks powerfully to the challenges and questions of our modern lives.

Dr. Sanders has accomplished something remarkable here. He has gathered not only over 286 Stoic quotes, but has also taken the time to carefully dissect and present them in a way that multiplies their meaning for the reader. He makes the wisdom of the past accessible, understandable, and applicable today. This is no small feat, for philosophy can often feel distant or academic; but Dr. Sanders brings it alive with clarity and heart.

For those who know Dr. Sanders, this comes as no surprise. He is not only a noted author and philosopher but also a martial arts master, a teacher, and a man who strives to live out the very values he writes about—honor, character, integrity, and purpose. His writings have inspired countless people around the world, winning awards for both their depth and their impact.

With over seventeen books to his name, each one a page-turner, Dr. Sanders has proven time and again that he is a true teacher of life, blending philosophy with his vast experience of human nature and life in general.

This book is more than a collection of wisdom; it is a guide, a companion, and a reminder that the wisdom of the ancients is still alive within us. Regardless of who you are, the lessons within these pages will speak to you. They will challenge you, encourage you, and strengthen your resolve to live a life of honor and meaning.

In *The Stoic Mindset*, Dr. Sanders offers us not just a philosophy, but a way of life. His words echo the timeless truth that wisdom is not merely to be studied but lived. For that reason, I encourage everyone, whether seasoned in philosophy or completely new to it, to open these pages and let them speak to your heart.

The wisdom contained in this book has the potential to be life-changing for everyone who reads it and applies it to his or her life. Dr. Sanders' way of taking ancient philosophy and applying it to today's world is nothing short of amazing. He understands how to take complicated issues and explain them so that everyone can understand them and apply them to their lives. His easy-to-understand analogies and examples make applying ancient wisdom to your life not only easier, but you will also understand why this wisdom is important to your growth and success in life.

This book is a true treasure, a masterpiece that bridges the ancient and the modern, the philosophical and the practical, the timeless and the timely. Dr. Sanders has once again given us a gift. May you find in these pages the same inspiration, strength, and clarity that I have.

With Aloha and Respect,

Sifu Al Dacascos
Founder of Wun Hop Kuen Do and Author of the Bestselling Book,
LEGACY: Through the Eyes of the Warrior

Introduction

As I began meditating on the topic of my new book, I knew that I wanted to write something that would help people live a better, more peaceful life. I wrote *The Stoic Mindset* as someone who has wrestled with life's struggles, disappointments, losses, uncertainties, and daily challenges that have greatly tested both my patience and character. In today's world, we have challenges that our forefathers could not have imagined, but the wisdom of the Stoics applies to our current challenges and problems just as well as it did 2,000 years ago.

We are surrounded by comforts our ancestors could not imagine, yet anxiety, depression, and stress are at all–time highs. Today, we live in a world bombarded by endless comparisons, political division, economic pressures, social media distractions, and a seemingly endless desire for more fame and wealth. But we aren't that different from our ancestors. Many people still wrestle with the same fundamental questions that have troubled people for thousands of years: *How do I live well? How do I endure hardships? How do I find peace in my life? How do I maintain my character and honor in a cruel world? How do I deal with other people's unacceptable behavior?*

These questions are not new. Long before our world of smartphones, social media, and twenty–four–hour news cycles, men and women were wrestling with the same issues that we deal with today. The Stoics of ancient Greece and Rome—philosophers such as Marcus Aurelius, Seneca, Epictetus, Zeno of Citium, and others—sought answers to those same questions. They searched for answers not in wealth, titles, or power, but in wisdom, rational thinking, virtue, and self–mastery. They discovered that while we cannot control what happens around us, we can always control our mindset and responses.

Stoicism is not an abstract philosophy meant to be debated by self-important philosophers or professors; it is meant to be a way of life. The Stoics had diverse backgrounds, from warriors, statesmen, slaves, emperors, teachers, and everyday people who applied timeless wisdom to their lives. They taught that the path to freedom is not through chasing pleasures or trying to avoid pain, but by cultivating a mindset anchored in wisdom, courage, justice, and temperance.

They believed that the highest good did not come from the external world, but from maintaining the correct mindset, attitude, wisdom, virtues, and inner peace. Living a good life is based on the things that you can control in your life and not worrying about the things that are outside of your control.

This book is written for you so that you can better deal with today's hectic world. You won't find any dense academic analysis or obscure philosophical debates or theories in *The Stoic Mindset*. Instead, you will find practical wisdom that is gleaned from universal truths, presented in clear, easy-to-understand language, and applicable to your life today. Each page begins with a Stoic teaching, teachings that have endured for centuries.

After each Stoic teachings, I expand on the lessons, breaking them down into plain language, with clear analogies and metaphors, and connecting them to the challenges we face in today: stress, uncertainty, relationships, work, loss, ambition, maintaining our honor and integrity, and even death. I also show how much of this same wisdom is taught throughout the ages and in many different cultures. *The Stoic Mindset* is not intended for entertainment, but for hardcore self-improvement.

It is also not intended to idolize the past, but to bring the universal wisdom of Stoicism into the present, to take what is useful, timeless, and true, and apply it to the life we live in our current society. No matter how ancient the teachings are, if those teachings do not improve your life, they are worth very little to you. The teachings in this book will absolutely change your life!

Stoicism is not about suppressing your emotions, becoming cold and indifferent, self-absorbed, getting rich, or controlling others; it's about balance and self-control. It's about clarity of thought, steadiness of spirit, and strength of character. The Stoic mindset is not unfeeling, but deeply rational; it refuses to allow our emotions to become storms that disrupt our inner peace and tranquility. Ultimately, Stoicism is about freedom—the freedom that comes from mastery over your mind, emotions, words, and actions.

In the pages of this thought-provoking book, you will learn how to:

- Cultivate a mindset of calm resilience during all trials and challenges.
- Practice moderation in a world that glorifies excess.
- Act with honor and integrity, even when no one is watching.
- Develop the courage to face challenges, suffering, and even death.
- Live with inner peace and calm tranquility in the middle of chaos.
- Live a life established in honor, character, integrity, and virtue.
- Face adversity with calm inner strength and rational thinking.
- Live by your principles instead of your impulses.
- Be resilient in a world of constant change and upheaval.
- Accept the reality of death without fear and live your life to the fullest.
- Live with wisdom, justice, courage, and temperance.

These are not abstract ideals, but practices that you must work to develop in your personal life. You will find wisdom for the small struggles of everyday life, the frustrations of traffic, the irritation of harsh words or rude behavior, the pressure of managing your family, job, relationships, and time—as well as for the profound realities of human existence: grief, mortality, and the search for meaning. Each Stoic teaching is a portal into deeper understanding, and each reflection is designed to make these truths practical for you today.

The Stoic Mindset does not promise you an easy life, but a life filled with freedom, inner peace, and calm tranquility. Stoicism does not teach us how to avoid hardship, but how to face it with inner strength. It does not tell us how to escape death, but how to live fully until that day comes. It is not a quick fix, but a lifelong practice. The Stoics remind us that philosophy is not merely in words, but is in self-control and personal action. It is not enough to read the wisdom of the Stoics; we must strive to integrate that wisdom into our lives.

As you read *The Stoic Mindset*, I invite you to approach each lesson not as mere theory or some ancient teaching, but as a challenge to put into practice. Read slowly, reflect deeply, and carry these ideas with you into your daily life. The measure of Stoicism is not in how well we understand it, not in memorizing a bunch of quotes, but in how consistently we use its wisdom to better our daily lives.

The world around you will always be unpredictable. People will disappoint you and betray you with their words and actions. Plans will fail; pain and challenges will come. And death will eventually call on you. However, if you cultivate the Stoic mindset, you will learn to live by wisdom, courage, justice, and temperance. You will realize why honor, integrity, rational thinking, and self-control can completely change your life. You will discover an inner peace that cannot be shaken, a freedom that cannot be stolen, and an internal strength that endures through every trial.

The Stoics left us scrolls of wisdom for living your life with freedom, honor, character, integrity, wisdom, courage, justice, and self-discipline. *The Stoic Mindset* is your guide for integrating all these traits and more into your daily life. If you study these teachings diligently, you will find they will have a deeply spiritual, mental, and emotional effect on every part of your life.

We must remember that at the time the Stoics were teaching their wisdom, it was meant for men. These teachings were written over 2,000 years ago, and the times and culture differed greatly from today's world. That being the case, I also want to stress that this book is not merely written for men, though some teachings apply more to men than to women. Be that as it may, the wisdom in *The Stoic Mindset* applies to anyone who is willing to apply it to his or her life. In addition, I use the words "man" and "men" to refer to everyone instead of writing "his or her" repeatedly throughout the book. This is merely to simplify the prose and to make it more readable. Have no doubts about it, the life-changing wisdom in *The Stoic Mindset* is for everyone who is willing to apply it to his or her life.

Moreover, *The Stoic Mindset* is not to be preachy or to give the impression that I am perfect, or that we should all be perfect. I am far from perfect, but I am better than I used to be and strive to be a better man every day. We must remember there are no perfect human beings, but each of us can work to be a better person than we were yesterday.

While we may never be able to reach the perfection of our character, we can certainly move closer to that goal daily. When you integrate the teachings in this book into your daily life, you will find the changes in your mindset will manifest faster than you may think, and soon you will notice how much your mindset, and your life, have changed.

This is your guide to personal freedom, a special kind of freedom that most people in today's society don't think about—the freedom to be in complete control of your mindset, your perceptions, your responses, your inner peace, and your life. These teachings are extremely powerful! Don't merely read them, but rather, slow down and digest each one and think about how it can apply to your life.

The Stoic Mindset provides you with the Stoic ideals to integrate into your life in order to fortify your spirit and mind in such a way that nothing can rob you of your positive mindset, calm mind, principles, honor, integrity, authenticity, or inner peace and tranquility.

My hope is that these teachings will steady you when life attempts to shake you, sharpen you when life challenges you, free you to be your authentic self, and lead you to a calm mind and spirit, inner peace, and tranquility. May you live with honor, wisdom, self-control, integrity, inner peace, and tranquility in a world that desperately needs more of these traits.

Bohdi Sanders, Ph.D.

The Stoic Mindset
Ancient Wisdom for Today's World

1

Waste no more time arguing about
what a good man should be. Be one!
Marcus Aurelius

Many philosophers, and those who love philosophy, like to argue and debate over their beliefs or the teachings of other philosophers. The Stoics also enjoyed debating various philosophies and using reason to prove them right or wrong. Just read Epictetus' writings and you see that he obviously enjoyed this.

I have no interest at all in such arguments or debates. I simply study philosophy and wisdom literature for actual wisdom, not to debate different philosophies or to appear wise. My philosophy is: I take what I find useful and integrate it into my life; and what I don't find useful, I simply disregard. That is just me.

It seems that Marcus Aurelius lived by this same philosophy. He stated that arguing about what a good man should be is a waste of time. I have no interest in arguing about what a good man should be; I simply do my best to be a good man. And I use the teachings and philosophy I study to help me in this pursuit.

Most of us know a good man when we see one. We don't have to argue about how he should act or what he should do. We know a good man lives his life by a specific code of honor. He lives with honor, integrity, courage, respect, and discipline. A good man does his best to keep his thoughts, words, and actions in line with the kind of man that he strives to be.

Justice, wisdom, and sincerity guide his actions. He is a loyal friend and has the courage to live his life according to his true beliefs, regardless of how anyone else lives or what anyone else thinks about it. A good man is courteous, benevolent, and helps other people as much as he can. He spends time in introspection to ensure that he is living as he should.

There is no need to argue or debate these things; we should simply integrate these traits into our lives. Don't concern yourself with how anyone else lives or behaves; just focus on improving yourself and becoming the best person you can be. Focus on being a good man, not arguing about what he should be.

2

First, say to yourself what you would be;
and then do what you have to do.
Epictetus

When you are going to go on a trip or a vacation, you first decide where you want to go, and then do what you must do to make it to your destination at a specific time. You don't simply start packing your clothes and then decide where you are going to go. That would be silly.

However, many people try to live their lives in this way. Think about it. Many college students go to college having absolutely no idea what they truly want to do with their lives. They simply try to figure out their lives as they go through the motions. How much better off would they be if they first decided what they wanted to be and *then* planned to do what they must do to achieve that goal?

The first step in changing your life, or becoming the kind of person you want to be, is deciding what you want. What kind of person do you want to be? What kind of life do you want to live? What values are important to you? You should take some time and think about the kind of life you want to live and the person that you want to be.

After you meditate on who you want to be and what you want out of life, you have decided on your destination or your ultimate objective. That is only the first step. Then, you must decide what you must do to achieve your objective. Make a roadmap for your life. You don't set out on a long road trip without a map and a plan to get to where you want to go, but many people live their lives with no plan to get what they want in life.

Your life is infinitely more important than some road trip, so don't take it for granted. Take your life more seriously! Take the time to decide what you want to achieve in life and what kind of person you want to be, then make a plan to achieve your goals. First, say to yourself what you want to be or what you want to achieve; then do what you must do to make your desired goals come true.

2

3

Difficulties strengthen the mind, as labor does the body.
Seneca

The German philosopher Friedrich Nietzsche stated, "What does not kill you makes you stronger." If you are well-versed in Stoic philosophy, you find that many of the wisdom quotes from modern philosophers and self-help gurus were already taught by the Stoics long ago. Some may consider that to be plagiarism, but it isn't. There are some thoughts that most wise men have in common. It is simply proof that all true wisdom is universal; it holds as true today as it did thousands of years ago.

Seneca taught that difficulties strengthen the mind, just as labor does the body. We all know that strength training strengthens your body. When you first decide to add weight training to your fitness routine, you may not be able to lift much weight. But after you have been lifting for a while, the weight that you couldn't lift when you first started training may become your warmup weight. That is because your efforts have strengthened your muscles.

Difficulties do the same thing for your mind *if* you approach them with the correct attitude. When a problem or challenge appears in your life, you have a choice to respond to it with the correct attitude and a rational mind, or to worry about it and allow stress to weaken your mind and body. Challenges will strengthen your mind, but only if you respond to them correctly.

Worry and stress are detrimental to your mind and body; they are also contrary to living with a Stoic mindset. If you allow yourself to worry about what is happening in your life, the stress can impair your memory, weaken your immune system, cause high blood pressure, sleep issues, hormonal imbalance, muscle tension and pain, and much more.

The Stoics taught that you should accept everything that comes your way just as it is. Don't worry about the situation; simply accept it and respond to it rationally. If you do this, the difficulties and challenges in your life will indeed strengthen your mind. When difficulties come your way, accept them as fate and address them rationally and stoically!

4

Man conquers the world by conquering himself.
Zeno of Citium

The majority of people in this world set out to conquer the world before they ever think about conquering themselves. This is completely backwards according to the teachings of Zeno. If you first conquer yourself, it will make achieving your other goals much easier. But what does it mean to conquer yourself?

Conquering yourself means that you have gained mastery over your own thoughts, emotions, desires, passions, impulses, actions, and speech. You refuse to allow anything to control you or to disrupt your inner peace and calm mind, whether it is your own desires or emotions, or external events or circumstances.

To conquer yourself, you must learn to control your fear, anger, greed, and excessive desires. These things can disturb your mind, inner peace, and lead to poor, irrational judgment. You must discipline yourself to stay calm despite what is happening around you.

To do this, you must develop your inner strength and a strong sense of independence. Always remember that external events are outside the realm of your control. While you have no control over external events, you always have control over how you respond to those events. This is one of the basic teachings of Stoicism, and I will cover this in extensive detail throughout this book.

It takes a lot of self-discipline to always respond in a calm, measured manner to whatever is happening around you, but it can be done. It just takes some practice and self-discipline. This is a major part of conquering yourself. Conquering yourself develops an inner strength that makes you less dependent on external circumstances for your happiness and peace of mind.

When nothing outside of your control can trouble your mind or disrupt your tranquility, then you have achieved true freedom. In a sense, you have conquered the world because it no longer has any control over your mind or your inner peace. You have successfully conquered yourself.

5

To live a good life…be indifferent to what makes no difference.
Marcus Aurelius

At first, this piece of wisdom from Marcus Aurelius seems obvious. After all, why would anyone care about something that makes no difference? But you must dig a little deeper to get the true meaning of this teaching. To truly understand this, you must understand what truly makes no difference in the world of a Stoic.

What made no difference to a Stoic was anything that was outside of his control. This means that the only things that are truly important are the things that are within your control. The things within your control include your mindset, character, your responses, your thoughts, your words, and your actions. Everything else is outside of your control, so you should regard those things indifferently and respond to them rationally.

Here, we also need to discuss what indifference means in Stoic terms. In Stoicism, "indifference" does not mean that you do not care about anything outside of yourself, but that you do not allow those things to affect you emotionally or to disrupt your inner peace. It is to say that certain things or events are neither good nor bad in themselves because they do not affect your ability to live a virtuous life. This takes quite a bit of self-discipline.

Being indifferent to external things doesn't mean that you ignore and neglect the things that you must deal with in your life, such as your job, providing for your family, etc. It simply means that you maintain a rational perspective. Do your best to maintain a calm, composed state of mind, no matter what is happening in your life.

By allowing things over which you have no control to disrupt your inner peace, it will be almost impossible to consistently maintain a calm, peaceful mind. There will always be something out there that will disrupt your inner peace *if you allow it to do so*. Don't compromise your inner peace by allowing the words or actions of other people to get to you. Remind yourself of the insignificance of most external things and always remain calm and controlled.

5

It is not what happens to you, but how you respond to it that matters.
Epictetus

This quote from Epictetus is one of the foundation stones of Stoicism, and it can be very hard for many people to grasp. The truth in this statement is closely connected to the last piece of wisdom I covered from Marcus Aurelius: "Be indifferent to what makes no difference."

On the surface, this statement may sound ridiculous. After all, doesn't it matter when something good or bad happens to you? Of course it matters—to a point. But what matters most to the Stoic are the things that are within his power to control—his responses and how he lives his life.

You have no control over the external things that happen to you, but you do have control over how you respond to them. You will see me discuss this truism many times throughout this book, as this thought is foundational to Stoicism. Living with a Stoic mindset means that you manage everything that happens in your life in a calm, rational manner, maintaining your inner peace and your virtue. To a Stoic, those are the things that truly matter.

It helps to keep in mind what things you can control and what things you have no control over. To truly be free, you must accept the things that you cannot control and focus on controlling the things that are within your control. When you release the desire to control external things, you free yourself from the mental and emotional stress that often accompanies the things outside of your control, and you have more energy to focus on the things that you can control.

By focusing on your response to external events, you will be better able to maintain your inner peace. The challenge is that we tend to forget that we have no control over external events or what other people do or say. This is especially true in the heat of the moment. You must continually ask yourself, "Is this something within my control?" If it isn't something you can control, accept it calmly. The quality of your life is determined by how you choose to perceive and respond to what happens, not by the external events themselves.

The greater the difficulty, the more glory in surmounting it.
Epictetus

Every warrior knows that there is more glory in defeating a powerful enemy than in defeating a weak enemy. This is exactly what Epictetus is teaching here. For someone with a Stoic mindset, hardships and obstacles are seen as opportunities for growth and improvement. Moliere, the 17th-century French poet and playwright, wrote essentially the same thing, stating, "The greater the obstacle, the more glory in overcoming it."

Facing monumental challenges or difficulties, and overcoming them, builds your character and spirit. The greater the challenge, the more it tests your ability, patience, and courage. And if you are striving to live with a Stoic mindset, it gives you vital feedback concerning how well you have trained your mind and spirit.

The greater the challenge, the more it tempts you to react emotionally to the external event. Think about it. It takes much more self-control and patience to respond stoically when some guy backs into your car and drives away than it does to respond stoically when you find some guy threw a soda can in your front yard. One is a much greater hassle than the other. Therefore, you have accomplished much more by responding calmly to someone putting a dent in your car than having to pick up someone's soda can.

In this example, you obviously had no control over either of these events. So, you should see them both as something external that you had no control over and respond calmly and rationally to each of them. Of course, one is no big deal, and the other will cost you time, money, and a hassle. But the Stoic would respond to each in a calm, rational manner.

After all, what good would it do to complain and throw a fit about either of these? Complaining and cursing would not change the situation. You would still have to pick up the can and get your car repaired. Getting frustrated and worked up will only rob you of your inner peace and accomplish nothing.

8

Begin at once to live, and count each separate day as a separate life.
Seneca

Many people go through life simply surviving, not really living. Each day, they go through the same routine, almost on autopilot. They get up at the same time, go to the same job, do the same thing at work, stop work at the same time, get home around the same time, eat, watch television, then go to bed, only to repeat the same sequence day after day. These people suffer through each day, looking forward to the weekend. They never give much thought to improving their lives. That is no way to live your life!

People who live like this never stop and think that they only get one life, one shot at seeing and doing all there is to do on this amazing earth. Of course, people must work to provide for their family, but that doesn't mean that they must go through life like zombies, working for the weekend. That is wasting much of your life.

The Stoic philosopher, Seneca, urges us to stop living our lives on autopilot and to see every day as important. He is encouraging us to be mindful of our lives, seeing every moment as something precious, something which if wasted, you can never get back. Treat each day as a special blessing from God. Make the most of every moment, every day.

Life is fleeting and unpredictable; don't postpone your happiness until "someday," as "someday" may never arrive. Begin really living your life and enjoy every day to the fullest. Don't wait! Don't procrastinate! You never know when this day will be the last time that you get to hug and kiss your loved ones. You never know whether today will be the last time you see your children or your friends. Every day could be your last!

Treat every day as a new beginning, a new life. If yesterday fell short, you get a new chance every day to live a better life. Each day is a new opportunity to live as you should, to be rational, helpful, and kind. Don't go through life like a zombie; be mindful of what a blessing every day is. Refuse to waste time or allow meaningless distractions to rob you of your precious time. Make it your goal in life to make every new day better than the day before. Each day is a special gift, so start living like you understand that fact.

If evil be spoken of you and it be true, correct yourself;
if it be a lie, laugh at it.
Epictetus

This piece of wisdom from Epictetus defines the Stoic approach to criticism and personal attacks. Think about it. If someone personally attacks you, either verbally or in writing, there are only two possibilities. Either what they say is true or it is false.

If what they are saying about you is true, then you have some changes to make. They are either pointing out something you have overlooked or not thought about, or they are pointing out something that you are already working to correct but haven't perfected yet. Either way, you shouldn't get defensive. Reflect on their words and take them as a reminder to improve the part of your life that needs some work.

The other possibility is that this person is an enemy or someone who wants to cause you problems, so they invent a lie, or lies, to damage your reputation. This happens much more often than you may think. In this case, Epictetus taught that you should laugh at their feeble attempt to hurt you.

While it is true that you should not allow other people's words to disrupt your inner peace, it is also true that we live in a very different world from that of Epictetus. In today's world, a libelous lie can be posted all over the internet and travel throughout the world in a matter of hours. This is definitely something that we must defend ourselves against.

That said, we must defend ourselves against it in the correct way, and without allowing it to disrupt our inner peace. It is a natural response to get angry when we see someone printing lies to hurt our reputation, but the Stoic mindset is about controlling those natural reactions. We can laugh at their pathetic attempt to destroy our reputation without allowing their words to make us angry.

Laughing at their lies demonstrates to those around you that you have the inner strength and the confidence to deal with what has been said without it upsetting you. You must accept things as they are and then respond. Do what you must do to protect yourself and do it with a smile on your face.

10

> It is not the man who has too little,
> but the man who craves more, that is poor.
> *Seneca*

This is a great example of the Stoic's view of wealth. The Stoics viewed wealth and poverty differently than most people. It is the man who is constantly unsatisfied with what he has who is truly poor. His insatiable desire for more leaves him in a continual state of struggle and unhappiness. No matter how much he may have, he still feels a sense of lack and a craving for something that is beyond his reach.

The Stoics believed that it is the person who is happy with whatever they have who is truly rich, because that person has a sense of contentment which eludes those who are constantly unhappy with their lot in life. Happiness comes from within. If you travel throughout the world, you will find people who have next to nothing who are happy, and you will see people who have an abundance of material things and money who are constantly unhappy.

This point of view challenges our conventional view of wealth and happiness. In today's world, people think that money and fame will make them happy. But if you observe many of those who have both money and fame, you will find that these people are not truly happy or content. Happiness has nothing to do with money or fame. You can be happy with nothing, just as you can be happy with an abundance of everything you can desire. It is your mindset, perception, and attitude that control your happiness or lack thereof.

True happiness is independent of external circumstances. The poorest people are those who are not content with their lives. Since the Stoics were focused on internal qualities and the things that were in their realm of control, this makes perfect sense. This doesn't mean that it is wrong for you to work to improve your financial life; it simply means that while you do, you should be happy and content with what you currently have. Remember, happiness and inner peace come from within; they *are* within your realm of control.

11

The best revenge is to be unlike him who performed the injury.
Marcus Aurelius

Marcus Aurelius urged us to take the high road in dealing with our enemies or those who seek to hurt us in some way. He is urging us not to retaliate or to seek revenge after someone has wronged us. This can be harder for some people than for others. Many of us have always been taught that when someone hurts us, we should make sure that we get even. But Marcus Aurelius urges us to keep our honor and integrity intact instead.

If you are a good person, the person who harmed you probably has inferior morals, or no morals at all. By being unlike this person, you are maintaining your own honor, character, and integrity. Again, we must remember that we should keep our focus on those things that are under our own control. You have no control over what others say or do; you only control what *you* say or do. Your duty is to maintain your own honor, not someone else's honor.

When people seek revenge on someone who has harmed them, they normally don't consider if what they are about to do is right or honorable. They simply want to punish or destroy the person who did them wrong. And in doing so, many will set their honor aside while they fight fire with fire.

This was not acceptable to the Stoic. You will not find any Stoic teaching that allows you to temporarily set your honor aside to get even with your enemy. Marcus Aurelius is urging us to do the exact opposite—to rise above the character and actions of the person who did us wrong and maintain our own character, honor, and integrity.

By accepting what has been done, you maintain your inner peace and self-control. This doesn't mean that you don't respond or take some action, but there is a big difference between seeking revenge on someone and taking action to defend yourself. Control what you can, accept what you can't control, and respond rationally. Decide what's right, then *do* what's right, and do it in the right way. As Confucius taught, "He who seeks revenge should start by digging two graves." Think about this.

12

It is the power of the mind to be unconquerable.
Seneca

If there is one thing that you have total control over, it is your own mind. As much as our society tries to control and manipulate your mind and force you to accept certain thoughts or beliefs as truth, they can't do it without your permission. They can try to manipulate you through peer pressure, putting certain messages in movies or advertising, but they can't succeed without you allowing them to be successful.

As Seneca wrote, your mind is unconquerable. You have the ultimate power over your mind. The problem is most people do not use this awesome power. They have surrendered this power to the media, television shows, movies, music, etc. Once you surrender your mind and allow yourself to be manipulated, you are no longer in control of your thoughts. You have allowed external forces to control something that was meant to be under your control.

The good news is that you can take back that control, and once you do, you can make your mind unconquerable. Only the power of a trained mind is unconquerable; untrained minds are merely potential power. And have no doubt about it, you must control your mind or someone else will. I wrote about cleansing your subconscious mind and controlling your mind in detail in my award-winning book, *The Art of Inner Peace*. If you are having issues controlling your mind, I highly recommend that you get a copy of that book.

Your mind is a lot like a computer; you can program it as you will. The problem is that most people don't understand this and never even consider that they must actually do some deprogramming and reprogramming of their minds to have a powerful mind that cannot be manipulated.

Today, we understand much more about how the mind and the subconscious mind work. While Seneca was right about the power of the mind being unconquerable, we now know exactly what must be done for you to take control of your mind. You have the power to make your mind unconquerable; the only question is—do you have the will to take control of your mind?

13

If you want to improve, be content to be thought foolish and stupid.
Epictetus

When you are truly ready to take control of your life, you will undoubtedly face judgments and ridicule from your friends, family, and others. Those who know you like the status quo; they don't want you to change your life too much. You will hear various objections to the changes that you are trying to make. Your friends may still want you to go out and party with them. Your family may think what you are doing is weird or against their chosen religion. They will have dozens of reasons to convince you to forget about "all those weird changes."

However, you were put on this earth to live *your* life, not anyone else's life; no one else has the right to decide how you should or should not live your life. Most people never really get serious about self-improvement. To them, the few people who do take self-improvement seriously appear weird or foolish. But Stoicism teaches that we should focus on our own goals and not seek approval from others. You will never get anywhere if you allow other people's opinions to influence your decisions.

The fear of appearing silly or foolish is tied to your ego. To improve your life, you must control your ego and trust in the process. When you have your ego under control, the opinions of other people won't matter to you. You won't care if others think you are stupid or foolish. Remember, other people have the right to think whatever they want, just as you have the right to think what you want and to ignore their opinions.

As long as they are not hindering your progress, endure their opinions as nothing more than meaningless chatter. However, if they start to hinder your progress, you may need to distance yourself from them until they have realized that your life is yours to live, not theirs. Commit to your progress and self-improvement. You will no doubt have some setbacks and make some mistakes along the way, but don't let that stop you! Whether or not others accept the new you is their business; your business is to work to perfect your character.

14

Associate with people who are likely to improve you.
Seneca

This is a fantastic continuation of the previous discussion. Once you start to make improvements to your life and begin to live a different kind of life, you may not want to spend as much time with the people who you used to enjoy. They may become a hinderance to your improvement. If you continue to spend a lot of time with people who do not support the changes that you are making, it will make it harder for you to make the changes you want to make. No doubt, Seneca understood this.

He urges us to associate with people who help us become better, who understand and want to see us move closer to our objectives. It is a universal law that you will become more like the people that you spend the most time with in your life. If you spend time with people with little to no ambition, their lack of ambition will rub off on you in different ways. That is why it is vital that you associate with people who will help you improve your life.

Everyone has different habits, different levels of knowledge, and different life goals. There are people who actually live the kind of life that you want to live. These are the people you want to spend time with and learn from; they have developed habits and do things that you may not have thought about before. Learn from them!

If you don't know anyone who lives with a Stoic mindset or who lives the kind of life that you want to live, find books or teaching videos by those who *do* live the kind of life you want to live. Spend time reading, studying, and learning from these people. You cannot have tea and talk to Marcus Aurelius, Epictetus, or Seneca, but you can spend time with their teachings and learn from them by reading their writings.

Who you associate with matters more than you may realize. The company that you keep will either hinder you on your journey or lift you up to a higher level of understanding and enlightenment. Be selective about who you spend your limited time with during your journey to develop the Stoic mindset.

We have two ears and one mouth,
therefore, we should listen twice as much as we speak.
Zeno of Citium

I am sure you have heard this saying dozens of times throughout your life. It is a popular saying and one that your parents most likely used to quiet you down when you were talking too much as a child. But chances are you were not aware that it is a Stoic teaching.

People love to hear themselves talk. It doesn't matter whether or not they have something important to say; most people have a hard time controlling their urge to speak. The next time you are sitting with a group of people, notice how uncomfortable people are with silence. Once nobody is speaking, it won't be long before someone will feel the urge to say something, anything to break the uncomfortable silence.

Let people talk as much as they want to. It makes you appear like a brilliant conversationalist when you keep the conversation going by asking them questions and then letting them talk about the subject. Most people don't understand how much others like to hear themselves talk. If you bring up a topic they are interested in, they will talk for hours.

By letting other people talk, you learn things you may not have known; when you talk, you are only repeating what you already know. So, encourage others to talk, and you will gather a lot of information about them and other topics, all while keeping your secrets and personal information securely hidden in your silence.

Anyone who talks more than they listen will inevitably expose information and secrets that are good to know. And if you are keeping good company, as you should, you will gain wisdom and knowledge that will help you on your journey. There is absolutely no value in entertaining others with information about your personal life when you could be listening and learning. You have two ears and one mouth, so always listen twice as much as you talk. It is the way of the Stoic.

> We are not given a short life, but we make it short,
> and we are not ill-supplied, but wasteful of it.
> *Seneca*

We are constantly bombarded with self-help gurus who tell us that life is short, so we had better do what we want to do now. Seneca had a different point of view concerning this. He stated that life is not short, but we make it short because we waste so much time. The truth lies somewhere in between.

Life is short when you look at the big picture. Life expectancy in the United States is only 76 years. When you consider that twenty years go by really fast, that will give you a little perspective about how brief life truly is. Seventy-six years is not that long at all. Both my grandfather and my great-grandfather lived much longer than that, and it still was not long enough for my liking.

In addition, when you consider how much of that time is wasted on meaningless things, Seneca is right; we do make our lives shorter by wasting so much of our precious time. Once you waste an hour, you can never get that time back; it is gone forever.

When you take the time to think about how much time you have to live on this earth, it truly is short. Consider the following. The average person spends about 21 days each year sick. If we sleep eight hours a night, that means we spend over 121 days sleeping.

The average person spends 3-4 hours a day watching television, 3-5 hours a day on their smartphone, and 1-3 non-work-related hours a day on their computer. If we take the lower number from each other those screen times, that is still seven hours per day, which is over 106 days spent on screen time. Now, consider that someone who works 40 hours a week spends over 86 days a year at work.

Add those up and they consume 91% of our time, which leaves us with only 31 days a year. Just consider what you could do with all that time if you spent it differently! I disagree with Seneca; I would say that life *is* short, and we *make it* much shorter by our lifestyle and habits. Think about this!

17

The good or ill of a man lies within his own will.
Epictetus

Epictetus believed that the essence of a man's happiness and virtue comes from how he responds to his circumstances. Therefore, what determines whether a man's life is good or bad depends entirely on his own choices and mindset. Your life is in your own hands; you are the captain of your own ship.

You may argue that if someone is poor or has major health issues, he doesn't have a good life. But to the Stoics, external events, things outside of our control, do not enter into the picture when it comes to living a good or bad life. What matters to the Stoic is how he responds to those external things. Therefore, if he responds rationally and virtuously, he is living a good life; his happiness does not depend on anything outside of his control.

How you live is your choice. If you depend on vices or external factors for your happiness, you are depending on things over which you have no control. True happiness always comes from within. You have total control over your happiness and how you respond to any external event or circumstance. That means that you are free to decide whether an event or circumstance will or will not "make" you happy, angry, sad, etc.

Remember, you have no control over other people, events, or circumstances, but you always have control over how you will respond to any and every situation in your life. By choosing to respond to life's challenges with rational thought, wisdom, patience, acceptance, and a calm mind, you can maintain your inner peace and happiness, no matter what else is happening around you.

However, the other side of that is also true. If you allow external things, which are out of your control, to upset you, anger you, or make you fearful, you are creating your own misery and disrupting your inner peace. This is why the Stoics believed that you must master your will in order to master yourself, and that mastering yourself is the only true freedom. The choice is always in your hands. How will you choose to respond to the challenges in your life?

18

Ignorant men differ from beasts only in their figure.
Cleanthes

As far as we know, humans are the only creatures on our planet that have the capacity for reason or rational thought. According to Cleanthes, that is what sets us apart from other animals. Additionally, he concluded that an ignorant man differs from other animals only in his body. Epictetus agreed with Cleanthes, stating, "Only the educated are free."

What Cleanthes was saying is that ignorance robs men of the unique capacity for reason; therefore, they are little better than animals. Their ability to reason and think rationally is what truly sets them apart from the animals. This reasoning comes from the fact that the Stoics define human beings by their unique ability to think rationally and make moral choices concerning their own lives.

Essentially, he was condemning ignorance. He felt that all true men should be educated because without knowledge and wisdom, people simply act out of their emotions and instincts, much like animals. Cleanthes taught that rational thought, wisdom, and knowledge were essential for all men.

Think about all the people in our prisons today. Most of those people are in prison for acting on their base instincts, just like an animal. Many are in prison for reacting to some external event instead of taking the time to think rationally about their actions. That is why I teach in my warrior books that the true warrior *responds instead of reacts*. When you respond, you are in control; when you react, the other person or event is controlling your actions.

Ignorant people, and people who do not control their temper, will react when provoked. If someone insults them, they reply likewise. Many people are in prison today for reacting violently to another person without thinking rationally about their situation. When they react in that way, they differ little from a cornered animal, which reacts defensively and attacks. This is just one example of how reacting instead of thinking rationally can invite misery into your life. Always respond instead of reacting; it pays big dividends!

19

He who laughs at himself never runs out of things to laugh at.
Epictetus

People who take themselves too seriously can never laugh at themselves. They always seem to take offense if someone laughs at their actions or words, which makes them look even more comical. Epictetus is urging us to stop taking ourselves so seriously. Lighten up! Don't take offense at the things that other people do or say.

If you do or say something, and people laugh at you, how have they hurt you? Have they harmed you in any way? Have they stolen something that belongs to you? No, of course not. The only thing they have injured is your ego, and that is only injured if you take offense at their laughter or their actions.

You must keep your ego under control. It can cause you more problems than almost anything else. Think about it. If someone makes a joke at your expense, he hasn't hurt you unless your ego is fragile. If you allow your ego to control your emotions, you will get angry at him about his joke. And if you allow your anger towards them to grow, it can easily turn into resentment or hatred, and eventually, that resentment or hatred will manifest through your actions, turning a simple joke into a major issue.

If someone makes a joke at your expense, laugh along with them. This neutralizes your ego and keeps your emotions in check. If they meant no offense by their joke, this will endear you to them. You will seem confident in who you are, and you will win their respect. If their joke was meant to invoke a reaction, you have successfully foiled their malicious attempt to get under your skin, and again, you have gained the respect of those who witnessed the event.

However, if you take offense at his joke, you have made his joke even funnier and exposed the fact that you have a fragile ego and some self-esteem issues. Again, how you respond to this situation is up to you. Respond rationally, and even if his joke was meant maliciously, you will have successfully defended yourself against his attempt to garner a reaction.

20

Is an emerald suddenly flawed if no one admires it?
Marcus Aurelius

We live in a culture that craves attention. It seems many people will do almost anything to get attention or to become famous. There are many examples of people who have "sold their soul" for fame and fortune, but why is that? Do they believe their lives are worth more if they are well-known? Those who have achieved fame and fortune will testify that their fame and fortune have not truly satisfied them. So why do so many people strive to achieve this attention?

Many believe that they have not really accomplished much if they don't have many admirers. Marcus Aurelius addresses that train of thought with this teaching. He emphasizes that someone's true worth does not depend on the opinions of others or any external validation. Just as an emerald does not lose its value if no one is noticing it, what others do or don't notice has no effect on your value.

The emerald in this teaching represents your intrinsic value; your value doesn't depend on being recognized by other people. If you live your life with character, honor, and integrity, you are a good person no matter what anyone else thinks about it. Their opinions mean no more than a blind man's opinion of a beautiful painting.

There is another quote along this same train of thought which is also attributed to Marcus Aurelius: "If an emerald falls into a sewer, it does not lose its value." This means that even when you fall short of your goal to live an honorable life, you still do not lose your intrinsic value. If you accidentally drop an emerald into a sewer, it is still an emerald. You don't discard it simply because it gets dirty; you simply clean it up and continue on your way.

Living a life of honor can be hard at times, and you will fall short from time to time as you endeavor to perfect your character. That doesn't mean you admit defeat. Every day is a new chance to start fresh and live the life you are meant to live. Clean yourself up and continue to fight the good fight!

21

Luck is what happens when preparation meets opportunity.
Seneca

Luck is pretty much a meaningless word in the grand scheme of things. Everything in life is based on cause and effect. Nothing appears magically, and nothing happens without a cause. People attribute events to luck simply because they cannot see the cause. If we could trace everything that happens in our lives back through the linked chain of events, we could understand the underlying cause of everything in our lives. But we don't have that ability, so we attribute things to good luck or bad luck.

In this piece of wisdom, Seneca is virtually saying there is no such thing as luck. By saying that luck is what happens when preparation meets opportunity, he is saying that what we call "luck" happens because we prepared ourselves and set a specific chain of events in motion. And because we did our part and prepared ourselves, we are ready to act whenever opportunities arise. Essentially, we set things in motion through our own thoughts and actions.

Think about this in terms of martial arts. If you were out on the town and some thug tried to mug you, his success depends on you, not on luck. If you have prepared yourself through self-defense training, you will be able to defend yourself and successfully walk away from that situation. But if you are unprepared, you will be at the mercy of the mugger.

You may be thinking that this event was not really your fault, that you had nothing to do with this guy trying to rob you. While it is true that you have no control over what other people do, you do have control over where you go, your environmental awareness, and your own preparation to defend yourself. You are responsible for the things that are *within your realm of control*.

There is no such thing as luck! Everything is based on cause and effect. Even if you cannot figure out what the cause of a certain event may be, there is always an underlying cause. Prepare yourself for the life you want to live. Control the things that you can control and be ready to respond successfully to unexpected events over which you have no control.

22

If it is not right, do not do it; if it is not true, do not say it.
Marcus Aurelius

Living a virtuous life with honor and integrity is not that complicated. Many people make it complicated because they try to control people or situations over which they have no control, or they allow their external desires to overpower their will. People complicate their own lives by focusing on the wrong things, things outside of their control, instead of keeping their focus on the things that they can control.

Many people seem to have trouble living a virtuous life; they make things more complicated than they must be. Marcus Aurelius really put things in the simplest terms, saying, if it is not right, don't do it; if it is not true, don't say it.

That brings us to the question of what is right and who decides what is right? Each person must decide what is right for themselves, but within the bounds of honor, integrity, virtue, and moral character. For example, one man may decide it is not right to eat pork because of his religious beliefs, while another man may believe that there is nothing wrong with eating pork. This is an example of a decision about what is right according to one's personal code. Eating pork is a personal decision, but it is not a universal law.

An example of a universal law would be, do not commit murder. Murder is not right, no matter what your personal beliefs may be. So, when I say that each man must decide what is right for himself, that does not apply to universal laws. There is no need to complicate things. Most people understand what is right and what is wrong.

The same goes for what is true and what is not. However, people seem to have more challenges when it comes to their speech. Today, many people think nothing of lying to get what they want or to get out of a trying situation. But lying for personal gain is not honorable, and it is not living with integrity. To have integrity, you must be a man of your word. Keep it simple! If it is not right, do not do it; if it is not true, do not say it.

23

If a man knows not to which port he sails, no wind is favorable.
Seneca

Seneca is telling us we must have clear goals in our life. He uses the example of being on a sailboat. If you are on a sailboat and you don't know where you want to go, it doesn't matter which way the wind is blowing because you have no destination anyway. Without a specific purpose or personal objective, there is no way to gauge your success; when you can't judge your success, you will simply waste time on meaningless things with no direction in your life.

If you have no objective, you will not prepare yourself for the right opportunities. Many opportunities may come your way, but it won't matter to you because you haven't prepared yourself to take advantage of them. Think about it. You may have the chance to interview for a high-paying job, but if you haven't prepared yourself to work in such a position, that opportunity is useless to you.

To get back to Seneca's example of sailing, if you don't have a specific intention to go somewhere, or a specific purpose for sailing, you might as well be sailing around in a circle in the ocean. And what is this if not a complete waste of your precious time?

Wise people have a purpose in everything they do. It is their purpose that gives their actions meaning. Without a purpose or the intention to do something specific, they simply drift through life, going whichever way the wind blows them, accomplishing nothing of value. Many people live their lives like this and then wonder why they never get anywhere in life.

If you want to live a good life, a life with purpose and meaning, you must get focused; you must have goals and objectives. Without objectives in your life, you're just going through the motions on autopilot as you inch closer and closer to death. Don't waste your life! Sit down and decide what you want out of life and what your purpose is. Then, pursue your purpose and do what you must do to make your life fulfilling.

24

No great thing is created suddenly.
Epictetus

Patience and perseverance are vital in developing the Stoic mindset. Most of the time, accomplishing your goals doesn't happen overnight; you must be patient and accept that some things are outside of your control. You can't force your goals to come to you on your timetable. Growth and mastery in any field take time. You must prepare yourself for the life you want; then, be ready to capitalize on the opportunities that come your way.

All great accomplishments are the result of a process and must be cultivated over time. You don't plant a tree today and get shade or fruit the next week; it takes time for that tree to mature.

Some people get all excited about a new venture, and they want it to be a success overnight, but that is not the way of the world. I had written seven books with little to no financial success. Most people would have given up after writing so many books and hardly seeing any success. It would have been extremely easy to give up and go back to working for someone else, but that was not what I wanted to do.

Instead of giving up, I re-evaluated what I was doing. I fired my publisher, bought the rights to my books back, turned down a couple of big publishers in New York and Dallas, and started my own publishing company. This took a lot of faith, as I had to borrow the money to buy the rights to my books back and start my own company.

I had to redo each book because my publisher refused to give me the rights to my book covers. So, I learned the business from the ground up. I republished my old books, changed my marketing plan, and wrote and published a new book. That book, *Modern Bushido: Living a Life of Excellence*, took off and hit #1 on Amazon, spent 107 weeks in the top 10 on Amazon's Bestseller List and won multiple book awards! Then, my other books started selling. If I had given up when my books weren't selling, I would have never experienced that success. Be patient and work to achieve your goals; never give up!

25

The willing are led by fate; the reluctant dragged.
Cleanthes

This piece of wisdom from Cleanthes emphasizes acceptance of the things that you cannot change. Getting upset, or refusing to accept circumstances that are outside of your circle of control, has never had any impact on the situation you are dealing with. When you get upset over the way things are, it only serves to rob you of your inner peace and add more stress to your life.

The Stoics taught that you should willingly accept the events and circumstances that occur in your life. They called these events and circumstances "fate." Whether you call these things fate or something else, the truth is you have no control over those things.

If something is beyond your control, then acceptance of it is the first step to dealing with whatever is happening. Many people simply choose to ignore what is happening, as if that will somehow magically make their situation go away. That is simply refusing to accept reality. You can't successfully respond to something if you refuse to acknowledge that it exists or creates a challenge for you.

While you may not want to deal with a bad situation or unfavorable circumstances, ignoring what is happening offers you no advantage. It is better to accept that things are what they are and then respond to them however you need to. Resisting reality only creates unnecessary stress and turmoil, because you are struggling in a fight that can't be won. If you have no control over an event or circumstance, struggling against it is a futile waste of time.

That is why it is important to understand what is in your control and what's not in your control. You can control your thoughts, actions, words, and responses, but you have no control over external events, the actions of others, and natural occurrences.

Marcus Aurelius taught that we should not only accept and bear what is necessary, but that we should love it. Things are what they are no matter how you feel about them, so why not embrace them with a calm, peaceful mind?

25

26

> When you get angry, you should know that you aren't guilty
> of an isolated lapse, you have encouraged a trend and thrown
> fuel on the fire…So, if you don't want to be cantankerous,
> do not feed your temper, or multiply incidents of anger.
>
> *Epictetus*

Most people don't give anger much thought. They simply feel happy when things are pleasing to them and feel anger when something rubs them the wrong way. But Epictetus rightly taught that you train yourself to be angry. He states that the more you encourage anger, the more you allow yourself to engage in angry outbursts, the more you will have a tendency to be angry again and again.

There is a scientific reason behind this truism. There are physical, psychological, and long-term consequences connected to anger. Anger triggers the body's stress response, releasing hormones like adrenaline and cortisol, and basically activates the fight-or-flight response. It increases blood pressure, your heart rate, and muscle tension. Anger also affects your breathing and can lead to hypertension, heart disease, and a weakened immune system.

Psychologically, it decreases your rational thinking process, and you begin to make decisions according to your emotions. And when you are angry, your brain intensifies negative emotions such as resentment, frustration, and hostility. It is never wise to allow your emotions to control your mind.

In addition, Epictetus touched on something that most people don't think about—anger is an addictive habit. The more you allow yourself to get angry about things outside of your control, the more you will continue to get angry. This is because of the hormonal cocktail that anger releases into your body.

Anger gives you a burst of adrenaline, and the more you get angry, the more you train your body to crave that adrenaline cocktail. So, if you want to be calm and in control of your mind and emotions, you must work at controlling your anger, or, as Epictetus taught, do not feed your temper. The more you control your anger, the less likely you are to lose your temper or get angry.

27

Be silent as to services you have rendered,
but speak of favors you have received.
Seneca

Seneca gives us great advice in this teaching. There is a teaching from the fourth century Taoist philosopher, Lieh Tzu, which states, "Those who do good because they want to be seen as good, are not good." This is what Seneca is urging us to avoid.

Too many people are quick to boast about what they have done for others or how much they give to charities. If they help a homeless person on the street, they like to take a photo and then brag about it on social media to hear people say how wonderful they are. At the same time, they keep the favors that they have received from others to themselves.

The Stoics taught to avoid boasting about the good deeds you have done for others, as it is self-serving and diminishes the value of what you have done. If you are truly giving from your heart, you don't need to have recognition or praise for your actions. Be humble and don't talk about the services you have rendered to others. Focus on the act, not the reward. Do good simply because it is who you are, and don't seek external validation for your actions.

On the other hand, be generous when you speak about what others have done for you. This cultivates a spirit of gratitude in your life. It reminds you of the favors that others have rendered to you, and it shows that you appreciate and recognize when others go out of their way for you.

In addition, you make others feel good when you recognize them for the good acts they have done. When you show others you appreciate what they do for you, you are also encouraging them to continue to do good deeds as they go through life. Too many times, people go out of their way to help others, only to be taken for granted. Always be grateful when someone helps you!

Be humble and discreet about the help you render to others, and openly acknowledge, and truly appreciate, what others do for you. This cultivates humility, gratitude, and selflessness within yourself and others.

28

The soul becomes dyed with the color of its thoughts.
Marcus Aurelius

Your thoughts are much more powerful than you may think. Your inner character, emotional state, and happiness are all deeply influenced by your thoughts. If you want to develop a Stoic mindset, you must discipline your mind. Remember, you must control the things that are in your realm of control, and your thoughts are one of those things.

The thoughts you entertain shape the person that you become. Positive, virtuous, and rational thoughts lead to a calm, peaceful mind. And when you think calm, peaceful thoughts, that is the kind of person you will become. Conversely, thoughts full of negative energy will cause you to be anxious, angry, and rob you of your inner peace.

You become what you think. This is not only a Stoic belief but is taught by sages throughout the world. Science has only just begun to learn how powerful the mind truly is. Your thoughts control your attitude, and your attitude shapes your perception of the world around you. If you maintain a positive mindset, rooted in integrity, wisdom, and justice, you will cultivate a spirit that is strong, rational, peaceful, and calm.

The good thing about this is that you have complete control over your mindset and what thoughts you allow yourself to entertain. While you can't control every thought that pops into your mind, you can control which ones you allow to remain there. You also have the power to change the thoughts that appear in your mind.

While you do have control over your mind, it takes discipline to master your thoughts. You must constantly be vigilant about what thoughts you allow. If you let down your guard, it won't be long until some negative event or some rude person tempts you to forget your mental discipline, and you will find yourself thinking negative thoughts of anger or resentfulness. When you protect your mind, you protect your inner peace. You must make mindfulness and self-awareness your way of life.

29

Very little is needed for everything to be upset and ruined, only a slight lapse in reason. It is much easier for a mariner to wreck his ship than it is for him to keep it sailing safely...In fact, he does not have to do anything—a momentary loss of attention will produce the same result.

Epictetus

Epictetus was spot on with this piece of wisdom. It takes very little to destroy something that is important to you. Many times, all you have to do is nothing; your neglect will allow things to disintegrate on their own. It doesn't matter if you are referring to your finances, your relationship with someone, your home, your yard, you name it. If you neglect to manage the important things in your life, eventually, they will start to spin out of control.

I will use finances as an example. To keep your finances in order and to increase your wealth, or to simply manage your family's finances, you must stay on top of your bills, your spending habits, your investments, etc. It takes very little for your finances to become a mess if you are neglecting your bills and your spending habits.

A splurge here or an unexpected expense there, and you can quickly find your finances are in a bind. You can't simply ignore your spending or your bills. This is something you must actively manage, or it will quickly spin out of control. It takes nothing more than doing nothing for your finances to become a giant mess.

On the other hand, it takes being frugal with your money, saving, and actively and consistently making good, wise investments to increase your wealth and keep your finances in good shape. It takes time, effort, and attention to manage your money wisely.

This is just one example, but if you think about it, this piece of wisdom applies to everything in your life. It only takes one stupid decision to ruin a relationship, but it takes constant effort to build a strong relationship. Think about this and manage the important things in your life wisely!

30

Set your own house in order. Cast out of your mind sorrow,
fear, lust, envy, spite, greed, petulance, and overindulgence.
Getting rid of these, too, requires looking to God for help,
trusting Him alone and submitting to His direction.
Epictetus

This teaching is the other side of the coin from the wisdom on the previous page. If you neglect your relationship, it will eventually fall apart. You must make your family and your relationships a priority in your life. And yes, this can be very demanding and difficult at times.

People are very good at critiquing other people's lives; they love to give advice concerning how others should live. But many people are not so judicious when it comes to setting their own house in order. They are eager to point out other people's shortcomings, while ignoring their own. This is just the opposite of what they should be doing.

Set your own house in order and stop focusing on how other people live their lives. God did not give you authority over anyone else's life. Stop criticizing how your friend, neighbor, or brother lives, and start focusing on your own shortcomings.

Jesus put it this way: "Why do you look at the speck that is in your brother's eye, but do not notice and acknowledge the log that is in your own eye?" Don't concern yourself with how anyone else lives when your life is not perfect. That is nothing more than hypocrisy! You have no control over anyone except yourself. Mind your own business and put your own house in order!

Epictetus urges you to pray and ask God for help in getting rid of whatever negative traits or shortcomings you may have in your life, as it can be difficult to get rid of some bad habits. Stop focusing on what others are doing wrong and focus on getting rid of your own issues. And if you are having trouble controlling some of your more challenging habits, look to God and ask for His help and His guidance. Remember, control what you have control over—your own personal life!

31

A gem cannot be polished without friction,
nor a man perfected without trials.
Seneca

Challenges make you stronger. If you have ever seen what it takes to polish a gem, you know that making that gem nice and smooth doesn't happen overnight. It takes many days of being rubbed and polished with different grits of fine sand to turn that rough stone into a beautiful and smooth gem. And once that process is finished, the gemstone is worth much more than it previously was.

The same principle applies to your life. There is no personal growth without challenges and self-discipline. Just as a gem must undergo the process of abrasion to become brilliant, you must face difficulties and adversities in order to develop your character, integrity, wisdom, and perseverance. After all, if you never faced any problems in life, how would you develop the skills to deal with adverse situations?

The challenges and obstacles in your life are essential to your becoming stronger and to your self-improvement. Without challenges in your life, you are much like an unrefined gem; your true worth remains hidden and untested. You don't know how you will respond to adversity. While you may think that you know what you would do in a certain situation, you really don't know because you have never had to deal with any adversity.

It is through overcoming adversity that you learn who you truly are and what you can do. Obstacles and challenges strengthen you if you work to overcome them instead of giving up. While this process of refinement may be painful, it builds your strength and self-confidence. It reveals who you truly are so that you can refine yourself into who you want to be.

Don't be resentful of challenges, obstacles, or hardships. Use them to your advantage by overcoming them and increasing your strength. Embrace them as part of your "polishing" process; they will shape you into the person you are meant to be. Refuse to allow anything to defeat or dishearten you!

31

32

Brave men rejoice in adversity, just as brave soldiers triumph in war.
Seneca

Instead of being resentful and angry because of some adversity that you are facing, see it as a challenge. Seeing obstacles and personal trials as a challenge reframes whatever is going on in your life. Instead of seeing something as a tragedy, see it as a challenge or an opportunity to demonstrate how strong you are. See it as a test of your courage, strength, and character, one that you must overcome to become the person you want to become.

Seneca compared adversity to a soldier's triumph in war. If you see the obstacles and negative events in your life as challenges, and yourself as a powerful warrior who is ready to overcome those challenges, it will give you strength. Instead of feeling depressed or defeated, feel challenged and tested. And refuse to allow this challenge to get the best of you.

If you were a warrior and some criminal was threatening your family, would you sit and feel sorry for yourself and give up, or would you summon all the courage, fortitude, and determination you have to rise up and defeat this threat? Of course, you would rise to the occasion with every fiber of your being and risk your life to defeat the threat to your family.

But so many people fall apart and give up when challenged by much less serious life challenges. They allow themselves to become depressed and defeated instead of rising up to overcome the challenge or trying situation. Refuse to surrender to any challenge or adversity!

Embrace life's challenges and adversities with the same vigor and determination that you would if that obstacle were someone threatening your loved ones. Instead of succumbing to defeat and depression, summon your warrior spirit! Warrior up! Not only to meet the challenge, but to completely obliterate any challenge that stands in your way. See every obstacle or adversity as a challenge to your character, honor, and inner peace, then rise to overcome it and show your true character and fortitude. Stand strong and be victorious!

33

Character is destiny.
Heraclitus

Your character ultimately determines which path your life takes; therefore, your character is your destiny. Character comprises a combination of traits that you develop in your life. A good character is built on traits such as honor, integrity, courage, uprightness, honesty, strength, and other virtuous character traits. A poor character would be the opposite of these traits and entail traits such as hate, fear, resentfulness, dishonesty, laziness, cowardice, etc.

The character traits that you develop will determine how you live your life, your outlook on life, and how you respond to life's challenges. As you go through life, you will have many challenges, heartbreaks, and various events and situations that you will have to deal with. The character traits that you develop will determine how you respond to those events and situations.

Each action you take, whether it is honorable or dishonorable, sets you on a specific path; and the path that you choose through your decisions and actions leads to your destiny. Many people see destiny or fate as something that is out of their control, but when you look at it in these terms, you find that you actually get to choose your destiny by how you live your life and the decisions you make.

Of course, there will be many events, situations, and circumstances in your life that you don't choose, but you always get to choose how you respond to them. And it is your character that determines how you will respond. Therefore, it is vitally important to strive to perfect your character. If you lack the character traits that make up a virtuous character, then you will not respond to life's challenges positively or without disrupting your inner peace.

Moreover, if you don't respond to life's challenges positively, your choice will set you on a completely different path, and that changes your destiny. Your destiny is not set in stone; you choose it by how you choose to live your life. Choose to live with honor and virtue, and you are choosing the path less taken—a path to a greater destiny.

34

> You may bind my leg, but not even Zeus
> has the power to break my freedom of choice.
> *Epictetus*

We often hear people say things like, "I have no choice" or "I had no choice; I had to do this." But those kinds of statements are never true. No matter what you are facing in life, you *always* have a choice. No one, no matter how powerful he may be, can take away your freedom of choice.

You may be thinking that this is absolutely wrong, that there are many times in life when you don't have a choice about what you must do. But you are confusing not having a choice with not having a *favorable choice* from which to choose. Those are not the same thing. You always have a choice concerning what you will or won't do, even if you don't like your options.

For example, you may need more money to make the payments on a new car you want, so you choose to get a second job. Most people would say, "I didn't have a choice; I had to have more money to make my payments." But that is not correct. They *did* have a choice. They could decide to get a used car, a cheaper new car, or to make other arrangements for transportation. Instead, they *chose* to get a second job because they wanted a specific automobile.

Just because you may not like the choices you have to choose from, that doesn't mean that you have no choice. You always retain your freedom of choice throughout your life. Again, you may argue, well what about the criminal who is sent to jail? He had no choice about going to jail. And once again, this is wrong. The criminal made his choice when he committed a crime. You are not referring to his choice, but to the consequences of his choice.

You are always free to choose, but you are not free from the consequences of your choices. Every choice you make carries with it a consequence of one kind or another. When you choose an action, you are also choosing the consequence that comes with that choice. The fact that you don't think about the possible consequences when you make your choice does not mean there are none. Make your choices wisely!

35

The impediment to action advances action.
What stands in the way becomes the way.
Marcus Aurelius

Everything in your life is connected in one way or another. If something is impeding your action, it is simply moving you towards some other action. As Marcus Aurelius wrote, the obstacle that stands in your way becomes the way. This is not to say that the obstacle in your path sets you on a different path, but only that it becomes a part of your path.

Everyone experiences obstacles as they go through life. You may have a specific plan for your life, but you will experience obstacles before you successfully get to where you want to be. Don't give up or decide to travel another path simply because you encounter some obstacle. It is there to challenge you, to see how you will respond to it.

Think about it. If you are hiking to the top of a mountain, and a storm has washed out the trail or blown a large tree down on the trail, that doesn't mean you have to give up and not hike to the top of the mountain. It simply means that you must take action to deal with the obstacle or find a way around it before you can get to the top of the mountain.

An obstacle in the path doesn't mean you must take a different path; it only means you must overcome the obstacle to continue on your way. If there is a large tree across the trail, you will have many choices to continue your hike. You can make a detour and go around the tree, or you can climb over the tree. You could take a saw and remove the tree from the trail. Initially, the tree is an impediment to your action, but it also advances different actions.

Everyone experiences obstacles as they travel through life. It is not the obstacles that matter, but how you respond to those obstacles. You can see the obstacles in your life as roadblocks and give up; or you can see the obstacles as challenges and warrior up. Will you give up, or will you rise to the challenge and refuse to allow anything to stop you from living the life that you want to live? The choice is yours. Choose wisely!

36

If I had followed the multitude, I would not have studied philosophy.
Chrysippus

The Norwegian playwright Henrik Ibsen stated, "The majority is never right. Never, I tell you! That's one of these lies in society that no free and intelligent man can help rebelling against." Chrysippus was essentially saying the same thing. The multitude of people do not seek wisdom or care for philosophy; they are perfectly content if given a comfortable life, food, and entertainment.

Truth, honor, and universal virtues are never determined by popular opinion or by the majority. Just because an idea or belief is held by the majority of people, that doesn't make it right or true. You must go your own way and follow your own path. Refuse to conform to what others believe is right or wrong. The majority often believe what is convenient, comfortable, or socially accepted, rather than what is true or right.

You must learn to think and reason for yourself. Study the wisdom of the Stoics and the sages to determine how you want to live your life and what is right and wrong. Don't be led by the majority. At the same time, don't rebel against something simply because the majority agrees with it. Learn to think for yourself and then have the confidence to act on what you believe is right. Have the wisdom to think for yourself and the courage to live what you believe.

Most people don't give much thought to wisdom or philosophy. They simply go through life working, paying bills, and entertaining themselves. Whether their actions are right or wrong rarely crosses their minds; their attention is on what they consider to be best for them personally. That is why you should be very careful in trusting others.

Refuse to live your life in that way. Seek to perfect your character and let others live as they will. You must concern yourself with *your life* and the things that you can control. You have no control over how anyone else lives, and if they are not hurting others, it is none of your business. Keep your focus on working to perfect your own character and live with honor and integrity.

37

The happiness of your life depends upon the quality of your thoughts.
Marcus Aurelius

There are many books on the market about happiness. People think that happiness is something that they must achieve or search for outside of themselves, but that is wrong thinking. Happiness does not come from anyone or anything external, but from your own thoughts, perceptions, and mindset.

Marcus Aurelius was absolutely right; the happiness of your life depends on the quality of your thoughts. You don't have to search for happiness; all you must do is adjust your mindset. What makes you unhappy is allowing external events, which you have no control over, to negatively influence your thoughts. If you learn to cultivate a Stoic mindset that is rational instead of emotional, you can maintain your inner peace and happiness no matter what is happening around you. I discuss this in detail in my award-winning book, *The Art of Inner Peace*.

How you perceive the things in your life determines your thoughts, and your thoughts determine your happiness. You must learn to control your thoughts instead of allowing other people, external events, and circumstances to control your thoughts and emotions. If your happiness depends on something external, it will be impossible to maintain your happiness or inner peace, because there will always be some person, event, or situation that will disrupt your tranquility and "cause" you to be unhappy or stressed.

However, if your happiness comes from within and you have mentally detached your happiness from external events, nothing can make you unhappy or disrupt your inner peace. It all boils down to your thoughts. If you determine you will be happy no matter what, your mindset will remain stable, and you will consistently be happy. If you allow external things to control your attitude, your happiness will ebb and flow like the waves of the ocean.

So, if you want to be continuously happy, calm, and at peace, you must practice controlling your thoughts. Happiness is a choice. Once you learn to maintain control of your mind, happiness will be your way of life.

TEMPERANCE · JUSTICE · COURAGE · WISDOM

38

Freedom is the only worthy goal in life. It is won
by disregarding things that lie beyond our control.
Epictetus

As a Roman slave, Epictetus' physical freedom was controlled by his master; yet he considered himself to be free. This seems strange until you understand the Stoic philosophy of true freedom. For Epictetus, freedom had nothing to do with his external circumstances. True freedom is freedom from the external things that enslave the mind—fears, desires, and the emotional control of things outside of our control.

The Stoics taught that true freedom is freedom of the mind. Human suffering comes from attempts to control things that are outside our control. We have no control over other people's actions, external events, external circumstances, and the outcome of our actions. The only things we truly control are our own thoughts, speech, actions, attitudes, and responses.

Freedom comes from focusing on those things that are within our control and letting go of, or accepting, everything else. By doing this, we achieve a state of internal and emotional freedom from everything outside of our sphere of control. Therefore, we must simply observe and accept what is outside of our control, and control those things within our control, in order to achieve true freedom.

If nothing outside of your control can disturb your mind or your inner peace, then you are truly free. Nobody has any control over you. This may seem to some to be a selfish state of mind. After all, if we refuse to allow anything outside of our control to negatively affect us, can we still be empathetic towards the struggles of others? Of course we can!

We can feel for others without allowing their pain to affect our overall mindset. The way to do this is through acceptance. Consider the Serenity Prayer—God grant me the serenity to accept the things I cannot change, the courage to change the things I can, and the wisdom to know the difference. The Serenity Prayer could be seen as the motto for Stoicism.

39

Life is very short and anxious for those who forget the past,
neglect the present, and fear the future.
Seneca

The only time we really have to live our life is today, this present moment. The past no longer exists, and the future has not arrived yet, and is guaranteed to no one. That said, we can make our lives seem shorter and less enjoyable if we do not use our time wisely.

Although the past is gone, we can still benefit from it through the lessons and experience we gained. When it comes to the past, we have three options: forget about it, dwell on regrets, or learn from it and enjoy our good memories. If we forget about the past, we lose all the wisdom and lessons that we have learned from it.

If we dwell on all the things that we regret, we not only waste time, but we are beating ourselves up over and over again for something that has already happened and which we cannot control or change. What we should do is learn from the past and enjoy the wonderful memories of good times, friends, and loved ones. Refuse to live with regrets or sorrow!

When it comes to the future, we only have two choices: we can worry and be anxious about what may happen, or we can prepare ourselves for the future, expecting the best out of life. The future does not exist yet; all we can do is plan for it, expect the best, and accept and respond to whatever comes our way.

What truly matters is the present. If you waste time regretting things from your past or worrying about what may happen in the future, you are truly wasting your life, because NOW, this present moment, is all you truly have to live your life. Live your life to the fullest in the present moment!

Discipline your mind to focus on and be happy in the present moment, welcoming whatever may come your way. Be grateful for your life and whatever it offers! Whether this moment offers something enjoyable or challenging, it is simply life; accept it as it comes to you, and do so with a happy, grateful, and peaceful heart.

40

It is not the things themselves that disturb people,
but their judgments about these things.
Epictetus

This piece of wisdom from Epictetus can be extremely hard for some people to grasp and is one of the basic tenets of Stoicism. It is hard for people to understand if they are not educated in the philosophy of Stoicism because they cannot fathom the fact that one can experience a very negative, heart-breaking event and not be sad or disturbed by it. But to the mind of the Stoic, whether an event is positive or negative doesn't matter, because it is an external event, and external events or circumstances do not affect the Stoic mindset.

The Stoic's mind focuses on the things that he can control, while cheerfully accepting the things that are outside of his control. This is what Epictetus meant when he wrote, it is not the things that disturb people, but how they perceive those things. Once you have disciplined your mind to the point where things outside of your realm of control cannot disrupt your inner peace, you can finally understand this truism.

Is it hard to get to this point? Absolutely! Almost all of us have spent decades allowing other people, external events, and circumstances to control our emotions. So, we have developed very strong habits when it comes to our judgment of external things, and habits developed over such a long period of time are very hard to break. But those habits can be broken and replaced with ongoing happiness and inner peace if we discipline our minds.

For example, the death of a loved one is one of the hardest events for us to accept with a cheerful heart. After all, we just lost someone very dear to us; how could we even think about being happy at such a time? The answer goes back to your perspective. You can be sad thinking about how you will never see that person again and how much you miss him or her, or you can be happy that you got to spend time with that person and only remember the good times you enjoyed together. It all depends on your perspective. When you change your perspective, you change your mindset and maintain your inner peace.

41

Thought is the fountain of speech.
Chrysippus

Although we often hear the phrase, "I didn't think before I said that," it is not truly accurate. What we say always starts with what we think, even if we don't give what we say much thought. When you say something like, "I didn't think before I said that," you generally mean that you didn't give it any deep, rational thought; you just voiced your opinion without thinking rationally.

What we say and what we do always begins with our thoughts. Our speech is a manifestation of our mental processes. The quality and wisdom of our words reflect the nature of our thoughts. Rational thinking leads to rational speech; angry thoughts lead to angry, hateful speech. That is one reason it is vitally important to cultivate rational, honorable thoughts. Since our words are so powerful, it is vital that we ensure our thoughts are those that originate from honor and integrity.

Our words are a window into our minds. If someone speaks harshly, you know that the prominent type of thoughts he has are harsh, angry, or resentful. If someone speaks in a very caring and loving way, you know that the majority of his thoughts are kind, loving, and happy.

It is important that we control our thoughts, not just because they are the foundation of our speech, but also because our thoughts are very powerful. If you remember, the thoughts you think, your perspectives, decide your view of the world and control your happiness and inner peace. If you have a Stoic perspective, you will be able to calmly handle most everything that you experience in life. But if you have a negative perspective, your happiness and inner peace will rise and fall as if you are riding a roller coaster.

In my book, *The Art of Inner Peace*, I discuss how important it is to reprogram your subconscious mind to control your thoughts. Around 95% of your thoughts, actions, and decisions are controlled by the subconscious mind. To make lasting changes to your mindset and speech, you must first do some reprogramming of your subconscious mind.

Manliness gains much strength by being challenged.
Seneca

The German philosopher Friedrich Nietzsche stated, "What does not kill me makes me stronger." That is basically what Seneca meant by manliness gains much strength by being challenged. When you overcome challenges and adversity, you become stronger, and your self-confidence increases.

Things in our public schools have changed, and not for the better. When I was in school, boys used to challenge each other regularly. There were fights quite often, but not like the fights we see on the news today. Back then, two boys would get in a fistfight over some issue, wind up with a bloody nose or bloody lip, and be back to being buddies the next day. This was part of growing up and learning to defend yourself. Today, if something like that happens at school, the inept school administrators would call the police, expel the boys, and put a permanent black mark on their school records.

Men need to be challenged and learn to deal with adversity; that is the way masculine virtues are formed, and self-confidence is developed. Today, there is a war on masculinity in our culture. It is much harder for boys to become masculine men today or to develop masculine virtues such as courage, honor, self-defense, etc. But that is a whole different topic.

The point is, adversity is not something to be feared or avoided, but something to be welcomed as a challenge to overcome. Overcoming adversity builds your self-confidence and self-esteem; it builds your inner strength and spirit. True character and courage are fortified by facing adversity, just as your muscles are strengthened through weight training.

It is through confronting and overcoming obstacles that men prove their mettle and grow stronger. The same goes for moral development. Many challenges require men to make tough decisions concerning moral choices and to stand firmly on what they believe is right. If your moral code is never challenged, how do you know whether you truly have integrity? Stand strong for what is right, no matter what adversity you face!

43

You can commit injustice by doing nothing.
Marcus Aurelius

When it comes to being just and doing the right thing, you can absolutely commit injustice by doing nothing. Cowardly people do this all the time. There are video after video where some elderly guy or some woman is being attacked or mugged on the street, and people just walk by, or stand there and video the whole thing, without lifting a finger to help the helpless victim. This is not only injustice, but cowardice and disgraceful!

It is not merely your words and actions that can be dishonorable and unjust, but your silence and lack of action as well. You must do your best to do what is right; this includes being a warrior when needed. Only a pathetic coward would stand by while someone is being abused or attacked and take no action. That is not the way of the Stoic mindset.

While it is true that you have no control over other people, you do have control over your own actions or lack of action. Not taking action when justice requires you to act is as wrong as committing injustice through your actions. Not speaking up against those who abuse or hurt others is also committing an injustice, not to mention cowardice.

Courage is one of the traits that the Stoics taught us to foster in our lives. If you look at the top of this page, courage is one of the Stoic traits that is printed on every single page of this book. Without courage, you are not living with a Stoic mindset; you are living the life of a coward!

You must ensure that you have the courage to stand up for what is right and to help others when you can. Never allow fear or a lack of empathy to control your mind or your actions. Act when honor requires you to act; speak when justice requires you to speak! C.S. Lewis wrote, "Every time you make a choice, you are turning the central part of you, the part of you that chooses, into something a little different than it was before." Every thought, every word, and every action matters. Bring everything you think, say, or do in line with the person you want to be!

44

It does not matter what you bear, but how you bear it.
Seneca

The Stoics taught that since you cannot control external events or circumstances, you should not only bear what is necessary, but you should love it as a part of your life. A little over a decade ago, I was having issues with my elbows from years of martial arts and weight training, and the doctor wanted to try PRP shots to heal them. I received dozens of extremely painful shots in each elbow during the process.

It was the most painful thing I have ever experienced, and I had to do this process six times. The pain was so intense that I threw up and then almost passed out. It was bad! But I went back to have it done five more times. During the second round, the doctor said, "You are more stoic today, Bohdi. Most people don't want to come back after the first time because it is so painful. It is okay to yell or curse; it is proven that cursing helps with the pain." But I remained silent, except when I asked for a break. I was not going to allow the pain to defeat me. After all, I made the decision to go in and have this procedure done; I was not going to allow it to get the best of me.

One way I deal with a painful procedure like that is to remember all the warriors of the past and the pain they had to endure with the archaic medical procedures of the day. They endured what they had to bear because they had no other choice, and we can also stoically bear what is necessary.

We all must deal with unwanted pain, deaths of loved ones, and negative events and circumstances during our lives. These things aren't unique to you or to me. Nobody wants to deal with these things, but these are some of those external things that are not in our realm of control.

Since we have no choice about whether we must deal with these painful events and circumstances, why not bear them stoically? Complaining and whining about them changes nothing but how others see you. Warrior up and bear what must be endured and do it stoically! Remain calm and stoic and let others see the Stoic character you have cultivated.

44

45

The more we value things outside our control,
the less control we have.
Epictetus

We already know that the Stoics urged us to stay focused on the things that we can control—our thoughts, words, actions, responses, behavior, attitude, choices, mood, and emotions. That said, there are a lot of things in our world that we have little to no control over. When we put too much value on the things that are outside our control, we have less control over our lives.

For example, if you put a lot of value on your popularity, something which you have very little control over, you have less control over your life. Your mood and emotions will fluctuate between feeling great about things and feeling down and depressed when your popularity wanes. Instead of spending your time controlling what you can control, you are continually trying to win the approval of other people, something you have little control over.

In doing this, you are giving other people more control over your life. When you give anything outside yourself control over your life, you will obviously have less control of your life yourself. Instead of working to improve your character and your life, you would waste time in a vain attempt to impress others, which really doesn't matter.

If you think about it, the more you value anything outside of your circle of control, the harder it becomes for you to control certain areas of your life. If you place too much value on politics, you lose a portion of your inner peace to stress and worry. When you place too much value on how others see you, you lose a portion of your self-confidence and self-esteem.

Everything in life has a price. When you place too much value on external things, you give away a portion of your control and inner peace. On the other hand, if you consistently value those things that are in your circle of control more than you value external things which you can't control, what other people think, say, or do won't affect you very much. Control what you can, accept what you must, and live your life your way!

46

What we do now echoes in eternity.
Marcus Aurelius

Your present actions have long-lasting consequences. Marcus Aurelius' own actions prove this to be true. When he sat down and wrote his thoughts and reflections, even in his wildest dreams, he would not have thought that his writings would be read by people almost 2,000 years later. But his writings have influenced people's lives for centuries.

What you do now will shape your legacy for years to come. Even after you're gone, your children and your children's children will remember you for your words, actions, and character. And some people, like Marcus Aurelius, will be remembered for centuries for their actions during their lifetimes.

The choices you make today have a ripple effect on those around you. Things you take for granted may mean more to others than you realize. Whether or not you believe it, people listen to what you say. They watch what you do, how you respond, and how you carry yourself.

While your reputation is something that you don't completely control, you can control your part of your reputation by conducting yourself as you should with honor and integrity. Leaving a good name for your children is something that most people don't consider in today's culture, but it is important. Your actions and behavior are more important than you might think.

Decide what kind of person you want to be and then conduct yourself in that manner. Even small virtuous actions can have a big effect on other people, people you may not even know. As a writer, I have received emails from people all over the world telling me how much my books and my philosophy have changed their lives.

And by changing one person's life for the better, you may be affecting all the people in that person's life as well. You never know just how far the ripple effect of your actions may travel. This is true for both your good and bad actions; so, make sure your thoughts, words, and actions are honorable and virtuous.

47

The wise man sees in the misfortune of others what he should avoid.

Seneca

There are three ways that you can learn what things you should avoid doing in life. You can read and study good wisdom literature and integrate what you learn into your life. You can learn through negative feedback, which is learning through personal experience. Or you can learn by observing others when they make mistakes, thus avoiding the painful consequences of making those same mistakes yourself.

A wise man will learn through his own studies and from observing the misfortunes of others. Learning by experience can have some harsh consequences that a wise man wants to avoid. As the old saying goes, "Experience is a hard teacher because it gives the test first, then the lesson afterwards."

Learning by observing the misfortune of others is like getting a copy of the test before the test is given. It is much easier to pass a test if you are familiar with the test beforehand. You can learn something from everyone; in this case, you would be learning what *not* to do because of the negative consequences that someone else has experienced.

A wise man will learn something from everyone. Now, you might be thinking that this is not true; after all, what can I learn from a homeless wino? Think about it. You can learn that if you don't manage your life and your finances, that could be you one day. Or if you allow something external to control your life, such as drugs or alcohol, you are playing with fire; they can destroy your life.

When you meet or observe someone, think about what you can learn from that person. What information does he have that could help you or improve your knowledge or your life? Some people will teach you things about yourself or how you should live; others will teach you important lessons about things you don't want to do or how you don't want to be. Either way, you can learn something valuable from them if you observe them and listen carefully.

48

Growing old is not so bad when you consider what the alternative is.
Cato the Younger

If you spend much time around elderly people, you will most likely hear them complain about the effects of growing older. You will hear them talk about regretting things they did or did not do when they were younger, or how this or that body part aches. But Cato the Younger gives you the perfect response to those complaints—growing old is better than the alternative.

When it comes to this life, you only have two choices: growing older or dying. If you don't die, then you are growing older every single day. Consider your body as a machine. How it functions depends a great deal on how well you take care of it, and give it high-quality food, water, rest, sleep, and exercise. But no matter how well you take care of your machine, someday it will wear out because the process of living puts wear and tear on your body, just like the process of driving a car puts wear and tear on the car's engine or other parts.

When you buy a new car, everything about it is fresh and works great; but after years of use, different parts wear out and must be replaced to keep the car running. This same principle applies to the human body; it grows old, and certain parts don't work as well as when they were newer.

To continue with my car analogy, ask yourself, "Would you rather have an old car that gets you where you want to go, even though it may not run as smoothly as it once did? Or would you rather not have a car at all?"

This is what you should consider as you grow older. Yes, you are most likely going to have more aches and pains, and some parts that don't work as well as they used to, but isn't that better than being dead and missing the things that life has to offer? Life is a blessing! There are so many amazing things to see, to learn, and to experience. Be grateful for every day that you get to experience more of this life. There are many people who were not as blessed as you, who would have loved to live to see old age, to have seen and experienced what you have. Accept the pain of growing older as the price for living a long life.

49

Don't explain your philosophy. Embody it.
Epictetus

When it comes to philosophy, whether it is Stoic philosophy or any other philosophy, there are two kinds of people—those who live their philosophy and those who just like to talk about their philosophy. Epictetus urges us to embody our philosophy instead of explaining it or debating it. Walk the walk, don't just talk the talk.

There are many people who love to debate and argue about different philosophies, and which is best, but they never seem to integrate the philosophy into their daily lives. Talking about your philosophy, or explaining your philosophy, does you little good; you must actually *live* your philosophy for it to benefit your life.

If you want Stoicism to improve your life, you must put it to work in your life. Simply explaining your philosophy, or talking about your philosophy, is like wanting to go swimming, so you go to the pool, but instead of getting in the water, you just sit by it and talk about how nice it is.

Anyone can sit and talk about Stoicism; it doesn't take much knowledge or effort to discuss something. But unless you are willing to put in the effort to live by Stoic principles, they are useless to you. Furthermore, when you only sit and explain your philosophy, you are not living a Stoic lifestyle. You are not controlling those things in your world that you can control. In a way, you are attempting to control or convince others to think like you, which is something that is outside of your realm of control.

Don't explain or debate your philosophy with others; live your philosophy! What others believe or think is none of your business. Of course, if someone comes to you and asks you to tell them about Stoicism, that is different. But other than that, focus on controlling your own thoughts and life, not on trying to convince others to believe as you do. Everyone has their own life to live, and it is not up to anyone else to tell them how to live. If they ask for advice, share your knowledge with them, but focus on your own life!

50

If we were to measure what is good by how much
pleasure it brings, nothing would be better than self-control.
If we were to measure what is to be avoided by its pain,
nothing would be more painful than a lack of self-control.
Musonius Rufus

There is a deep connection between self-control and virtue. Self-control enables us to avoid impulsive actions and harmful desires, which could cause us problems. A lack of self-control has destroyed many lives. Just think about how many people are in prison today because they acted on impulse or uncontrolled emotions instead of thinking rationally about their situation. That is an example of a lack of self-control.

It only takes a single moment of allowing your emotions to control your actions, instead of pausing and thinking rationally, to destroy your life. Once you allow yourself to act on impulse instead of rationally controlling your actions, you could be setting yourself up for a lifetime of pain and regret. If you look at it like that, a lack of self-control is truly something that can cause you tremendous pain.

Self-control enables you to avoid such grief and will lead to a more fulfilling life that is filled with happiness and inner peace. You will also find that the pleasure you get from mastering your life through self-control will be more enduring than some external pleasure or action that is short-lived and may lead to years of regret.

A lack of self-control cultivates a life full of emotional and psychological turmoil, whereas a life based on self-control and wisdom leads to satisfaction and inner peace. It is impossible to live with a Stoic mindset if you lack self-control. Every part of the Stoic mindset depends on your self-control. Self-control brings about a higher form of pleasure, that of inner peace and contentment; but a lack of self-control leads to an erratic life of uncontrolled desires and actions, ultimately leading to regret and pain. The Stoic mindset is one of continual self-control.

51

Do not let the force of the thought, when first it hits you, knock
you off your feet; just say to it, "Hold on a moment; let me see who
you are and what you represent. Let me put you to the test." Oppose it
with some good and honorable thought and put the dirty one to defeat.
Epictetus

You have no control over what thoughts pop into your mind, but you do
have control over which thoughts you entertain or allow to remain there. The
thoughts that appear in your mind depend on many factors, such as your mood,
your emotions, your physical activity, and what you are feeding your mind
through your senses.

The average person has over 6,000 thoughts per day. Obviously, many of
these thoughts will not be thoughts you want to foster or dwell on. You must
be selective when it comes to which thoughts you allow yourself to meditate
on and to remain in your mind. This is one reason you should be watchful
concerning what you feed your mind.

It is very easy to become distracted by angry, hateful, resentful, or
inappropriate thoughts, and before you know it, you have allowed those
thoughts to take root in your mind. As Buddha taught, "The mind is everything.
What you think, you become."

This means that you can control what you become or what you experience
in your life by controlling your thoughts. Epictetus taught that you must not
let an inappropriate thought unbalance you. When a negative or inappropriate
thought appears in your mind, ask yourself, "Is this thought moving closer to
my goals or further away?" If it is not the kind of thought that you want to
dwell on, mentally replace it with a positive thought.

This is not hard to do, if you catch the negative thought as soon as it appears
in your mind. Simply say to yourself, "No, I refuse to think that," and then
replace that thought with a more constructive thought. This takes some
practice, but you can control the thoughts you allow to take root in your mind
if you are consistently mindful of your thoughts.

52

Choose not to be harmed—and you won't feel harmed.
Don't feel harmed—and you haven't been.
Marcus Aurelius

This passage by Marcus Aurelius is another way of saying that your perception and responses to external events determine the meaning that those events have in your life. For example, if you are returning something to the store, and that customer service rep is rude to you, you can see that in two ways. You can choose to ignore it and not allow it to upset you, or you can allow it to irritate you and put you in a bad mood.

If you choose to overlook the employee's rude behavior and just go on with your day, you are choosing not to allow that person to affect you. "If you choose not to be harmed, you won't feel harmed; and if you don't feel harmed, you haven't been." It all depends on your perception and how you perceive that person's behavior.

Many people *decide* to be offended by the behavior of others, become irritated and upset, snap back, and remain upset for hours. This is because they *choose* to feel harmed, disrespected, or offended. They are allowing the actions of someone else, who they do not control, to upset them, instead of just writing it off as someone who is having a bad day. This is a good example of allowing something or someone outside of your circle of control to control your mood and your actions.

How you perceive someone's rude behavior doesn't change what he said or did; his words and actions are now in the past. But how you choose to perceive his words or actions affects you. Just choose to focus on responding in a positive way and don't allow things outside of your control to affect you. That will make your day more productive and peaceful.

When you learn to control your mind, and how you perceive things outside of your control, you will have more control over your life and more inner peace. Never allow the words or actions of someone else to control your mood or disrupt your inner peace.

53

While we wait for life, life passes.
Seneca

This is a deception that affects many people's lives. You only have a short time to live on this earth. Every minute not used is a minute that never returns; it is wasted and gone forever. If each of us had a large hourglass and each grain of sand in that hourglass represented one minute of our life, we could comprehend just how fast our life passes. You would see exactly what it means to waste time.

In addition, unlike the hourglass, you can't simply turn it upside down and start over again. Once those minutes, hours, or days are gone, they are gone forever. Time continues to pass whether you use it wisely or waste it, and it never slows down to let you catch your breath.

Many people put off living their life fully until they have more money, the kids are older, or they retire. They are waiting for their life to start, while it continues to pass them by. They have all these plans about how great their life will be *someday*, but someday never seems to arrive. Someday is always in the future; meanwhile, every day continues to pass by barely noticed.

While they make plans for someday, they fail to realize that the only time that truly exists is today, this present moment. While they plan and wait for their life, it is passing them by daily, unappreciated and wasted. This happens to everyone at one time or another because it is so easy to forget this fact.

That is why it is a good practice to be grateful to God every morning when you wake up, and not to waste time being angry, resentful, upset, or allowing external things to control your mental state. Refuse to allow anything or anybody to control your life!

You only have one life to live, one chance to experience all this amazing planet offers. Don't waste it! Live the life you want to live now. You will always be able to find some excuse or reason that you must wait until this or that happens; but that is exactly what Seneca is saying. While you wait for life, your life is passing you by. Live your life every day!

54

We should always be asking ourselves:
"Is this something that is, or is not, in my control?"
Epictetus

This small piece of wisdom from Epictetus is a great practice if you want to live with a Stoic mindset. One of the fundamental Stoic principles is to control the things within your realm of control, and to accept the things over which you have no control. By asking yourself, "Is this something that is, or is not, in my control?" you keep this principle fresh in your mind.

What is under your control? Your own thoughts, speech, actions, perceptions, and responses. What is not under your control? Everything else—external events, what others think, say, or do, circumstances around the world, and the outcome of your actions.

By continually asking yourself whether something is under your control, you are reminding yourself not to allow anything that is not in your control to disrupt your inner peace. This helps you to develop habits that will free you from unnecessary stress or worry. If something is not under your control, don't waste time trying to control it or being upset about it.

This practice leads to a calm tranquility because you develop the habit of testing whether something is in your control, and if it isn't, you simply breathe in, breathe out, and move on, refusing to allow it to aggravate you or disrupt your inner peace.

Moreover, this practice is not just for physical events or situations. You must evaluate your thoughts as well because our thoughts tend to dwell on worries about the future or on regrets of the past. When you find yourself in the grips of fear or anxiety, ask yourself if what you are worried about is something you can control. If it isn't, then stop worrying about it!

You must develop the mindset of refusing to worry about things that are out of your control. Refuse to allow fear to dwell in your mind! You must replace negative thoughts with calm, rational thoughts. Develop the habit of refusing to be stressed or upset with anything outside of your realm of control.

55

The man who tries to find out what has been said against him,
who seeks to unearth spiteful gossip, even when engaged
in privately, is destroying his own peace of mind.
Seneca

This passage from Seneca will hit home for many people and continues with my teachings on the previous page. Most people gossip and talk about other people; many even do so maliciously. But whether it is malicious gossip or just bored busybodies, all gossip has one thing in common—it is outside of your circle of control.

We all have a natural curiosity concerning what other people say about us or what others think of us. The older you get, the less you care about this, but all of us have experienced this at one time or another. The Stoic mindset has the perfect remedy for not allowing gossip to "make" you angry, resentful, or upset—refuse to allow *anything* that is not in your control to bother you or to disrupt your inner peace.

When someone finds out that others have been talking about him or her, it is natural to want to know what was said, and, up to a point, it can be useful in protecting ourselves from fake friends, unknown enemies, etc. But few people can listen to what others say against them without allowing it to disrupt their inner peace or "make" them angry or resentful.

This is what Seneca meant in this passage. If you are actively trying to find out what negative things other people are saying about you, be prepared to have the calm tranquility of your mind challenged. It takes someone who is advanced in living with a Stoic mindset to hear negative, spiteful gossip about him without allowing it to disrupt his inner peace.

Once again, you must ask yourself whether what others think or say is something that you can control. The answer, of course, is "no." You have no control over what anyone else thinks or says about you, or about anything else, as far as that goes. Unless you have a specific, strategic purpose in finding out what is being said about you, you are simply disrupting your own inner peace.

56

Never let the future disturb you. You will meet it, if you have to, with the same weapons of reason which today arm you against the present.
Marcus Aurelius

If you are allowing thoughts of the future to disturb your inner peace, you are engaged in worrying about things that you can't control. While you can prepare yourself to successfully meet future challenges, you can't control future events or circumstances. If you have no control over the future, don't allow it to disturb your inner peace; just trust in your own ability to manage the future just as you have handled every other day in your life.

What are the weapons that Marcus Aurelius is referring to in this quote? They are rational thought, logic, emotional control, wisdom, and knowledge. And it is these same weapons that have enabled you to deal with everything that has happened in your life. Why, then, would you worry that these same weapons would not be enough to successfully deal with the future?

Instead of worrying about what may or may not happen in the future, have confidence in your own ability to rationally respond to whatever happens. While it is okay to have concerns over what may happen, and to rationally prepare yourself the best you can, it is never wise to worry about the future. Worry has never made any situation better and never will.

Worry is simply allowing your mind to dwell on difficulties or trouble. It is giving up rational thought and allowing anxiety and fear to control your mind. Where rational thought and wise preparation prepare us for future events, worry is worse than useless. Worry not only does nothing to help you prepare for the future or maintain your inner peace, but it robs you of your precious time in the present moment.

When you really take the time to think rationally about worry, you will refuse to allow it to dwell in your mind ever again. Not only does worry rob you of your tranquility in the now, but it cultivates stress, irrational fear, and uses your imagination against you. Whenever you find yourself worrying about something, ask yourself if it is something you can control.

57

Life, if well lived, is long enough.
Seneca

This quote from Seneca is another way of saying that it is the quality of life, not the quantity, which matters. A well-lived life is a good life whether it is 30 years long or one hundred years long; just as a wasted life is a wasted life, no matter how long it is. So, what is a well-lived life?

A well-lived life is a life filled with purpose, virtue, wisdom, happiness, and inner peace. If you stop and think about it, all of those are things that are absolutely in your control. Your purpose in life comes from within you, just like your happiness and inner peace. You decide what your purpose is, and your mindset controls your happiness and inner peace. Wisdom and virtue come to those who actively seek them, and you control what you seek.

Seneca felt that those who chase wealth or material things are wasting their lives and allowing distractions and trivial things to disrupt their inner peace. Those people are constantly stressed and seem to feel as though they never have enough time. Of course, we all need a certain amount of money and material things, but that shouldn't be our sole focus in life.

Instead of stressing over material things, spend more time focusing on your personal growth, meaningful relationships, and ensuring that your own thoughts, words, and actions are wise and virtuous. When you live your life in such a way, you realize that the key to feeling that life is long enough is living fully in every present moment.

If you live fully in the now, making the most of every moment and aligning your life with honor, integrity, and other higher character traits, you are living a full life, no matter how long your life is. You determine how you live, but you have very little control over when you die.

Yes, you can live a healthy lifestyle, exercise, and maintain a positive outlook on life, but there are many unforeseen events and circumstances that you don't control. Live fully, and you will live long enough. Don't concern yourself with how long you live, but with *how* you live.

58

The wise man considers in silence whatever anyone says.
Cato the Younger

Many people voice their opinions about everything under the sun, and most of them do so without ever giving any rational thought to what is being said or to the subject at hand. It is unwise to speak without thinking; doing so can cause you many unforeseen problems, as well as having a negative effect on how others see you.

Cato the Younger emphasized the importance of considering what other people are saying. This takes wisdom and self-control. Most people will immediately give their opinion without stopping to think about what is being said or why it is being said. If you react emotionally or impulsively to what is being said, you are not taking the time to strategically consider what is being said and why.

Don't allow your mindset or speech to be controlled impulsively by your emotions. Discipline yourself to rationally consider what is being said. Don't jump to conclusions or engage in meaningless debates. Take the time to think about what is being said, even if you must save your response for a later time. There is no shame in taking time to think about what has been said.

Be restrained in your conversations; value listening over speaking. Not only does this keep you from speaking without thinking, but it allows you to better understand what the other person is trying to say. No matter what the other person is saying, maintain your calm composure. Don't give the other person control over your emotions or your responses.

Remaining rational, deliberate, and restrained in your conversations enables you to gain information, to clearly understand what is being said, and to avoid misunderstandings. This allows you to think rationally about what is being said and why, and to respond wisely, if you decide to respond at all. Remember, you are not required to respond to everything that somebody says. You don't have to have an opinion about everything, nor do you have to join every conversation. Silence is golden!

59

It is not death that a man should fear,
but he should fear never beginning to live.
Marcus Aurelius

If you enjoy warrior movies, like I do, this quote from Marcus Aurelius may sound familiar. In the movie Braveheart, Mel Gibson's character, the Scottish hero, William Wallace, makes the comment, "Every man dies, not every man really lives." That is just another way of saying what Marcus Aurelius said many centuries earlier.

As you study wisdom literature or self-help authors, you will find that much of the wisdom contained in these books has been taught by the Stoics or the sages of the past. Then, over the years, that wisdom gets attributed to the modern author instead of the person who originally taught it. But for our purposes, who originally taught a concept is not as important as the concept itself. I am more interested in integrating the actual wisdom into my life than in arguing about who said what.

Marcus Aurelius was trying to teach people to stop fearing death and to fear that we are not truly living our lives to the fullest. It is a waste of time to worry about, or fear, death. Death comes to every individual and every living thing; it's simply a part of life.

The wise person will not fear death, but rather, will fear wasting the short time he or she has on this earth. When you have this attitude, you strive every day to live your life to the fullest. Some fears are useful, and this is one of them. When you catch yourself wasting time in some meaningless way, remember this fear and remind yourself that you are wasting precious time.

Refuse to waste time, for time is what your life is made of; when you waste time, you are wasting a portion of your life. Remind yourself of this truism every day and start living your life to the fullest. Make it your goal in life to live your life to the fullest, to experience as much as you can during your short time on earth. You will be glad you did!

60

*Humanity is the quality which stops one from
being arrogant towards one's fellows or being spiteful.*
Seneca

Humanity is the condition of being human. True humanity involves a deep sense of empathy, humility, and a recognition that we all share the same desires, pains, feelings, urges, etc. We all have the same basic needs in life. Maslow's Hierarchy arranges human needs from the most essential to the least essential.

He stated that we all have specific needs.

1) Physiological needs such as air, water, food, shelter, clothing, sleep, and the urge to reproduce.
2) Safety and security needs such as personal security, financial security, health and well-being, and safety nets against illnesses and emergencies.
3) Social and belonging needs such as love, friendship, family bonds, and a sense of belonging with a community or group.
4) Esteem needs such as self-esteem, recognition and respect, status, and prestige.
5) Self-actualization needs such as pursuing personal goals, realizing your potential, creativity and self-expression, and self-improvement.

Seneca taught us we should be compassionate and humble towards others; he urged us not to view ourselves as superior. When you view yourself as superior to others, it creates a gulf and a lack of connection between yourself and the other person. This lack of connection will lead to a disregard for others' feelings and perspectives.

He also mentioned that your humanity will stop you from being spiteful to other people. Spitefulness is a form of malice often rooted in bitterness or envy and can even drive us to want to harm the other person in some way. Seneca urged us to treat other people with the same respect and understanding we would want from them. Stay grounded in your humanity.

61

> You should be especially careful when associating with
> one of your former friends or acquaintances, not to sink
> to their level; otherwise, you will lose yourself.
> *Epictetus*

Once you begin to make changes in your life, it is not uncommon for your friends, or former friends, not to understand what is going on with you. Some friends will want you to stay the same way you have always been because they don't want you to change your life, which may distance you from them.

For example, if you are used to going out drinking and partying every weekend, but start to see the emptiness of this way of life, and want to change your life for the better, many of your friends will continue to try to get you to fall back into your old lifestyle. It is not that they don't want you to improve yourself, but rather, they don't want their own lifestyle to change. They want their friends to continue partying with them every weekend and to keep them company.

A common example of this is when one guy in the group develops a serious relationship with a girl. He then spends more and more time with his new girlfriend, and less with his buddies. His goals and desires change, and he is no longer that interested in going out partying with the guys. His life changes significantly, but his friends are still living the same empty lives.

On the occasions when he spends time with his friends, they will continue to try to get him to party with them like he used to, even though he is no longer interested in this kind of lifestyle. If he is not careful, they will convince him to go out with them, and he will gradually slip back into his old ways, causing himself issues in his relationship and with his new lifestyle.

Epictetus advises us not to sink to the level of others, but to continue striving to live with a Stoic mindset. Many people won't understand your new mindset and may try to get you to give up on your new life. You must have the courage and discipline to refuse to sink to their level, or you will lose yourself. A divided house can't stand; you must stand strong in your convictions!

62

You will earn the respect of all if you
begin by earning the respect of yourself.
Musonius Rufus

Musonius Rufus is stressing the importance of self-respect as the foundation of earning respect from those around you. You will never earn the respect of everyone; there will always be those with different values who have no respect for anyone or anything. But you will earn the respect of those who are living a good life by first developing genuine self-respect for yourself.

Developing true self-respect involves living in alignment with your own values and code of honor, having self-discipline, and living with integrity. Basically, when you develop and live by your own code of ethics, or code of honor, self-respect is the result. You are taking charge of your life and living your life your way, with honor, integrity, courage, and discipline. Any man who lives this way will develop a high level of self-respect.

Once you have mastered your code of honor, you will act in ways that demonstrate honor, integrity, and moral strength. And have no doubt about it, others will notice your behavior, and it will inspire admiration and respect from them. Once this happens, you will find that people trust you and have faith in what you say. If someone says derogatory things about you, those who know you will not believe them, because they see how you live your life.

External respect naturally follows internal respect. When you respect yourself, you act differently. You project confidence and authenticity in your actions, and others see this. Your self-respect inspires a calm confidence in everything you do. You won't be losing your temper or allowing yourself to be overtaken with anger or malice.

This is a large part of the Stoic mindset. The Stoic mindset emphasizes the importance of your inner character over seeking the approval of others. If you focus on living a life of honor, character, and integrity, you will maintain your self-respect, and you will find that the respect of other people will naturally follow. When you truly respect yourself, others will respect you as well.

63

So, what oppresses and scares us? It is our own thoughts, obviously.
What overwhelms people when they are about to leave friends,
family, old haunts, and their accustomed way of life? THOUGHTS!
Epictetus

Epictetus taught that everything begins with our thoughts. It is our thoughts that oppress us; it is our thoughts that scare us. It is our thoughts that overwhelm us. Everything in your life begins with your thoughts. Once you master your mind, making changes in your life becomes easy.

Let's examine the fear of public speaking as an example. The fear of public speaking is the most common fear today; it is even more common than the fear of dying. This fear is rooted in concerns about being judged, making mistakes, or failing in public, and it can be so strong that it can mentally paralyze someone who must deal with this fear.

The strange thing about this fear is that it completely resides in your mind—your thoughts. Some people have a fear of heights or a fear of snakes. Both of these have to do with the fear of death, which is also a common fear. But nobody has ever died from public speaking; it only has power because your thoughts give it power. It exists solely in your mind.

Remember, your mind is one of the things that you have power over and can change. When the thing that scares you resides solely in your mind, you can absolutely remove that fear, because you control your mind. And this goes for any fears that originate solely in your mind.

Those who have a fear of public speaking simply must reprogram and change the thoughts they have about public speaking. It is only your negative thoughts and lack of self-confidence that make you scared to speak in public. So, change your thoughts! Convince yourself that speaking in public is no different from speaking to your friends. Speaking is simply communicating with others in a way that they can understand your thoughts. The more you realize this, the more your self-confidence grows, and the more your mental fear subsides. When your thoughts are the problem, change your thoughts!

64

There is no evil in things changing, just as there
is no good in persisting in a state of change.
Marcus Aurelius

If there is one thing that is constant on this planet, it is that everything changes. In fact, everything is in a perpetual state of change all the time. Marcus Aurelius is teaching us that change is neither good nor bad; it's simply life. Nothing stays the same, even if you can't see the change. Change is not good or bad; it simply is the way it is.

Change is a fundamental aspect of our universe, and resisting change is futile. When it comes to change, we have two choices: we can gripe and complain about it, or we can calmly accept it and adjust our lives along with it. What we can't do is stop it.

Complaining about change has never stopped anything from changing. It only invites negativity into your life. You can hate change, protest it, complain about it, resist it, but none of that affects it; change is independent of your feelings, wants, or desires. It is outside our realm of control.

Life, nature, and the world around us are in a continuous state of flux. To fight against change is to struggle against nature. It is as futile as trying to resist the constant flow of a river. You can try to stop the flow of a river to the sea, but you will never be successful. All you will accomplish is to frustrate yourself and disrupt your inner peace.

Remember, you will never maintain your inner peace if you are trying to control things that are outside of your control. The key to maintaining your inner peace is to control the things that you *can* control, and to accept those things which are outside of your control.

Marcus Aurelius is saying that we must find balance and acceptance in our lives. We must recognize change for what it is, embrace it with our inner peace intact, and find stability within ourselves, rather than constantly fighting against change. Your outer life is constantly changing; your job is to maintain balance, consistency, peace, and tranquility in your inner life.

65

An angry man opens his mouth and shuts his eyes.
Cato the Younger

Anger can be one of your worst enemies if you don't control it. It may surprise you to learn that anger is one of the things that is in your realm of control. You absolutely *can* control your anger. Some people would argue that they have no control over their anger, that things outside of their control "make" them angry. But this is totally flawed thinking.

External things cannot "make" you angry; you *decide* to be angry. Nobody can make you do anything outside of your own will. External things can present you with temptations and opportunities to be angry, but ultimately, you are the one who decides whether you will allow some external event, circumstance, or somebody's words or actions, to allow anger to enter and exist in your mind. This can be hard for most people to understand.

Remember the things that are within your circle of control. Your thoughts and emotions are definitely within your control; thus, you can decide not to be angry, just as you can decide to be angry. You may be thinking, "I don't decide to be angry; it just happens automatically."

What seems to be automatic is really just happening so quickly that you don't give it any thought; you have allowed your anger to go unchecked so many times that it simply bypasses your conscious thought process. But that doesn't mean that you have no control over your anger. You have allowed anger to go uncontrolled so many times that it has become one of your habits. You must start consciously controlling your anger instead of allowing your anger to control you.

Anger, like any other habit, can be controlled and changed. Cato the Younger is telling us that when you are angry, your anger is in control of your mouth, not your mind. Instead of using your freedom of choice, you are *allowing* anger to take control and speak for you. This can cause you more problems than you think. Break the habit of anger and control what is in your circle of control. Refuse to allow negative habits to control your life!

66

Don't seek for everything to happen as you wish it would,
but rather wish that everything happens as it
actually will—then your life will flow well.
Epictetus

Expectations have a way of disappointing us and making us sad, angry, or disappointed. But there is an easy way to put a stop to the cycle of expecting or hoping for something to happen the way you want it to, then getting disappointed when it doesn't happen that way. All you have to do is stop wishing for things to happen a certain way, and, as Epictetus wrote, wish for everything to happen as it will.

This is a hard piece of wisdom to master! We all have our preferences concerning how we would like our life to go or how we would like the events around us to unfold. But Epictetus tells us that this is one of the causes of unhappiness and that it can disrupt our inner peace.

Think about it. If you have no preference concerning the outcome of the things around you, then you will have no reason to be upset, angry, or disappointed when things don't turn out how you wanted them to. When you have this mindset, you simply respond to what is and make the best of whatever comes your way.

Although this is extremely hard to do, once you adjust your mindset, nothing external, or outside your circle of control, can disrupt your inner peace. You simply determine that you will be calm, happy, and tranquil no matter what. There are always options when things don't go as planned. That is what Epictetus meant by "your life will flow well."

Instead of allowing external things or other people to affect your life, learn to go with the flow and make the best out of every circumstance. Refuse to allow anything outside of your control to affect your mood or your happiness. Remember, happiness comes from within, and nothing and nobody has any control over that but you. Instead of being rigid about everything, learn to be flexible and happy, no matter what comes your way.

67

Death smiles at us all; all we can do is smile back.
Marcus Aurelius

Every living thing on this earth dies at one time or another; that is just a fact of life. None of us in our right mind actively seeks death, but we all know that eventually, at a time undisclosed to us, we will die. It doesn't matter if we are not ready to die or don't want to die; it is not up to us.

One of the foundations of Stoicism is accepting those things that we have no control over, and not simply accepting them, but embracing them. Death is one thing that we do not control. We may have some control over how long we live if we exercise, eat nutritious foods, and avoid things that are detrimental to our health; but even then, we will die someday.

Although we have no control over the fact that we will die, we have complete control over our attitude about dying and whether we accept our death with dignity, honor, and courage. Too many people take pains to protect the reputation up until the time of their death. When death is near, they figure that their reputation no longer matters, but that is faulty thinking. Your reputation continues even after your death in the form of your legacy.

Your legacy is the lasting impact you leave behind after you are gone. It is composed of your actions, values, choices, how you helped others, and the work you created while you were alive. It reflects what you have accomplished during your lifetime and the respect that those who knew you best have for you. Your legacy echoes through the things that mattered the most to you and the impression that you leave on those who knew you or who knew your work.

How you approach and accept death is the final building block of your legacy. It is the last chance you have to teach those around you how to face life with a Stoic mindset and to demonstrate your wisdom and courage. Death comes for us all, and a man of wisdom, knowing he cannot control the hand of death, accepts his death with courage and the conviction that he has done his best in life. He doesn't stress, cry, or wish for more time, but rather he sees death as the final chapter in a life well lived.

68

He suffers more than necessary, who suffers before it is necessary.
Seneca

How many times have you been stressed about something that may happen, only to find out that you were worried for no reason and the thing you were stressed about never manifested? Many people do this constantly, forgetting that worry never changes anything except for their mental state, health, and inner peace.

Seneca wrote that going through that exercise is causing you to suffer unnecessarily. Even if what you are worried about does come to pass, it doesn't do you any good to sit and waste time worrying about it. All you have done is cause yourself extra suffering.

Instead of worrying and suffering unnecessarily, take action. If you are concerned that something bad is about to happen in your life, instead of moping around worrying about it, do what you can to prepare for it. A good example would be if you lived on the Florida coast and the meteorologists predicted you were in the path of a hurricane.

In this case, you would have two choices. You could sit around worried that your house is going to be destroyed, and you are going to lose all your belongings, or you could see what may be coming your way and take action to prepare for the storm the best that you can. Being concerned about something is not the same as being worried about it.

Worrying about something is a pointless, stressful, mental exercise which accomplishes nothing; while being concerned about something is foreseeing what could happen and then taking steps to prevent it from happening or to minimize the damage. The latter is the way of the Stoic mindset.

Of course, you have no control over the weather or whether a storm comes your way. But you have complete control over how you perceive the news of an approaching storm, and what you do to prepare for it to keep yourself, your family, and your property as safe as possible. Remember, control what you can control and accept the things that you have no control over!

69

"But we must stick with a decision."
For heaven's sake, man, that rule only applies to sound decisions.
Epictetus

Many times, we hear parents say something like, "My son chose to take piano lessons, so he must continue them. You must finish what you start." While the intent behind the parent's decision may be honorable, the decision is certainly questionable.

As Epictetus taught, sticking with a decision only applies to sound decisions; it does not apply to every decision you make. Let's continue with the example of a child deciding to take piano lessons. How would a child know if he enjoys playing the piano before he tries it? He wouldn't! You must be willing to explore and try new things in order to know whether or not you enjoy a certain activity.

If you make a child continue to do something that he tried and found that he disliked, he will be hesitant to continue to try new things. After all, he tried playing the piano, found he didn't like it, but was made to continue his lessons simply because his parents said he must finish what he started. Wouldn't it be better if the child felt he could try something new without getting roped into continuing with it if he didn't like it?

The same principle applies to you. You may have started a project and later found that the project was nothing but a pain and you hate every second that you spend on it, only to continue to work on the project because you were taught that you must finish what you started. Why continue to waste your time on something that you dislike and no longer see the value in doing?

Have you ever considered that maybe your decision to work on that project was not a good decision? Maybe it sounded good at first but turned into nothing but a nightmare. You don't have to stick with something simply because you started it; that is not a rational decision. If you see the value in continuing, then by all means continue to work on it. But don't continue to do something simply because you *once* thought it was a good idea.

70

> He who fears death will always be a slave…True freedom
> comes from accepting the inevitable and finding peace within it.
> *Seneca*

As you should already know by now, Stoicism teaches us to accept what is inevitable and to respond to it the best that we can. This also applies to death. I already discussed how we have no control over death; everyone who lives dies. It does you no good to fear something that is inevitable. All that does is cause you unnecessary stress and suffering.

Seneca taught that if you fear death, you will be a slave to death. Death will constantly be on your mind, but not in a constructive way. There is a way to think about death constructively, without fearing it, and without your thoughts causing you distress.

One practice the samurai practiced was to keep their death constantly on their mind. This may seem like a morbid practice, but it had a specific purpose. The samurai were commanded by their feudal lords, and their lord could command the samurai to go to war, or to commit suicide, at any time he pleased. So, the samurai had to be at peace with the possibility of his own death at any time.

The samurai kept the thought of their own death on their minds daily to be at peace with their fate. They did not sit around and worry about dying or when they might be commanded to take their own life. Rather, they kept their death in mind to be prepared for it. They understood the importance of keeping their lives in order and planning for their family.

While no one can command you to take your own life, the time of your death is just as unpredictable as the samurai's. Keeping that fact in mind helps you to be at peace with death and causes you to appreciate the life you have. It also reminds you of the value of each day and the importance of keeping your affairs in order. Refuse to fear death! Keep in mind that true freedom comes from accepting the inevitable and finding peace within it. Face what must be faced with a calm, courageous spirit!

71

Vice cannot be removed completely,
nor is it right that it should be removed.
Chrysippus

Chrysippus was one of the most influential Stoic philosophers. And although he believed that vice, the moral weakness or character flaws in a man, could not be entirely eliminated, he was okay with this fact. He felt our vices help us recognize and aspire to live a virtuous life by teaching us to accept certain limitations, while seeking to perfect our character.

By observing or experiencing vices, we are able to understand and appreciate what it means to live a virtuous life. He saw vice as a contrast to virtue, making virtues like justice, courage, and self-control stand out. Chrysippus saw vice as a normal part of being human because we are all imperfect and are constantly learning and growing.

Said another way, this argument means that if there were no vices in our world, we would not have the opportunity for personal growth or moral development. After all, if there were no vices, there would be no need to develop our moral strength. It is the mistakes we make, or others make, that push us to strive for the perfection of our character.

Moreover, the Stoics believed that everything in nature has a purpose, and vice is a natural part of being human, so our vices must have some fundamental purpose. Trying to eliminate vice completely is a practice in futility, as it contradicts our underlying nature. And since certain imperfections are natural and unavoidable, they must be accepted.

That said, it is important to understand that Chrysippus did not teach that we should embrace vice, but rather that we should strive to perfect our character, while accepting that vice is a part of our human nature. Acceptance of this doesn't mean that we excuse bad behavior, but simply that we accept the fact that certain vices are a part of human nature, and we must work to overcome them to live a virtuous life. We can aspire to the perfection of our character, even if we cannot attain that objective.

72

Our life is what our thoughts make it.
Marcus Aurelius

The idea that our life is what our thoughts make it is not unique to Stoicism. Buddha taught this same philosophy in the *Dhammapada*, stating, "We are shaped by our thoughts; we become what we think." The Bible also contains several passages that teach that our thoughts shape our lives. In the *Book of Proverbs*, we find the following passages: "Above all else, guard your heart, for everything you do flow from it," and "For as he thinks in his heart, so is he." There are several more passages in the Bible which follows this same thought.

More recently, the teachings of Transcendentalism and the New Thought Movement taught this same philosophical thought. Ralph Waldo Emerson taught, "The ancestor of every action is a thought." And James Allen, in his book, *As a Man Thinketh*, taught, "A man is literally what he thinks, his character being the complete sum of all his thoughts."

This train of thought can be found throughout the world in many religions and in the teachings of many sages. I wrote extensively about this philosophy in my award-winning book, *The Art of Inner Peace*. It is clear that a person's thoughts have power and matter more than most people realize.

How you perceive the words and actions of the people around you, and the events and circumstances in your life, directly affects how you will respond to them; and how you respond to them directly affects your life. We know that happiness comes from within, which means your thoughts create or hinder your happiness and overall satisfaction with your life.

Think about it. Two different people can see the same event or prediction, and one of them will be worried and stressed about it, while the other is completely at peace with it. What separates them? Their personal perceptions concerning what they heard or saw. You have complete control over which thoughts you allow yourself to dwell on; therefore, you are in control over the direction of your life. Your thoughts are more important than you may think!

73

Circumstances don't make the man; they only reveal him to himself.
Epictetus

It is a popular saying in today's culture to "fake it until you make it." While it is true that you can fool other people, you can't fool yourself. You always know who you truly are, even if you choose to ignore it. However, ignoring who and what you truly are only works as long as things are going smoothly in your life. If you run into hard times, the "fake it until you make it" attitude completely falls apart and reveals who you truly are.

While circumstances may not make the man, they do cause his mask to fall off, and the true man is revealed. For example, if someone wants others to think he is calm and rational, he may be able to fake those character traits when everything in his life is going smoothly. However, if he is faced with a major emergency, his calm and rational disposition suddenly disappears and is replaced by panic and irrational thinking and behavior. His true character will be revealed.

Inevitably, he will blame circumstances for his actions, but it is not really the circumstances that cause this change; they simply revealed his true nature. He wanted people to see him as a calm and rational man, but instead of truly cultivating those character traits, he simply tried to fake it until he made it; this is akin to a man bluffing in a card game. The bluff only works if no one calls his bluff. If someone calls his bluff, the truth about his weak hand is revealed.

Circumstances do not have the power to change you. You may argue that going through hard times or a bad situation makes you stronger and develops your character, but this is incorrect. Circumstances have no power over you unless you give them power over you; they are only occurrences in your life. Although you may classify a certain circumstance as good or bad, it is still only an event, and events do not have control over you.

You decide how you will respond to the events and circumstances in your life. You can use them to strengthen your character, or you can use them as an excuse for your undeveloped character. The choice is always yours!

74

He who has learned how to die has unlearned how to be a slave.
Seneca

Seneca taught that the fear of death enslaves a man and limits his freedom to live a full life. He believed that whoever fears death would not accomplish great things in his life because he is only half alive, always allowing his fear to dictate his actions in some way. Therefore, the man who has learned how to die has freed himself and is no longer a slave to his fear of death.

The fear of death is a type of mental enslavement, and the more one fears death, the more enslaved he is. If someone is a slave, then he has a master who owns him and controls what he can and cannot do. When you have a powerful fear of death, that fear masters you and prevents you from living your life to the fullest.

Everyone must come to terms with his or her mortality. Nothing you can do will change the fact that one day you will eventually die. Once you accept this fact, you free yourself from one of life's most common fears. Remember to always strive to accept whatever is outside of your circle of control.

When you learn to accept the things that are outside of your circle of control, they no longer control you; you free yourself. This is why Seneca taught that once you come to terms with your death, you have freed yourself and are no longer a slave to that fear.

How do you get to this point in your life? You meditate and accept the fact that one day you will die. Every living thing eventually dies; it is simply a part of life. So, why should you meditate on your death?

Meditating on your death keeps this truth fresh in your mind and will cause you to live your life more fully, freely, and gratefully. It will change how you perceive everything in your life. You will start to see things differently when you realize how wonderful and short life truly is. Once you come to this realization, you will live in inner peace and tranquility, and you will be grateful for each and every day.

75

Better to trip with the feet than with the tongue.
Zeno of Citium

This short piece of wisdom from Zeno demonstrates just how powerful your words are. If you physically trip and fall, you may get bruised up, or even break a bone, but bruises and broken bones heal. The accident is quickly forgotten as your body heals, and you simply move on with your life. But saying the wrong thing can have consequences that can last a lifetime. This is what Zeno was trying to get across to his students.

Your words are powerful, and you should be careful when it comes to what you say. They can have a haunting impact on your friendships, relationships, and your life. Therefore, you should use wisdom and self-discipline when you are speaking. This is especially important when you are upset or angry.

Most people have a habit of shutting down their verbal filter when they get angry or very upset. When angry, many people stop caring about the consequences of their speech and just blurt out whatever is on their mind, regardless of the possible consequences. They will say and do things during such times that cannot be taken back.

And have no doubt about it, once words are spoken, there is no taking them back. You may apologize profusely for what you said or did in anger, but that does not erase your words or actions from the minds of those who were there. Your words can ruin your friendships, damage your reputation, destroy the trust others have in you, and can hurt those you love most.

The *Book of Proverbs* states, "He who restrains his words has knowledge; and he who has a cool spirit is a man of understanding." If you want to live with a Stoic mindset, you must be self-disciplined and maintain a calm spirit.

Anyone who allows anger to control his speech has completely lost control of his calm, rational mind. He has allowed his emotions to take control of his mind; and it is never smart to allow yourself to be controlled or guided by your emotions instead of your rational mind. Always remain mindful of the power of your words and be thoughtful about what you say.

76

The first thing to learn is that God exists, that He governs
the world, and that we cannot keep our actions secret,
that even our thoughts and inclinations are known to Him.
Epictetus

This teaching from Epictetus is extremely powerful and will completely change your life if you stay mindful of it. If you continually remind yourself that God is in control, and that you cannot keep secrets from God, you will start to become much more purposeful in your thoughts, speech, and actions. If God knows even your thoughts and inclinations, then there is nothing you can hide from Him.

Many people conveniently forget this truism. In fact, they never give God much thought unless they are dealing with a serious situation in which they are fearful of and pray for God's help. At that time, they may start to doubt that God will help them because they remind themselves of all the unvirtuous things they have done.

So many of the unwise things that many of us do in life could be prevented if we were more mindful. If we keep the fact that God sees and knows everything we do and think fresh in our minds, it will change the things we think about, the words we speak, and the things we do. We would be much more mindful of everything we think, say, and do. However, most people get busy with their work, bills, family, hobbies, and life's stress, and forget that God knows everything.

Moreover, that is simply the second part of this teaching from Epictetus. Some people forget about the first part as well; God does exist, and He governs the world in ways we can't understand. Being mindful of this should help those seeking to live with a Stoic mindset not to worry about the things they cannot control. After all, if you believe God is in control, why would you worry?

Staying mindful of this teaching will help you remove worry from your life. Control the things that you have control over, and trust that God is in control of the things that are outside of your sphere of control.

There could be no justice, unless there was also injustice; no courage, unless there were cowardice; no truth, unless there were falsehood.
Chrysippus

Chrysippus believed all virtues derived their meaning from their opposites. For example, how can people truly appreciate living in a safe environment if they are completely unaware of criminals and crime? If they did not know about the horrible things that criminals do, they could not appreciate the safe, peaceful life that they live.

We can understand certain qualities such as courage, truth, and justice by observing and contrasting them with their opposites—cowardice, lies, and injustice. To the Stoics, all virtues are based on duality. This means all virtues are important because they counteract their opposites, which are negative. The presence of negative character traits is necessary because without them we could not truly understand the values of positive character traits.

If we never observed how pathetic cowardice is, we could not truly appreciate the courage of the warrior; if we had no knowledge of how unfair injustice is, we could not place such a high value on justice. Without the many vices we see throughout the world, we would not fully appreciate the virtues of good men and women.

So, what is the value of this wisdom in your life? Think about it. This insight urges you to see the problems and challenges in your life as necessary building blocks for your own growth and your moral development. This goes back to the truism that you can learn something from everyone. While you may think that you couldn't possibly learn anything from the wino lying on the sidewalk, in actuality, you can learn many lessons from him.

Seeing him lying there in his dirty clothes and drunken state should teach you that you never want to find yourself in that condition. It teaches you the value of self-discipline and the importance of continuously taking care of your affairs. He can teach you what *not* to do and how *not* to live your life. Always find a way to learn from everyone who crosses your path.

78

> Only an absolute fool values a man according to his clothes,
> or according to his social position, which after all
> is only something that we wear like clothing.
> *Seneca*

Do you value a man who dresses in a suit and tie more than you value the man who dresses in jeans and a t-shirt? Do you value the president of a large company more than the skilled carpenter who builds homes, or the doctor more than the teacher? According to Seneca, if you do, you are an absolute fool.

A man's social position or how he dresses doesn't truly reveal anything about the man's character or integrity. Most conmen dress in nice clothes; after all, they wouldn't be very successful at conning people out of millions of dollars dressed like a lumberjack. Likewise, the world is full of examples of men and women who have held high social positions, but who were later exposed to be little more than criminals.

The true value of a man is not in the clothes he wears or his position in life, but rather in his underlying character; but most people in this world are impressed by superficial appearances. Why do you think so many people look up to celebrities or entertainers when underneath the expensive clothes and their carefully scripted persona, there is nothing more than another flawed human being?

Many of these people work hard to maintain an outward appearance to conceal their flawed character. The façade is meant to foster the illusion that these people are somehow more important than the average person. And there are plenty of absolute fools in this world who buy into the illusion.

Just think about how many politicians use celebrities to influence voters to vote for them, as if a celebrity somehow knows more about the needs of a country than the working man. Only a fool would be influenced by these people. Don't allow the social position, clothing, or celebrity status of other people to impress you. See it for the pretense that it truly is. Keep your focus on what truly matters—a person's true character, integrity, and honor.

79

There is a limit to the time assigned you, and if you don't
use it to free yourself, it will be gone and never return.
Marcus Aurelius

Everyone on our planet has an expiration date, and none of us knows when that day will come. You only have so much time on this earth, so you should use it wisely. Once it's gone, you can never reclaim it; it is gone forever. While we all know this to be true, unless we purposely keep it fresh in our minds, it is very easy to forget.

Marcus Aurelius wrote his teachings as he was contemplating the reality of his own death. No doubt, he looked back at many parts of his life and realized that he had wasted a lot of his time on meaningless things, just as all of us probably do. There is an old saying that you never truly realize the value of something until it is gone. I believe this was the mindset that Marcus Aurelius had as he authored his famous book, *Meditations*.

His writings were never meant to be published for others, but simply a man recording his own thoughts towards the end of his life. *Meditations* is a rare glimpse into the mindset of an honorable ruler who truly valued wisdom and the Stoic virtues in his life.

When you are young, it seems like you have all the time in the world; the days even seem longer. Young people rarely think about life being short or the fact that they should appreciate every day and get the most out of every hour of their lives.

Once people become adults, life becomes so busy that most people rarely slow down enough to meditate on the true value of time, or on the fact that their time is limited. It is not until later in life that most people start to look back and realize how fast the years have gone by and how little time they have left to enjoy our amazing world or their friends and family.

None of us knows how much time we have been given to enjoy life. Stop taking your time for granted and begin to appreciate every day! You don't want to wait until it is too late to realize that life goes by faster than you think.

80

Wealth is the slave of the wise. The master of the fool.
Seneca

Wealth can be both a blessing and a curse depending on your perspective. If you are wise, your wealth will serve you because you can use it as a means to an end. Wealth should be a resource for you, an aid to help you meet your goals and provide for your family. When a good man gets wealth, others also benefit from his good fortune because he willingly helps those around him.

Wise men do not allow money, or the pursuit of wealth, to dictate their mindset, values, or actions. To them, money and wealth are nothing more than tools that can be used to make their lives better and to help others. The wise understand that, while wealth can buy a certain amount of freedom, true freedom in this world comes from being content with what you have and mastering your own desires. Money doesn't buy contentment; contentment must come from within each of us.

The fool is the opposite of the wise man. When a fool gets wealth, it becomes his master. He allows his wealth, and the pursuit of greater wealth, to control his thoughts, actions, and emotions. He doesn't truly live his life because he is constantly focused on keeping the money and possessions that he has and increasing his wealth.

Foolish men measure their worth by their possessions and wealth, constantly pursuing more wealth to maintain their flawed self-esteem. To these men, their wealth is the most important thing in their lives, and they willingly sacrifice their inner peace, happiness, and integrity for their love of money. They become a slave to their pursuit of wealth, even to the point of sacrificing their honor and integrity to increase it.

The wise man knows that true inner peace and happiness come from being content with whatever you have in your life, while you work to increase your wealth and provide for those around you. To the wise man, honor, wisdom, and self-control are more important than riches, so he refuses to be a slave to the love of money.

81

> He who is running a race ought to endeavor and strive to
> the utmost of his ability to come off the victor; but it is utterly
> wrong for him to trip up his competitor, or to push him aside.
> So, in life, it is not unfair for one to seek for himself what may
> accrue to his benefit; but it is not right to take it from another.
>
> *Chrysippus*

Chrysippus taught that it is good to strive to improve yourself and to try your best to win when you compete, but you must win with honor. If you are running a race, do your best to win. Train hard to be victorious. But don't allow your desire to win to cause you to lower your standards or set aside your honor. Maintain your character and integrity, even if it means you don't win.

Losing with honor is better than winning with dishonor when it comes to competitions or life in general. It is not wrong to seek the best that life has to offer; but it is wrong to achieve your goal by dishonest means. By all means, try to increase your wealth and improve your life, but do so honorably. It is better to live without something than to achieve it dishonorably.

If you achieve your goal, whether it is wealth or a higher position in life, by dishonest means, you have achieved nothing other than lowering your standards and dishonoring yourself. When you want something so badly that you cheat, swindle, lie, or steal from someone else, you are being controlled by your desire; you have traded your honor and inner peace for something much less valuable.

Work to benefit yourself and your family, but always do so honorably, with character, honor, and integrity. Never trade something that is eternal and priceless for something that is temporary. No man would trade his life for any material possession, but in a way, that is exactly what you are doing when you lower your standards to achieve something by dishonest means. Remember, although honor is something that no man can take from you, you can lose it through your own actions. Never trade your character, honor, and integrity for titles, material things, riches, temporary pleasures, or anything else!

82

The mind that is anxious about future events is miserable.
Seneca

I am sure that we have all experienced being worried about something at one time or another in our life. It is not a pleasant experience, is it? Worry causes stress, mental issues, and physical ailments in your body. In addition, it is a total waste of time. No matter how much you worry about what may or may not happen in the future, it changes nothing; what will happen will happen, whether you worry about it or never consider it.

So why make yourself miserable by worrying about something that you have no power to change? Refuse to worry about anything! If what you are concerned about is within your realm of control, then get up and do something about it. If it is outside your realm of control, then no amount of worrying will change that fact. All you are doing by worrying about it is making yourself miserable.

Worrying about future events always causes unnecessary suffering. When you worry about what might happen, you are wasting the present moment. Remember, time wasted is time that you can never get back. Instead of worrying about something that is out of your control, get busy doing something that *is* within your control. Living consciously in the now is the antidote for worry. You cannot live fully in the present moment and worry about the future at the same time.

The future only exists in your mind; only the present moment is real. The past is only a memory, and the future is only an expectation. All we truly have is the present moment. Another thing to consider is that by constantly thinking and worrying about some negative situation that *may* happen in the future, you could be attracting it into your life.

Science is proving that our thoughts are much more powerful than we may think; thoughts contain energy. What you focus on with emotion, whether that emotion is positive or negative, you are attracting into your life. Maintain your inner peace and live with contentment in the present moment!

83

Wealth consists not in having great
possessions, but in having few wants.
Epictetus

The Stoics taught that true wealth is being content with what you have in
your life, whether that is great wealth or very little. You can be just as happy
with a little as you can with a lot. Epictetus taught that true wealth is not
measured by how much you have, but by being happy and content with
whatever you have in your life.

This sounds completely backwards to most people in our materialistic
society, but it is true. You can be just as happy in a small house with very few
material things as you can be in a mansion with everything your heart desires.
While this may sound ridiculous to you, it is true, nonetheless.

True happiness comes from within; it has nothing to do with material
possessions. Your happiness is one of those things that *is* within your circle of
control. And since it is under your control, you can decide to be happy
whenever you want to be happy.

There are many people on this planet who have mansions, every material
thing you can think of, and more money than most people can even imagine,
but who are unhappy and not content with their life. They are constantly
striving for more wealth or another expensive toy; they are constantly stressed
about their next big deal or making sure they don't lose what they have.

Epictetus taught that true wealth is limiting your desires to what you have,
while you strive to improve yourself or your position. If you limit your desires
to what you really need, instead of what our society works hard to convince
you that you need, you will find that there is very little that is necessary for a
fulfilling, happy life.

Be grateful for all the things you have in your life and prioritize
contentment over material desires. Simplify your life! Place higher importance
on your inner peace and self-mastery than you do on material things. Focus on
what is truly important in your life and be indifferent to the rest.

84

You have power over your mind—not outside events.
Realize this, and you will find strength.
Marcus Aurelius

This truism by Marcus Aurelius is very simple, but also very easy to forget. It is something that you must continually remind yourself of daily, and sometimes, several times a day. As I have stated before, this is one of the fundamental teachings of Stoicism; there are some things that you can control, and some things that you have no control over at all.

When stressful or irritating events arise in your life, calm yourself down and mentally remind yourself that you have no control over external events. All you can do is control how you respond to those events. In addition, most of those external events don't require any kind of response from you whatsoever. Just maintain your calm mind, observe what has happened, and then move on.

As Marcus Aurelius wrote, once you realize the truth in this, you will find strength. Realizing that there is nothing you can do to affect the situation, distances you from whatever is happening. This doesn't mean that you won't feel empathetic toward those involved or that you don't care; it simply means that you comprehend that there is nothing you can do about what is happening.

There is no reason to become irate or angry about an event that you have no control over. When you find that some external event is really starting to get to you, pause and remind yourself that getting angry over what is happening changes nothing. All it is going to do is disrupt your inner peace and raise your blood pressure. It won't do anything positive for you.

It is easier to deal with these types of events if you simply see them as a test of your self-control and determination to remain cool, calm, and collected, no matter what is happening around you. Getting angry will only cause you additional problems. See negative external events as a challenge to test your resolve and be determined to win that challenge! Refuse to allow anything outside of your control to get the best of you. Warrior up!

85

No man is free who is not master of himself.
Epictetus

Epictetus was born into slavery during the Roman Empire and spent his entire early life as a Roman slave. If you know anything about life as a Roman slave, you know that many of them were badly mistreated and had a very hard life. Even though he eventually obtained his freedom, Epictetus taught that no man is free who is not the master of himself.

Slavery comes in many forms. If you are not free, that means that you are a slave in one form or another. Some people are slaves to their uncontrolled anger or their quick temper. Others are slaves to their vices, whether it is alcohol, drugs, gambling, sex, etcetera. The list of things that can rule over a person is never-ending.

Being a freed slave, his experience with slavery shaped Epictetus' teachings about freedom and being the master of your own life. Having experienced the horrors of slavery, Epictetus was determined not to allow anyone or anything to control him. He realized that no man is truly free if anyone or anything has the ability to control him in some way.

To be the master of yourself means you refuse to allow anyone or anything to control you. Most of us would violently oppose allowing anyone else to control our life. However, when you allow someone to anger you or to cause you to lose your temper, they are controlling you. If someone can "make" you angry, that person can control you anytime they choose to do so; thus, you are like a slave in that circumstance.

Of course, the truth is that no one can "make" you angry; you have complete control over whether or not you allow yourself to be angry. When you say that someone *made* you angry, what you are truly doing is attempting to place the blame for your anger on someone else instead of yourself. You are offering yourself as a type of slave to that person. Stop giving other people control over your emotions and free yourself! Control the things that are in your power to control; never give that control to anyone outside of yourself.

86

> We are more often frightened than hurt; and
> we suffer more in imagination than in reality.
> *Seneca*

Do you remember a time when you were very stressed about something bad happening in your life? Maybe you were stressed that you were going to lose your job for some reason, but it later turned out to be a false alarm. Or maybe you were stressed that a medical test was going to come back positive for a terminal disease, but it came back negative.

These are both examples of what Seneca wrote about in this teaching. The thing that you were worried about did not hurt you at all. What caused you to suffer was your worry and uncontrolled imagination concerning the issue. You suffered unnecessarily when you could have controlled your mind and not have been worrying to begin with.

If you think back over your lifetime, you can probably think of many times when you were anxious and stressed about something, but the thing that you were worried about never came to pass. In these situations, you suffered because of your negative thoughts and uncontrolled imagination. It was your *perception and fear* of the external events that caused you to be stressed, not the events themselves.

Stop worrying about things that you cannot control! If something is not in your realm of control, then you can't do anything about it, so there is no reason to worry about it. Don't allow fear of what *may* happen in the future to cause you to spend the present moment worrying and upset. Never allow fear to control your mind or to dictate your actions!

Your mind can tend to exaggerate potential negative events and make them seem much worse than they truly are. Control your mind and stop meditating on potential negative events. The Stoics taught us to focus on what is within our circle of control. I know I repeat this a lot, but it is vitally important to the Stoic mindset. If you keep your focus only on the things within your control, you will reduce your stress and maintain your inner peace.

87

Dwell on the beauty of life. Watch the stars,
and see yourself running with them.
Marcus Aurelius

Marcus Aurelius wrote this passage as he looked back on his life. Those who have lived long lives can often look back on their lives and see things much clearer than they did when they were younger. Here, Marcus Aurelius is urging us to dwell on the beauty of life instead of all the negative things we experience in life. He is encouraging us to appreciate the beauty of life and enjoy all the magnificent wonders this world has to offer.

Many people have allowed life to jade them, causing them to focus on all the negative aspects of life instead of being grateful for all the beauty that this planet offers. Negative thinking can become a habit if it is not controlled and replaced with more positive thoughts. If you replace your negative thoughts with thoughts of gratitude and appreciation, you will start to see things from a different perspective.

How you look at the world around you determines your attitude and what you see. If you look at the world with wonder and appreciation, you will begin to see everything in a different light. You will see the same beauty and the same negativity that everyone else sees, but you won't allow the negativity to control your mind.

The overall shift in your perspective will allow you to maintain your inner peace and calm demeanor, even in the most trying of times. You will develop a more balanced view of life instead of allowing the world's negativity to affect you. In addition, you will find joy, even in the simplest of things.

Marcus Aurelius is urging us to look at the stars and to allow our imagination and wonder to fill our minds. He is inviting us to live with a mindset of gratitude and to focus on our own connection to the universe. If you practice this mindset, and stay focused on the present moment, you will find yourself less stressed about the concerns of the world, and more inspired to live a life of serenity and inner peace.

88

Live out your life in truth and justice,
tolerant of those who are neither true nor just.
Marcus Aurelius

You must have the confidence to live according to your moral principles regardless of what anyone else does or how anyone else lives their life. Not everyone is going to agree with your moral principles or code of honor. You will have to deal with many who don't care about truth, justice, or honor. Just remember, you are not responsible for how other people live their lives; you are only responsible for how you live your life.

Make a firm decision to live your life by your own code of honor. Always do your best to align your actions with the principles you hold dear. Live truthfully and pursue wisdom, honesty, and authenticity, while respecting others and their right to live as they see fit. Be tolerant of those who do not live by the same principles as you and remember, not everyone knows what you know or has had the same experiences that you have had.

Instead of getting upset with those who are neither true nor just, practice tolerance and compassion for them. It does no good to get angry or resentful because of how they live; how they live is not in the realm of your control, nor is it any of your business. You are not here to pass judgment on others, but to live *your* life the best that you can.

It is all too easy to judge others who do not live as you think they should, or to look down on those who do not share the same moral principles that you hold dear to your heart. Keep in mind that everyone has their own struggles in life, struggles which have shaped them into the person he or she is now. You do not know why they behave as they do, and it is not your business to know.

Who are you to sit in judgment of other people when you have not perfected your own character? Stop passing judgment on others and start focusing on perfecting your own character. You have plenty of work to do on your character; waste no time critiquing the character of other people. Live your life with honor and integrity, and allow others to decide how they will live.

WISDOM · TEMPERANCE · JUSTICE · COURAGE

89

I am a citizen of the world.
Diogenes

It is fairly common to hear someone declare that he or she is a citizen of the world in today's culture, but this was a revolutionary idea in 155 BC. Diogenes was the head of the Stoic school in Athens before he was sent to Rome and was notorious for making controversial statements and for his philosophical stunts. Stating that he was a citizen of the world instead of a citizen of Greece or Rome would have been very radical during this time period.

Consider that in ancient Greece, a man's identity was closely tied to the city-state in which he lived. Being a citizen of Athens or Sparta entitled him to certain privileges. By stating he was a citizen of the world, Diogenes was rejecting his loyalty to either Greece or Rome, and demonstrating his belief that he was a part of a larger community—that of simply being a human being.

He believed that being a human being transcends the boundaries of any city-state or empire. Diogenes was known to push the limits of societal norms and rejected classifying people by where they were born or where they lived. He believed people should be judged according to their wisdom and virtues instead of considering where they were born or their social status, which they did not earn, but were simply given by birth.

Diogenes was also making a radical statement about societal norms. By stating that he was a citizen of the world, he was also stating that he was free from the societal constraints under which others lived. He was declaring that he was free to live by his own code, which for a Stoic was according to nature and reason. He was also declaring that he was not bound by the laws or customs of either Greece or Rome, which was also a very radical idea.

In today's terms, it would be like someone saying, "I live by my own code, and my code is more important to me than society's norms or unjust political laws." This is the way of the true warrior, whose code is more important than arbitrary rules or laws. He doesn't live according to what everyone else believes, but by his own code of honor, which is based on what's just and right.

90

Ignorance is the cause of fear.
Seneca

Many people allow fear to control their lives. Seneca taught that fear is caused by ignorance. While that might seem untrue, when you get down to the root cause of most fears, it makes perfect sense. Fear often stems from our imagination or lack of fully understanding the situation. Let's use the fear of snakes as an example.

Most people are very fearful of snakes because they have some knowledge about how deadly some venomous snakes are. They have seen nature shows on television and have heard the snake handlers talk about how quickly a bite from this snake or that snake can kill a man. But they have little knowledge or experience with snakes other than that. Their fear of snakes is based on a lack of fully understanding snakes.

They may have seen a snake handler discussing a Gaboon viper or an Eastern Diamondback rattlesnake, and it scared them so much that they developed a fear of all snakes. What they fail to understand is that not all snakes are venomous. But their ignorance of which snakes are deadly, and which are not, causes them to fear all snakes.

Another major fear is the fear of dying. The Stoics believe that ignorance causes fear, and when it comes to dying, unless one has really given the topic some in-depth thought, they are completely ignorant concerning death. This fear stems from the unknown.

Seneca taught we can conquer fear by gaining knowledge and self-awareness. For example, if you meditate and come to an understanding of what you truly believe about death, you can overcome your fear of death. When you understand that death is simply a part of life, and something which is not in our circle of control, we can be at peace with the concept of death.

Remember, we must accept what we cannot control. If you have a specific fear, educate yourself concerning that fear, and then face your fear head-on. In doing so, you will overcome your fear.

Riches are a cause of evil, not because of themselves, they do any evil, but because they goad men on so that they are ready to do evil.
Posidonius

Long before the Apostle Paul stated, "the *love* of money is the root of all evil," Posidonius taught riches are the cause of evil, not because they do us any harm, but because they goad men on so that they are ready to do evil. So, what does it mean that they "goad men on so that they are ready to do evil"?

Neither Posidonius nor the Apostle Paul said that money and riches are evil or bad, but that the *love* or desire for money can move men to do evil to gain riches. There is a big difference between being evil and wanting something so bad that you are willing to commit an evil act to acquire it.

Many people have misquoted and misunderstood these teachings, even though both Posidonius and the Apostle Paul made it clear that money is not evil on its own. Gold, silver, and money are inanimate objects; they are no more evil than any other metal or means of exchange.

Let's look at an analogy. A gun is an inanimate object. It is not evil and does nothing to hurt or kill anyone. The fact that a gun can be used to commit murder does not change this fact. It is not the gun that commits murder, *but the man who uses it* who is to blame.

If you read the two quotes in the first paragraph carefully, you see that this is exactly what Posidonius and Paul are saying. It is not money or riches that are evil, but the uncontrolled and erroneous desires of some men that are evil. The real issue here is not money or wealth, but the nature of men who do not live as they should; it's a moral problem, not a money problem.

This is not a warning about being rich or desiring more money, but rather a warning against allowing external things, whether it is money or anything else, to corrupt your internal virtues. No matter how much a virtuous man would like more money, he will not set his honor or integrity aside to get that money. Always place more importance on your honor than your wealth!

92

There is one road to peace and happiness:
renunciation of externals; regarding nothing as your
own; handing over everything to fortune and to God.
Epictetus

Epictetus taught that true peace and happiness come from within. In this quote, he is saying that we should not place too much importance on external things or events, but rather, we should trust that God is in control of the things that we cannot control. However, he goes even further and states that we should hand over everything that we cannot control over to God.

Worry and stress will disrupt our inner peace and happiness if we do not take steps to distance ourselves from them. No one who is constantly worried about external things is truly living in peace and happiness. But if we surrender the external things to God, instead of worrying about them, then we will be on the road to a more peaceful and happy life.

Let go of the things that you cannot control and trust that God is looking out for you. When you do this, it removes the worry and stress that you have concerning those things. You must realize that you cannot control everything, no matter how much you would like to be in control. Trying to control things that are outside of your realm of control does nothing but add stress to your life. It is an act of futility! Control the things that are in your realm of control, and trust that God is in control of the rest.

Epictetus also urged us to renounce external things. This means that we must detach ourselves from the things that are outside of our circle of control. This includes things such as your reputation, the opinions and actions of other people, events, circumstances, etc. Make a firm decision not to allow anything outside of your control to disrupt your inner peace or happiness.

That doesn't mean that we should neglect or ignore external things, but that we should not allow them to control our actions or our mental state. We live in this world; thus, we must deal with external circumstances and events, but we do not have to internalize them or allow them to control us.

As is a tale, so is life: not how long it is,
but how good it is, is what matters.
Seneca

Seneca gives us a great analogy in this excerpt from his writings. At first glance, it seems like nothing more than an obvious statement of fact. It doesn't matter how long a story is, but how good it is; it is the same with life. But hiding in this analogy is one of the important principles of Stoicism—we can't control how long our life is, but we can control how good it is.

We don't control how long we live; that is, unless we purposefully take our own life. Even though we can take steps to increase our health and our life expectancy, we still have no control over the unforeseen things that could cut our life short.

Although we have no control over how long our life may be, we can control the quality of our lives. We have control over what we think, believe, say, and do, and those things determine the path we travel during our lifetime. Every decision is akin to coming to a crossroads and choosing which way we will go. This is the way you should approach the important decisions in your life.

Everything matters! Every thought you choose to entertain is programming your subconscious mind. Every decision you make guides your life in one way or another. Take your life seriously and refuse to waste time on things that do not add to the joy, peace, happiness, or improvement of your life.

Take inventory of your life. Ask yourself, "Would your life make a good movie or a good story?" If you could see your life as a movie, would you be the hero, the villain, or would you simply be one of the extras in the background watching the action, but not adding much to the story?

This is something that is absolutely within your realm of control. You are the writer and director of your own movie. If you aren't satisfied with your movie script so far, then it is time to make some changes to the script. Don't be satisfied with just being in the background; step up and make your story a good one!

94

Everything we hear is an opinion, not a fact.
Everything we see is a perspective, not the truth.
Marcus Aurelius

At first, this appears to be an enormous generalization, but upon further examination, we find that Marcus Aurelius was spot on with this realization. We don't see or hear everything. What we hear is limited both by our physical abilities, which can hear only a small fraction of the sound frequencies that exist, and by our interpretation of the sounds we hear. And, to further complicate things, the words we hear other people speak are skewed by their opinions, hidden meanings, or perceptions of what is or is not true.

The same goes for what we see. Humans can see only a tiny fraction of the visible electromagnetic spectrum. Moreover, what we can see is colored by our brain's perspective; someone else may look at the exact same thing but see something different. Thus, everything we see is our perspective, not necessarily the truth.

Consider the fact that humans can only see frequencies from 430—790 THz and can only perceive sounds between 20 HZ—20 kHz. These ranges are just a tiny portion of the entire spectrum of light and sound that we know about. This means that most of what exists on our planet is entirely invisible to us.

Also, when we consider what we see as far as human actions, we must consider all the factors that we don't see, such as other people's intentions and motivations. We don't really know what's in someone's mind. Taken as a whole, there is truth is the old saying, "there's more to it than meets the eye."

The absolute truth always lies hidden beneath the surface. I believe that Marcus Aurelius was trying to say that understanding and perception go much deeper than what we hear or what we see. The truth is much more complex and lies somewhere below the surface of our perceptions. Appearances can be deceptive. Never accept appearances as the complete truth. Always remember that you are not hearing everything and that you are most likely seeing only what someone else wants you to see. Be careful what you believe to be true.

95

If you know you are in the right, why fear those who misjudge you?
Epictetus

One of the principles of Stoicism is to strive to always do what's right and to stand strong on your principles. In this quote, Epictetus is urging us to act when we know we are right, and not to be swayed by the opinions of others. Other people may attack you, misunderstand your intentions, or slander you for your actions, but none of that matters if you know you are in the right.

Marcus Aurelius taught the same thing, writing, "Do the right thing. The rest doesn't matter." When you know for sure that you are right and you need to act, do it! Don't allow the fear of what others may think about your actions to cause you to stand down.

Will others possibly misjudge you? Absolutely! Do the right thing anyway. Will your enemies and those who want to see you fail spin your actions to mean something other than what they are? You bet! Do the right thing anyway. Will it possibly cost you in some way? It could! Do the right thing anyway. Never allow the opinions of others to prevent you from doing the right thing! I urge you to take a few minutes and go read the poem attributed to Mother Teresa titled, *Do It Anyway*.

Doing the right thing should be all that matters to you, not what other people think about it. You are not responsible for what other people think, nor do you have any control over what other people think. Remember, if you can't control something, accept it, respond to it if you need to, and move on. Other people may misjudge your intentions, but as long as you know inside that you did what's right, your conscience will be clear.

One more thing to consider is not only should you do what you know is right, but you must also do it at the right time and in the right way. Doing the right thing can turn out badly if you do it in the wrong way or at the wrong time. Take everything into consideration and do the right thing, at the right time, and in the right way. Then, what others think about it won't matter to you at all.

96

No matter whether you claim a slave by purchase or capture,
the title is bad. They who claim to own their fellow men, look
down into the pit and forget the justice that should rule the world.
Zeno of Citium

Throughout the history of the world, there have always been good men and evil men, and there most likely always will be. Although living by the Stoic principles focuses on improving yourself and controlling the things that you have some control over, you will still have to deal with other people. Some of those people will undoubtedly not be men of honor and integrity.

Never allow yourself to believe that someone wouldn't be underhanded or that he wouldn't act in a dishonest or hateful way. There are many examples of evil men doing horrific things every day all around the world. Though you are not responsible for the actions of other people, you still must be wise and protect yourself against those who would do you harm.

It is all too easy for those who live with honor and integrity to believe that no one would lie, cheat, steal, or murder other people, but we must remain aware that there are many evil men in this world. Those men do not care about justice, honor, integrity, or the lives of others.

Living with a Stoic mindset does not mean that you don't need to be wise and keep yourself and your family safe from those who do not live by the same principles. While you aren't responsible for the actions of others, you are responsible for keeping yourself and your family safe from those who would do you harm. The Stoic mindset is aware, not naïve.

Don't get so involved in improving your character that you forget to be wary of those with malicious intentions. Work to perfect your character, to control those things that are within your circle of control, and to be unmoved by those things that are outside your circle of control, but continue to be wise and aware of what is going on around you. While we don't control the actions of others, we still must be aware of their actions and do what must be done to keep ourselves and our families safe. Think about this.

97

*If you see someone fond of externals, someone who values
them over their own moral integrity, you can be sure that he is
vulnerable to thousands of people who can frustrate or coerce him.*
Epictetus

When someone depends too much on externals, things that are outside his circle of control, he will be vulnerable to those who want to control him. If he is dependent on factors outside of his control, he is easily coerced to do or say things that are not in line with his character or principles.

For example, if someone values his wealth over his principles, he is vulnerable to being manipulated where his finances are concerned. Someone who places too much value on advancing in his workplace may compromise his principles to get a promotion.

This is one reason Epictetus taught that being self-sufficient is necessary to be truly free, and that those who want to be truly free must be grounded in honor, integrity, and other personal traits which nobody can take from them. A man who values his honor over any external temptations cannot be pressured or intimidated because he already has what is most important to him—his honor and integrity.

If you place too much value on things that you can't control, you are placing your inner peace and happiness in the hands of other people or other forces. The only way to be the master of your life is to be self-sufficient and value your honor and integrity more than anything outside of your control. Placing too much value on things outside of your realm of control opens you up to a life filled with anxiety and fear, and even manipulation and being controlled by others.

Protect your honor and integrity by being detached from external temptations such as money, wealth, or fame. Focus on the things that you can control. True freedom means you can't be manipulated or compromised by others because you don't place a high value on the things they try to use to manipulate you. Be morally self-sufficient!

98

Throw me to the wolves, and I will return leading the pack.
Seneca

Stoic philosophy is a philosophy of resilience, positivity, courage, and the ability to turn adversity into strength. If someone throws you to the wolves, they are placing you in an extremely challenging and hostile environment, an environment in which one would expect to be ripped apart and defeated.

Seneca's words not only express the philosophy of a Stoic, but also the philosophy of a warrior. Stoics embrace challenges and refuse to give up or to allow external situations to defeat them. They use challenging situations to test their courage and emerge stronger after their victory, just as warriors do.

The Stoic mindset has a lot in common with the mindset of the warrior. "Throw me to the wolves, and I will return leading the pack," is definitely the mindset of the warrior. Warriors don't give up; they find a way not only to survive, but to overcome and conquer. No matter how dire the situation may be, warriors rise to the challenge. And this is exactly what Seneca is expressing in this quote.

Seneca is expressing great confidence in himself and his inner fortitude. He is saying that external hardships and challenges cannot defeat or break him because he has cultivated the inner strength and mindset of a Stoic warrior. Throughout his writings, Seneca referred to external challenges as being powerless against the Stoic mindset.

This powerful quote demonstrates the Stoic mindset of not allowing anything external to disrupt your inner peace. It is a resolute determination not only to survive any external challenge, but to thrive and use the situation to your advantage.

After all, if someone throws you to the wolves, they have the expectation that you will be destroyed and disheartened. Saying you will return leading the pack means you will not only return victorious, but that you will return with the power to turn the tables on those who tried to destroy you. See challenges as a test of your character and REFUSE TO LOSE!

99

Prefer enduring satisfaction to immediate gratification.
Epictetus

The Stoics taught that true happiness and personal satisfaction come from leading a virtuous and disciplined life. If you align your actions with virtue and honor, instead of chasing temporary pleasures, you will find greater happiness in the long run.

How many times have you given in to the temptation of immediate gratification, only to regret your decision as soon as the pleasure of the moment or the new purchase has passed? Think about it.

If you are trying to lose weight and you are in the checkout line at the grocery store where there are all kinds of candy bars and drinks full of sugar, and you give in and buy a candy bar and soft drink, you may enjoy it for a short period of time. But later, you must deal with the disappointment and regret of giving in to that temptation instead of pursuing your overall goal.

Epictetus is urging us to prefer the satisfaction of self-discipline and controlling our temporary desires or impulses. Those with a Stoic mindset prefer delayed gratification as opposed to immediate, short-lived gratification. Anytime you have a goal that you want to achieve, and something or someone tempts you with something that moves you further away from your goal, use that situation as a chance to strengthen your resolve and your self-discipline. Don't give in to the temptation of immediate gratification!

Each time you discipline yourself to delay gratification, you are strengthening your resolve and your self-mastery. Think of it in terms of strength training. If you want to develop muscle mass and definition, you must stick to a training schedule, but there will be times when you are tempted to skip your workout.

Skipping your workout would be an example of immediate gratification. But if you resist the temptation to skip your workout, you will have more satisfaction than you would if you opted for the immediate gratification of being lazy. Choose long-term satisfaction over short-term pleasures!

100

Do not act as if you were going to live ten thousand years. Death
hangs over you. While you live, while it is in your power, be good.
Marcus Aurelius

It is very easy to put the fact that someday you are going to die out of your
mind. Most people are busy and don't want to think about that subject, but it
would benefit you to keep this truism fresh in your mind. You will not live
forever, at least not in your current body. You only get one chance to do what
you want in this life and to be the kind of person you want to be.

The time to be who and what you want to be is now—in the present
moment! The future is uncertain and not promised to anyone; the time to act
and get your life on the right path is NOW! If you want to improve your life
and start living with a Stoic mindset, there is no better time than today.

It is easy to justify not making the necessary changes to improve your life;
excuses are a dime-a-dozen. You could reason that you have done too many
dishonest things, or that it is too late for you to live an honorable life. But those
are nothing more than justifying the fact that you don't want to put in the effort
to improve your character and live a life of honor and integrity.

It is never too late to change your life! You have the power to stop living
your current lifestyle at this very moment. All it takes is making a firm decision
to begin to live the rest of life with character, honor, courage, and integrity.
Start taking your life more seriously. Discipline yourself to live as you were
meant to live!

Focus on living a life of wisdom, honor, and integrity; that is what gives
your life true meaning. It doesn't matter what you have done or how you have
lived up to this point. You can start right where you are and decide that you are
going to be a man or woman of honor and integrity. That is the basis of Stoic
philosophy.

Someday is nothing more than an illusion; the time to do what's right is
NOW! Reject complacency and embrace wisdom, honor, integrity, and
courage. Think about what truly matters in your life!

101

The art of living is more like wrestling than dancing.
Marcus Aurelius

Marcus Aurelius obviously had a lot to manage in his life as the Emperor of Rome, so it is easy to see why he would make this analogy of life. If you are dancing, you are carefree and not really thinking about anything but enjoying the music in the present moment. But if you are wrestling, you are constantly under attack by your opponent and continually must make adjustments to keep from losing the match.

When you are wrestling, you must deal with something external, something that you do not control—your opponent. Your opponent continually tries to defeat you, coming at you with unexpected moves that you must constantly counter to maintain control and win the match. You have no control over what your opponent will throw at you next; all you control is how you respond to his attacks.

Wrestling, like life, requires that you stay ready; it requires continual effort, strength, and never-ending perseverance. You can't be passive, or you will lose your chance to overcome your opponent and be victorious.

This is a great analogy of life. You never know what roadblocks life will throw at you next; you must continually be mindful and disciplined to be ready to meet life's next challenge. Living a life of honor and integrity is a constant battle where you will have one chance after another to compromise your integrity.

Once you begin to live your life by Stoic principles, you will have many victories, along with some days where you may lose the battle and fall short of your expectations. What you must remember is that losing a battle is not the same thing as losing the war. If you fall short of your Stoic goals one day, you don't give up; you simply get up, dust yourself off, and continue to strive to perfect your character. Each day offers a new opportunity to start fresh and to be the person that you want to be. The more victories you have, the better prepared you will be to meet and overcome the next challenge.

102

All things are part of one single system, which is called nature;
the individual life is good when it is in harmony with nature.
Zeno of Citium

Zeno of Citium was the founder of Stoicism, and one of the foundational principles of Stoic philosophy is that all things are connected, and we should live in accordance with nature. He believed the universe is rational and has a specific order that is governed by natural law. This belief led him to see every individual, and even everything in the universe, including every event, as an important part of the whole with its own purpose.

He believed that our well-being depends on purposely aligning our lives, our thoughts, words, and actions, with the natural order of the universe itself. This is one reason the Stoics taught that we must accept the things that are outside of our control, and not only should we accept them, but that we should embrace them because they are a part of the natural course of the universe.

Zeno also taught that seeking to perfect our character is the true path to happiness, and that reason and a rational mind should guide our actions, instead of our uncontrolled emotions. We should recognize our emotions but keep them in check with our rational mind, while we strive to increase our wisdom and self-discipline.

In addition, his philosophy teaches that we are all connected since we are all part of the same universe. This belief leads us to believe that our well-being is connected to the well-being of other people, so we should work, not only for our own best interests, but for the best interests of the community.

When you work to perfect your own character, honor, integrity, courage, and sense of justice, you are helping the community as a whole, as well as staying in harmony with nature and the universe. Knowing this, it is obvious why prominent men such as Marcus Aurelius, Epictetus, and Seneca all adopted Stoicism as their own philosophy of life. Maintain harmony with nature and respect all life on our planet. This thought is found in sagacious teachings throughout the world.

103

The man who has anticipated the coming of troubles
takes away their power when they arrive.
Seneca

As a martial artist, this wisdom from Seneca makes perfect sense. If you anticipate what is coming your way, and prepare for it, you absolutely take the power away from whatever trouble is coming. This is one of the main reasons that people practice martial arts; they want to be prepared for any physical attacks that may come their way.

Here is another great example. If you stay informed about the weather and see that a major winter storm is forecast for the weekend, you can anticipate what is coming. You know you may be snowed in, so you can go out and stock up on food, water, and supplies that you may need. Since you know you might lose electricity, you may buy a generator and make sure you have candles, flashlights, and lamps ready. And you get your snow gear and warm clothes out and have them ready to go.

Since the winter storm is outside of your realm of control, you don't worry about it; you accept it is coming, and you prepare for it the best you can. While your preparations won't stop the snow and hassles from coming, your anticipation of the coming troubles will take away some of their power to completely disrupt your life.

I'm sure that you can think of many other examples that prove Seneca's point. The key here is to anticipate what might happen. This means that you must stay informed. Accepting everything that is outside of your realm of control doesn't mean that you simply throw your hands up and declare that whatever happens will happen. That is the mindset of a victim.

While you must accept the events that are out of your control, that doesn't mean you simply rest on your laurels. You accept things as they are, and then you rationally decide how to best *respond* to what is happening. You are an active player in the game of life, not a victim! Think rationally and respond wisely to the events and circumstances outside of your circle of control.

104

He is most powerful who has power over himself.
Seneca

As we already know, one of the central tenets of Stoic philosophy is centered on self-discipline and self-mastery. Those of us who have tried to reach a goal that takes a lot of self-discipline, such as dieting and losing weight, know that the biggest challenge is disciplining your mind and your desires. It takes a lot of self-discipline to eat a fresh salad or drink a protein shake when what you really crave is a cheeseburger and French fries.

Seneca taught that true power comes from mastering your own thoughts, words, actions, emotions, and desires. This makes perfect sense. Think about it. When you try to master external things which are outside of your control, you have some successes and some failures, and you always know that you can justify your failures by saying, "There was nothing I could do about it; it was just outside of my control." However, you don't have that excuse when it comes to having power over yourself, because you are the only one who truly has power over yourself.

So, what does it mean to have power over yourself? It means that you are in control of your thoughts, emotions, desires, words, and actions. Seneca taught that self-mastery, or power over yourself, is the foundation of your character. Power over yourself means you can control your thoughts and impulses, and when faced with a decision, you choose to act with honor, integrity, and wisdom.

This is the power that enables you to resist temptations and distractions, to remain calm when you face adversity or aggravations, to be rational instead of impulsive or emotional, and to stay true to your honor. Having power over yourself means you are truly free and can't be manipulated by other people or swayed by outside forces. Power over yourself means you are in control of the things that truly matter—your virtue, character, honor, and integrity. And when it comes to things outside of your control, you are able to respond rationally, not emotionally. That is true power!

For it is not death or pain that is to
be feared, but the fear of pain or death.
Epictetus

If something is inevitable, there is no reason to fear it. Fearing the inevitable does not prevent it from happening; all it does is rob you of your inner peace and of time that can be more wisely used. That is what Epictetus is trying to tell us in this quote. Death and pain are both a part of life for everyone; there is no reason to fear either. Simply deal with each of them with the same honor and fortitude as you do with the other things in your life.

Fear will not only rob you of your inner peace, but it will also rob you of many of life's experiences. When someone has an overwhelming fear of death, it prevents them from living their life to the fullest. They are constantly passing up different experiences and opportunities because of their irrational fear.

Furthermore, their fear persistently lives in the back of their minds, attacking their thought process anytime they consider trying something new and adventurous. When they see something that looks like it would be fun to try, their fear immediately jumps to the forefront, brainstorming every possible reason why this new activity is too dangerous to experience.

To live life to the fullest, you must take control of your fear instead of allowing your fear to control your mind. If you allow your fear to control your actions, it will absolutely rob you of many of life's pleasures. Many people have become so fearful that they refuse to leave their house or even associate with people. That is not truly living!

You must discipline yourself to control your fears. Fearing death or pain has never stopped death from coming or removed pain from your body. Accept the fact that death and pain are a natural part of the human experience and refuse to allow fear to control you. Once you conquer your fear of death, you will be amazed at the freedom you will experience. It is your destiny to die. The question is not whether you will die, but how you will spend the time you have been given to live on this earth. Choose wisely!

106

When jarred, unavoidably, by circumstances, revert at once
to yourself, and don't lose the rhythm more than you can help.
You'll have a better grasp of the harmony if you keep on going back to it.
Marcus Aurelius

We all must deal with unavoidable situations and heart-wrenching events during our life. It could be the unforeseen death of a loved one, a financial emergency, losing your job, a divorce, or some other life-jarring event. These things are unavoidable, and you have no control over them; but you do have control over how you choose to respond to them.

Marcus Aurelius is urging us to remember to maintain our inner peace, self-awareness, and composure during these times. It is all too easy to completely forget the Stoic wisdom that you have studied during an emergency or some heartbreaking event, but those are the times that you are challenged to maintain your balance and inner peace. Living the Stoic lifestyle is not worth much if you cannot maintain your calm, rational mind and inner peace in trying times.

These are the times that test your resolve and your self-discipline. When Marcus Aurelius wrote you should at once revert to yourself, he was urging us to immediately go within when faced with these external challenges and emergencies. Go within and remind yourself that you have no control over what has happened; you only have control over how you respond to it and whether you maintain your inner peace.

Many people immediately lose their inner peace and their composure during these trying times. They allow the situation to overcome their peace of mind and then start reacting to what has happened instead of calmly responding to the situation.

In trying times, discipline yourself to immediately go within and remind yourself that you will not allow an external situation, which you have no control over, to control you. Remind yourself that you *refuse to allow anything to disrupt your inner peace and calm*. First, calm your mind, then respond as you need to and maintain your inner peace.

107

He has his wish, whose wish can be to have what is enough.
Cleanthes

When you are never satisfied with what you have, it is hard to maintain your inner peace. We should all strive to be the best we can be and work to obtain the life that we want to live, but at the same time, we must be content with who we are and what we have in the present moment.

This is hard for some people to grasp. They question how someone can be perfectly content with their current life and still be motivated to strive for more. After all, isn't being unsatisfied with what you have or who you are the catalyst that motivates people to strive for more? While it's true that trying situations can motivate people to improve their lives, that doesn't mean that they can't be happy and content with life while they work to improve their situation.

You can always be happy if your goal is to be happy and content with what you have in your life, while you work to improve your life. This is what Cleanthes is trying to get across to us. If you wish for the right things, in the right way, you will always be content with what you have, whether it is a little or a lot.

You have probably heard of people who have won millions of dollars in the lottery saying how winning the lottery ruined their lives. When we hear someone say that we are dumbfounded; after all, they just won enough money to buy whatever they want and to be financially secure for the rest of their life. How could they say it ruined their life?

The truth is that winning the lottery did not ruin their lives; their actions ruined their lives. They thought that money would make them happy, but happiness is never dependent on external things. Happiness and contentment come from within. You can be just as happy with little as you can be with a lot.

A person who is content with having enough will always be content. Don't get sucked into believing that you will be happy when this or that happens. Be happy and content NOW! Don't make your happiness dependent on external circumstances.

108

> You can tell the character of every man
> when you see how he receives praise.
> *Seneca*

A man's character shows in how he receives praise or power. An honorable man will be humble and grateful for the praise he receives. He understands that others are under no obligation to give him recognition or praise. They praise him for his actions or accomplishments because they can recognize he has done a good job or gone out of his way to help others.

Honest praise is an honor that someone gives you, and you should receive it as such. Don't feel the need to be embarrassed or to put yourself down in some form of false modesty; just be sincerely grateful for the honor that you are given.

I used the term "honest praise" because there is also dishonest praise and flattery designed to manipulate you in some way. Always be suspicious when you know that someone is flattering you, as this is different from sincere praise. The difference lies in the intent and authenticity of the person giving you a compliment.

Honest praise is authentic and based on your genuine qualities or achievements. It highlights your actual accomplishments or strengths, with the intent of sincerely recognizing what you have done or accomplished. Sometimes it's hard to distinguish between honest praise and flattery. You must look beyond the obvious to discover the truth.

Flattery often compliments you for things which may not be entirely true and is intended to please you in order to manipulate you or soften you up for the other person to manipulate you later. The underlying intent is not to sincerely honor you, but is self-serving.

Either way, receive praise humbly and gratefully, but always remain aware of what is truly going on. True praise must be based on reality and is an honor. But beware of flattery and recognize it as a manipulation tactic. Keep your ego in check and don't allow it to make you susceptible to flattery.

109

If you want to be a writer, write.
Epictetus

Epictetus was very plainspoken and direct. If you read his actual writings, instead of a few quotes taken from his writings, you will find that he seemed to have very little patience with some people. He was blunt and quick to call people out for their shortcomings. He was also blunt in his teachings.

What he is saying in this quote really has nothing to do with writing, but he is bluntly urging us to be what we want to be in life. Epictetus is saying if you want to be something, then do it. Don't sit around and wish for it or daydream about it; simply do it.

If you want to be a writer, write! If you want to be an investor, then work towards that goal now. Take action to do what you want to do in life. Your years on this earth are numbered, and you only have one life to live. There are no do-overs. If you have a goal to be something or to do something in life, do it now. Don't waste time wishing for it or dreaming about it; just do it!

When I first decided to start writing and brought up the topic of writing a book to some of my colleagues (I was a history teacher at the time), I was told, "You can't do that. There are way too many authors out there. It would be way too hard for you to get your foot in the door."

But I didn't listen to the negativity. I simply started writing a blog on social media. I quickly developed a following, and a small publisher came across my work and contacted me about authoring a book. From there, I ended up publishing several books with him. Then, I found he was not a good fit for me, so I bought the rights to my books back and went in another direction. After that move, I wrote my award-winning bestseller, *Modern Bushido: Living a Life of Excellence.*

Now I have published eighteen books and have written several as a ghostwriter. None of those books would have been written or published if I had simply wished I could be a writer or dreamed about being a writer. If you want to do something in this life—do it! Take action to achieve your dreams.

110

If anyone can refute me—show me I'm making a mistake or
looking at things from the wrong perspective—I'll gladly change.
It's the truth I'm after, and the truth never harmed anyone.
Marcus Aurelius

Many people are offended when someone points out their mistakes or
shows them they are wrong about something. Because of their overblown egos,
they seem to want to defend their opinions, even if you show them that they
are misguided. They dig in and double down on their erroneous perspective,
defending it at all costs.

They are not concerned with the truth, but with maintaining their egos.
These people are sincere about what they believe, even though they are wrong.
Never forget that someone can be sincere while at the same time being
completely wrong. And if they are not open to hearing the truth, they will
remain stuck in their erroneous beliefs until they are finally forced by
circumstances outside of their control to realize the error of their ways.

You should never allow your ego to impede your understanding of the truth.
Keep your ego in check! If you don't, it will always stand between your
inaccurate beliefs and the truth. Your ego lives in your mind and subconscious,
where it uses your emotions to convince you that any information that is
opposed to your beliefs is an assault on your intelligence. It influences how
you think, how you make decisions, and your overall worldview. It is also tied
to how you view yourself.

If allowed, your ego will always defend your beliefs, regardless of whether
those beliefs are right or wrong. You must discipline yourself to always seek
the truth, rather than defending or maintaining your ego. A disciplined ego is
healthy and balanced, whereas a defensive ego can get in the way of your
acceptance of the truth. Preserve an open mind and always be open to listening
to a different opinion or a different way of looking at the world. Be open to the
truth no matter where it may take you. As Marcus Aurelius taught, the truth
never harmed anyone, well, other than a liar.

111

> To bear trials with a calm mind robs
> misfortune of its strength and burden.
> *Seneca*

Challenges, trials, and difficulties are a part of life. Everyone has their own challenges to deal with in life. Seneca taught that if we bear those challenges and difficulties with a calm mind, it takes away some of our burden associated with those hard times.

Many people get frustrated and lose their temper when some unexpected difficulties come into their life. They not only have to deal with the issue at hand, but they increase their difficulties by losing their temper or panicking. When they lose their temper, they may say or do things they will wish they had not said or done. They are adding to their misfortune because they do not discipline themselves to control their minds and maintain their calm demeanor.

Things are what they are. Getting upset about how something is has no effect on the situation; it only agitates your mind even more. When you are very upset, stressed, or irate, you can't think clearly. Getting upset and yelling or cursing has never solved any problem or made any situation any better. It only demonstrates your lack of self-control and robs you of your inner peace.

Seneca taught that if you maintain a calm inner peace during a trying situation or misfortune, it can help you deal with what is going on in your life. Maintaining a calm mind enables you to think clearly and rationally to solve the problem at hand. Panicking only makes everything worse. While many people believe that panicking, falling apart, or losing their temper over some misfortune is a natural reaction, it is not the Stoic mindset.

You must maintain your inner peace and calm mind no matter what you are facing externally. Don't panic and don't allow yourself to lose your temper. Refuse to allow anything, no matter how horrible it may be, to rob you of your inner peace and rational mind. Whatever you must face, face it with a calm, rational mind! Bearing your trials with a calm mind not only helps you deal with your burdens, but also earns you the respect of others.

112

It is in virtue that happiness consists, for virtue is the state
of mind which tends to make the whole of life harmonious.
Zeno of Citium

Zeno, the founder of Stoicism, taught that you must align your mind and actions with the natural order of things. He believed that virtue was the key to inner peace and happiness. Zeno's teachings taught that happiness comes from inside of you, from cultivating virtue, not from wealth, material things, or anything outside yourself.

Virtue comprises qualities such as honor, wisdom, integrity, courage, justice, temperance, etc. Zeno taught that living a virtuous life would promote inner peace and happiness throughout your life. It is virtue that will help you live as you were meant to live and help you maintain a balanced, rational mindset and a calm, peaceful life.

According to Zeno, it is the harmony between your calm, rational mind, your virtuous actions, and how you respond to the external world around you, that brings you true happiness. He taught that happiness was not simply some momentary emotional state brought on by pursuing pleasure, but rather a constant state of mind that is rooted in your own personal integrity, honor, and character.

When your happiness comes from within and is rooted in your own code of honor and integrity, which has become your way of life, you are not happy now and then, but consistently. It will show through your countenance, your thoughts, your speech, and your actions. Furthermore, since your happiness is an internal state of being, nothing external can rob you of your happiness; you have total control over your inner peace and tranquility.

Therefore, it is important for you to live a virtuous life. Maintaining your character, honor, and integrity is for your own good. It is not something you do to feel superior to others, but to be at peace within yourself. Your conscience will be at peace if you are living according to your own code of honor, no matter what is happening externally. Think about this.

113

There is only one way to happiness, and that is to cease
worrying about things that are beyond the power of our will.
Epictetus

Would you be happier if you never worried about anything outside of your
control? How would your life change if you were never concerned with
external things that you can't control? What things are totally within your
circle of control?

These are questions you should ponder and come to terms with if you want
to live a happy life full of tranquility and inner peace. Epictetus taught that if
we stopped worrying about things which are outside of our realm of control,
we would have no problem being happy. Let's examine that thought a bit
further.

What things are inside your circle of control? Your thoughts, your speech,
your actions, your attitude, the desires you choose to entertain, your will, what
you value, what you choose to listen to, read, or watch on television or the
computer, your opinions and views, how you respond to other people,
situations, or circumstances outside of your control, your values, your
boundaries, who you associate with, what you choose to put in your body, and
how you spend your time. This list clearly shows that you have control over a
lot of things in your life.

However, there are many more things that you don't control. You have no
control over how other people act, what others think, say, do, or believe, the
traffic, the weather, death, the past or the future, the outcomes of your actions,
or any external events outside of your personal realm of control.

Keep your focus on the things that are in your circle of control and don't
allow things that are outside of your circle of control to disrupt your inner
peace. The more you work to perfect all those things that you *can* control, the
happier you will be, but only *if* you refuse to allow the things outside of your
control to rob you of your inner peace. This means that you may need to change
how you respond to things outside of your control.

114

There is no genius without a touch of madness.
Seneca

The people we consider to be geniuses in their field of study are rare. People with exceptional insight and creativity, who are extremely brilliant in their field of study, are usually unconventional people who think and act in ways that are outside the norm. To many people, they may be perceived as a little crazy, as they do not live as most people live.

Many times, these extraordinary individuals will challenge the status quo and push intellectual boundaries. Their unique style of thinking may make them seem eccentric or even irrational to other people because they think, act, and speak differently than the average person. They have a different perspective from the average person, so they think about life differently; their priorities and focus are different.

If you look back at those individuals who we consider to be geniuses in their field, you see that many lived a life that absolutely seemed strange, or even a bit crazy to others who did not see the world as they did. In addition, their brilliance often rubbed the authorities of the day the wrong way.

But it was this so-called "madness" which fueled their passion and drove them to relentlessly think about and study their subject until they discovered insights that others could not see or comprehend until decades or centuries later. Without these individuals, we would not have the extraordinary innovations that we take for granted in our modern world.

So, what does this Stoic teaching have to do with your life? It urges you to be who you truly are—be yourself. What others think about what you do, how you dress, or how you live is none of your business, and you should not worry about their opinions. Remember, you have no control over what other people think, do, or say. Just be you! Don't worry about fitting in with everyone else. Discover what excites your spirit, and then do what you were meant to do on this earth. Stop worrying about what other people think about how you live your life! Live your life your way regardless of the opinions of others.

We must concern ourselves absolutely with the things that are under
our control and entrust the things not in our control to the Universe.
Musonius Rufus

I have discussed focusing on the things which are under your control a lot
so far in this book, and will probably discuss it even more, as it is one of the
fundamental principles of Stoicism. It is an easy topic to understand, but it is
not as easy to integrate into your daily life because most of us have lived our
entire life allowing external things to worry us or control us in some way.

Musonius Rufus gives us a tip that can make it easier for us to stop worrying
and reacting to things outside of our circle of control. He tells us we should
concern ourselves *absolutely* with the things that we control and leave the rest
to the Universe or to God.

Let's look at the first half of this quote first. If we concern ourselves
absolutely with the things under our control, that means we focus on those
things unconditionally and completely. Focusing totally on the things we
control doesn't leave any time for us to concern ourselves with the things
outside of our control.

You might think, "Yeah, but some of those things outside of my control do
actually affect my life." And you would be right; we live in a world where
some things outside of our control do affect our lives. The Stoics never said
that those things would not affect your life, but that we should not allow them
to affect our happiness or inner peace. Either way, you still have no control
over the things that are outside of your control.

So, what should you do about the things that affect your life but are outside
of your circle of control? Rufus taught us we should leave them to the Universe
or to God. If you have faith that God loves you and is looking out for you, then
trust Him to take care of those things. You don't need to understand what His
plan is or why He allows something to happen. Just trust that He is taking care
of the things that you don't control. Focus on what you can control and trust
God or the Universe to take care of the rest.

116

Be tolerant with others and strict with yourself.
Marcus Aurelius

We all make mistakes, lose our temper from time to time, and fall short of the perfection of character that we should be pursuing. Nobody's perfect! That said, it can be much easier for us to see others' faults than it is to recognize our own faults. Marcus Aurelius urges us to be tolerant of the faults of other people, but to be strict with our own.

If we are focusing on the things that are in our circle of control and leaving those things outside of our circle of control to God, then we are not spending much time focusing on the faults of other people. Even though others can be aggravating at times, we should be tolerant of them.

One way to remember to be tolerant of others is to remind yourself that you don't really know what is going on in the lives of other people. The woman who speaks rudely to you at the store may be dealing with a major life crisis and is at the end of her patience. It may be completely out of character for her. The guy honking his horn, screaming, and cursing in his car may have just gotten screwed over by his boss and lost his job.

The reasons behind people's rude behavior are endless. While this doesn't excuse their behavior, Marcus Aurelius tells us we should be tolerant of the shortcomings of others. Remembering that they could be dealing with major problems in their life will help you remember to be tolerant of their rude behavior.

At the same time, Marcus Aurelius tells us to be strict with ourselves. This means that you should work to improve your character and your shortcomings, not simply ignore them. Also, he says to be strict with yourself, but not to beat yourself up when you fall short of your goal of perfecting your character. Be strict with yourself as you work to perfect your character, but don't speak negatively about yourself. You wouldn't constantly call a child a loser or a horrible person when he or she makes a mistake; likewise, be patient with yourself as you strive to become the best that you can be.

Death is not an evil. What is it then?
The one law mankind has that is free of all discrimination.
Seneca

Many people see the laws in their country as sacred, but they neglect to stop and think about where those laws originate or why they exist to start with. While many think the laws of man are somehow sacred and must be obeyed no matter what, they see the politicians in their country as corrupt liars who will say and do most anything to line their pockets with money.

What they fail to realize is that it is these same men and women, whom they have little to no respect for, who write and pass these laws that they feel are so important. The truth is all laws are written and voted on by politicians, and many of our laws are passed for less than honorable reasons. Years before the birth of Jesus, Seneca knew this and referred to this.

The fact is that laws are not sacred. They are made by corrupt politicians who are influenced by lobbyists and the ultra-rich who can afford to buy off politicians to pass the laws that they want passed, and to write the laws in such a way that it benefits their businesses or their families. There is nothing sacred about that!

Of course, this doesn't apply to every single law. There are some laws that are written to protect the people from criminals and those who would take advantage of them. Other laws are passed to protect the state or country. Either way, every law has an underlying reason for existing, and many of them make little to no sense for the population.

Seneca knew this and pointed out that there is one law that applies to all mankind regardless of their standing, political power, or riches. That is the universal law of life and death. Every human will eventually die, no matter how much they may try to avoid death. Death comes to us all; all we can do is decide how we will live and how we will spend our time until that day comes. How will you live your life? This is a question that you should answer right away because you don't know how long your life will be.

118

The more we value things outside
our control, the less control we have.
Epictetus

Seeing how much of Epictetus' teaching revolved around distinguishing between the things you can control and the things that are outside of your control, should tell you how important this simple concept truly is. While it is easy to understand, it can be difficult to actually put this into practice on a daily basis.

"The more we value things outside our control, the less control we have," is a universal truism. It is just as true in the United States as it was in ancient Rome, or anywhere else in the world. The more value you place on external things, the more out of control your life will be because you are basing your happiness on things which you can't control.

When someone places too much value on external things, those things have power over his emotional state, and thus, his mental well-being. External things such as the behavior of others, wealth, the weather, fame, and the thoughts and words of other people will cause you stress and rob you of your inner peace and happiness if you place too much value on them.

You may argue that we must care about these things because they affect our lives. However, while some of those things do influence your life, placing too much value on anything outside of your circle of control will rob you of your inner peace. Therefore, you should focus your attention on the things that you can control.

By focusing on the things that you can control, you take back your power and can maintain your inner peace, happiness, and Stoic mindset. The more you let go of your attachment to external things, the more control you have over your mind and emotions, and that leads to greater inner peace. It also sets you free from the control that external things have over your life. Take control of your life by focusing most of your attention on the things that you can control!

119

> I don't know what treason is, if it is not
> betraying the liberty of your own people.
> *Cato the Younger*

Wow, Cato the Younger did not hold back with this teaching. One of the main purposes of governments is to protect the rights and freedoms of their people. According to Cato the Younger, if a government is not protecting the freedom of the people it serves, it is committing treason.

Every government is established to protect the rights and freedoms of it citizens, to maintain order to protect citizens and their property, to provide public services for it citizens, to set up a fair and just legal system to punish those who infringe on the rights of its citizens, to regulate the economy to benefit its population, and to defend its citizens from outside threats from foreign militaries. In short, governments are supposed to support, protect, and answer to their citizens.

However, as we know, many governments around the world commit treason, according to Cato the Younger's definition. They infringe on the freedom of their citizens in many ways. Many who are elected to protect and serve the citizens of their country are corrupt men and women of low character and no honor. They use their position not to benefit the citizens of their country, but to increase their personal wealth at the expense of the citizens they swore to serve and protect.

These politicians beg for the people's support while making empty promises about how much they are going to do for the country's citizens. But once they are in office, they serve their own agenda, which is often not in the best interest of the country or its citizens, and act as if they are above those in the general population. Those who beg for your vote, once in office, seem to feel as if they are now royalty. I agree with Cato the Younger. If this is not treason, I don't know what it is. Be very careful when it comes to trusting any politician! History proves repeatedly that most of the politicians in the world cannot be trusted.

120

Difficulty comes from our lack of confidence.
Seneca

A lack of confidence can cause you many difficulties in life. Your perception of difficult situations depends on your self-confidence and overall mindset. A self-confident person has a totally different mindset than someone who does not believe in himself or who lacks self-confidence.

Most challenges in life are not insurmountable, but they can feel that way to someone who lacks self-confidence. Self-doubt prevents many people from living the life they were meant to live. When you doubt your ability to perform a certain task or to manage a specific situation, you are telling your subconscious mind that you can't do it. And your subconscious mind will remind you of this repeatedly.

While self-doubt is not an emotion, it causes feelings of fear, anxiety, frustration, and insecurity, and these emotions cause many people to hesitate to try new things or difficult tasks. A lack of self-confidence will make many things seem more difficult than they are.

Those with a lack of self-confidence will judge external challenges as being much larger or much more insurmountable than they are. When you recognize doubt as a natural part of being a human being, you can then evaluate your self-doubt rationally and calmly and better evaluate life's challenges.

By focusing on developing your inner strength and self-confidence, you can transform your perception of the challenges you will encounter in life. This is one of the benefits of developing a Stoic mindset. The more confidence you have in yourself, the better you can manage the external challenges in your life.

This will reduce your stress and give you greater courage to try new things with a calm, confident attitude. The more you successfully take control of the things that are in your control, the more your self-confidence will grow. And the more self-confidence you develop, the easier it will become for you to deal with the external challenges of life.

121

Do not let thoughts sweep you off your feet. It is a great battle…
It is a fight for autonomy, freedom, happiness, and peace.
Epictetus

Learning to control your thoughts can be one of the hardest things to master. It takes persistent awareness and self-discipline to consistently control your thoughts and bring them in line with the person you want to be, but it absolutely can be done.

This doesn't mean that you will be able to totally stop unwanted thoughts from popping into your mind, but that you will be able to recognize those thoughts as they appear. When an unwanted thought appears in your mind, you have the power to cancel it immediately and not entertain it or allow it to remain in your mind. Just mentally say to yourself, "No, I refuse to think this or to allow this negative thought to remain in my mind."

As Epictetus taught, it is a great battle that will absolutely throw you off your game if you are not careful. That is why you must remain aware of your thoughts. The moment you are careless concerning what thoughts you allow to remain in your mind, those negative thoughts will start to snowball and produce more mental negativity until you completely lose your inner peace and tranquility.

To live with a Stoic mindset, you must learn to control your mind. No man is truly free if he cannot control his mind and bring his thoughts in line with who and what he wants to be. Your thoughts have the power to keep you calm and rational, or to completely rob you of your inner peace. Thoughts can calm your spirit or cause you to panic. All actions began as a thought, so do not take this battle lightly; it is one of the greatest battles you will have to fight to live with a Stoic mindset.

Make a firm decision that you are going to control your thoughts, then keep this battle fresh on your mind. It is very easy to get busy and forget to maintain Stoic thoughts until after you have allowed your mind to spin out of control. Stay vigilant and maintain your inner peace and happiness!

122

Think of the life you have lived until now as over and, as a dead
man, see what's left as a bonus and live it according to Nature.
Marcus Aurelius

Many cultures and religions throughout the world have taught the concept
of dying before you die, just as Marcus Aurelius taught. Marcus Aurelius wrote
his now famous book, *Meditations*, during the latter years of his life, so it is
only natural that he would have many thoughts about death. But this is not just
a Stoic teaching.

Buddha taught that being mindful of your death would bring you peace and
clarity about what is truly important in your life, leading to a life that is free
from attachment and suffering. The samurai meditated on death daily and
believed that by doing so they would free themselves of the fear of death and
that it would help them maintain their honor. The samurai book, *Hagakure*,
states, "Meditation on inevitable death should be performed daily."

Tibetan Buddhism, in the *Tibetan Book of the Dead*, encourages its
followers to meditate on their own death and to see death not as an end to one's
life, but as a transformation. They consider this preparation for a path of
enlightenment.

Early Christians also meditated on their own mortality and used symbols
such as skulls to remind them of their own death, and the eternal life they
would have through their belief in Jesus. Some of the underground tunnels
where these Christians gathered and hid for safety are lined with skulls.

The mystical Islamic sect, the Sufis, used the phrase, "die before you die,"
as a way to transcend the ego and detach themselves from worldly concerns.
They believed this would help them reach a spiritual awakening and bring
them closer to God. This practice was to prepare them for the afterlife.

Keeping the fact that you will eventually die fresh in your mind will help
you focus on the things that truly matter to you. Your life is no more guaranteed
than that of the samurai. People die every day in unexpected ways. Today is
the day to come to peace with the fact that tomorrow is not promised to anyone.

123

He who fears death will never do anything worthy of a living man.
Seneca

This teaching by Seneca is a perfect continuation of the previous teaching by Marcus Aurelius. Seneca taught that you must accept the reality that death is an inevitable part of life for us all. Coming to terms with the fact that death is simply an aspect of life for every human being is essential to your well-being, as well as living life to the fullest.

As I discussed on the previous page, one of the best ways to overcome the fear of death is to meditate on your death daily and keep the fact that you will die fresh on your mind. None of us knows the day or time of our death, but we all can be assured that we will die, and so will everyone in your life. Don't take your life, or the time you spend with your loved ones, for granted. You never know when this day will be the last time you speak to those you love.

Coming to peace with this not only frees you from the fear of death but also reminds you to make every minute of your life count. You don't have time to waste! Even what is considered a long life for people today is still very short; time will go by much faster than you expect. And that is if you actually live to an old age. People die every day who leave their home without a care in the world, only to never come back home again.

Keeping this in mind will help you maintain the correct attitude towards those you love. When you focus on your death or the deaths of those you love, it will cause you to speak more lovingly to those who are important to you. It will help you be more patient with those who cross your path. And it will increase your inner peace, as it will inevitably cause you to decide what you truly believe about death and what happens after you die.

This frees your mind to live as a man of honor, character, and integrity, because you know that your time on this planet is short. If there is anything you want to accomplish or do in life, now is the time to do it. Tomorrow never really exists except in your thoughts. The only time you really have to live is now. Come to terms with your death!

124

Do every act of your life as though
it was the very last act of your life.
Marcus Aurelius

When I started writing this book, I began by reading and researching the writings of the Stoics and highlighting the quotes which spoke to me for the book. I asked God to guide me in order to make this book useful to those who read it.

Then, I added the quotes in no specific order. The only thing I really tried to do, as far as the order of the quotes went, was to not have too many quotes by the same Stoic too close together. As I am writing this, I am amazed at how the last three quotes have all fit together perfectly.

In this teaching, Marcus Aurelius encourages us to do everything as though it were the last act of our life. I have already discussed how you should come to terms with your death and how short and precious life truly is. This teaching takes you one step further—you should do everything as if it is the last thing you will ever get to do.

If you do this, you will stop wasting your precious time. You will start taking your life more seriously; you won't procrastinate when it comes to making sure you have everything in order in case you unexpectedly die tomorrow.

Take some time to consider what things you would do differently if you started doing every act as if it was the very last act of your life. Would you speak to your loved ones differently? Would you finally take care of the will that you have been putting off writing? Do you think you would stop allowing meaningless annoyances to irritate you as much? How would this change your life?

This mental exercise helped the Stoics focus on what truly mattered to them. It helped the samurai to perfect their skills. It helps spiritual people to stay focused on their true beliefs and live as they should. And it will help you achieve excellence in everything you do. Apply this wisdom to your life.

It is more necessary for the soul to be cured than
the body; for it is better to die than to live badly.
Epictetus

The French philosopher and Jesuit priest, Pierre Teilhard de Chardin, in his teachings on the spiritual evolution of humanity and the interconnectedness of the spiritual world and the material world, taught that you are not a human being having a spiritual experience, rather a spiritual being having a human experience. But almost 2,000 years before his teachings, Epictetus taught that the health of your soul, or spirit, is more important than the health of your body.

The Stoics did not have a specific belief about life after death, and their views on this topic varied from one Stoic to another. The Stoic teachers focused mostly on living a rational, virtuous life in the present. But by digging deeper into their teachings, like this one by Epictetus, we can get an idea of what they believed.

Epictetus also wrote, "You are a distinct portion of the essence of God; and contain a certain part of Him in yourself." Taken together with the teaching above, it is obvious that Epictetus believed in the soul or spirit. Chrysippus believed that the soul might live temporarily after death, but ultimately returns to God, or what he called "Divine Logos."

Most of the Stoics believed that what happens to someone after his death is unknowable and is irrelevant to living a life of integrity and honor. As Marcus Aurelius put it, and was reworded and used in the popular movie, *Braveheart*, "It is not death that a man should fear, but he should fear never beginning to live."

However, if we read between the lines, we can see that the Stoics believed the soul is important. Epictetus states that it is better to die than to live badly. There can be only one reason for this belief—the soul or spirit is more important than your physical life. This is the entire basis of every religion or spiritual belief. Is your soul healthy and ready for death?

126

Man seems to be deficient in nothing so much as he is in time.
Zeno of Citium

We all have the same amount of time in each day, but some people seem to be able to use their time more efficiently than others. Even over 2,000 years ago, Zeno noticed that many humans fail to use their time wisely, wasting hours every day that could be used to better meet their needs or accomplish their goals.

When you ask someone to do something or invite them to dinner or a get-together, it is very common today to hear people say, "I don't have enough time." This is an indication that this person is not using his time wisely, as he has the same amount of time in a day as everyone else.

While it is true that some people are much busier than others, it is also true that most people do not manage their time wisely. Stating that you don't have enough time to do something is simply saying that the event or the person asking for your attention is not a high priority to you.

We all make time for the things that are important to us. There is always time to watch your favorite television show, go to the beach, watch your favorite sport, etc. It is only the events, gatherings, or activities in which we are not very interested that we seem "not to have time for." If you think about this, you will find that it is true.

Time is the most valuable resource we have, and that is what Zeno was referring to in this teaching. We can always make more money or buy more material things, but no matter how much we would like to, we cannot buy more time. Many people waste time on worthless distractions or worrying about external things over which they have no control. These distractions rob them of their most valuable possession—time.

Instead of wasting time on various distractions, we need to prioritize our time on the activities and thoughts that move us toward our goals. Most people live as if their time on this earth is infinite, neglecting to appreciate the present moment until it is too late. Your time is not infinite; use it wisely.

127

No man can escape his destiny, the next inquiry being
how he may best live the time that he has to live.
Marcus Aurelius

Marcus Aurelius added to Zeno's teachings on the use of time, urging us to accept the inevitable while using our time wisely. Think about how much time you have wasted over the years worrying about something that you had no control over.

Refusing to accept things as they are and worrying about them, or trying in vain to change them, only leads to frustration and mental anguish. It is also a complete waste of time. You must accept that certain things are out of your control, respond to them the best you can, and move on.

Worrying about how things are or what may happen is one of the worst ways to spend your valuable time. Not only does it accomplish nothing of value, but it robs you of your inner peace as well as your time.

If you remind yourself that your time is the most valuable thing you have, you will absolutely refuse to spend your time worrying about things that you can't control. Instead, focus on how to best spend your time.

What truly matters is how you choose to use the time that you have. When you are tempted to veg out on the couch and hypnotically scroll on social media, start asking yourself, "Is this really the best use of my limited time? Is this going to move me closer to my goals or help me perfect my character?"

By asking yourself these questions throughout the day, you find you can better manage your time and accomplish more of the things you want to do. Focus on how you can best use your time to perfect your character and move yourself closer to your goals, rather than wasting it complaining, worrying, or on some mindless activity.

Think about your overall objectives and what kind of legacy you want to leave for your children or family. Refuse to allow pointless wastes of time to hypnotically lull you into a semi-meditative state while you mindlessly put your mind on autopilot. Mindfully stay aware of how to best use your time.

128

When someone is properly grounded in life, they should
not have to look outside themselves for approval.
Epictetus

This is a very important teaching for our modern society. So many people
are worried about whether or not others will approve of what they think, what
they say, or what they do, that they are afraid to express themselves or take an
action without first gauging whether their words or actions are politically
correct. This is being dishonest, and it shows a lack of self-confidence.

To Epictetus, being properly grounded in life meant living with wisdom,
courage, self-discipline, integrity, and justice—the Stoic virtues. The Stoics
taught that these character traits are the foundation of a good life and that when
someone integrates these traits into their life, they will have self-confidence,
mental and emotional clarity, and inner peace in their life.

Those who have developed these traits have no need for external approval.
Remember, the approval of others, or their disapproval, is outside of your
control. And since it is outside of your control, it should be irrelevant to your
self-esteem and self-confidence. Refuse to allow the opinions of others to
trouble your mind or affect your life.

Ground yourself in honor, wisdom, and integrity, and neither the approval
nor disapproval of others will affect your decisions. This is a freedom that most
people never achieve. When you value the approval of others, it makes you
dependent on their fluctuating opinions. This is not true freedom, nor is it a
wise way to live your life. It will foster stress, anxiety, and disrupt your inner
peace.

Be self-sufficient and get your validation from within your own spirit,
based on what is right and honorable. Don't worry about societal expectations
or the opinions of others. When you know your words or actions are honorable
and just, it will give you a calm sense of internal peace, no matter what anyone
else thinks about what you say or do. What is right takes precedence over their
approval or their opinions.

129

It takes a wise man to discover a wise man.
Diogenes

Diogenes was probably the most cynical of all the Stoics. In this teaching, he says that only someone who has cultivated wisdom in his life can distinguish between a wise man and a fool. His statement can also be said as, a fool cannot distinguish between a wise man and a fool because he lacks the wisdom and insight to discern the qualities of true wisdom.

As we already know, the Stoics associated wisdom with virtue, integrity, and living according to nature. Diogenes believed that if a person was lacking in virtue, honor, integrity, and character, that his lack of knowledge concerning these traits would prevent him from being able to fully understand or comprehend the value of wisdom or to distinguish a wise man from someone who lacks wisdom.

Most people judge people only by their social status, appearance, or achievements, none of which is of much value in determining whether someone is wise. Wisdom is an internal quality and cannot be ascertained from external appearances, titles, or achievements. It takes someone with at least some wisdom to look beyond the veil and discover the true character of another person. You must look beyond the superficial to discover true wisdom.

Diogenes' statement also speaks to the rarity of true wisdom. The average person may lack the perspective to distinguish genuine wisdom from cleverness or a quick wit. It is the act of mistaking cleverness or a quick wit for wisdom that allows charlatans and conmen to take advantage of those who are seeking wisdom, but who lack the wisdom to distinguish a wise man from a charlatan. The *Book of Proverbs* states that fools mock wisdom when they hear it.

True wisdom is a rare quality, and because it is so rare, it is hard for the average person to recognize. The wise man has cultivated wisdom in his life and can easily recognize and appreciate it when he finds it. The average man mistakes clichés and repeated quotes for wisdom.

130

It never ceases to amaze me: we all love ourselves more than other people, but care more about their opinions than our own.

Marcus Aurelius

In this teaching from Marcus Aurelius' book, *Meditations*, he points out a very interesting, odd, and true observation about most people. No one would argue that most people love themselves more than anyone else. At the same time, most people care more about the opinions of others than their own. When you see this truism in writing, it seems very odd. Why would you love yourself more than others, but care more about other people's opinions than your own? The answer is that most people do not have enough self-confidence, so they look for validation through the opinions of other people.

There is nothing wrong with listening to different opinions or getting advice from someone who knows more than you about a certain subject. Expert advice is one thing, but when it comes to your life and how you live, you should value your opinions more than anyone else's opinions. No one knows more about your true desires, goals, and what is right for you than you do.

The self-confident man, while he may listen to the opinions of others, will not value those opinions more than his own. He listens to the opinions of others and uses whatever he finds to be valuable in their words, but in the end, he always looks at all the angles and decides for himself. Self-confident people don't need, nor want, others to make their decisions for them; they are confident in their own ability to make the important decisions about how they want to live their lives and what is best for them.

The wise man makes his decisions based on what is right and virtuous, not according to the opinions of others, especially those whose opinions are not based on honor, character, or integrity. He does not look for external validation of his thoughts, words, or actions; he simply does what is right according to his code of honor. Everyone has an opinion on almost everything, but not everyone's opinions matter. If you need advice from others, make sure that you are getting advice from someone who knows what he or she is talking about.

131

I start to speak only when I'm sure that
what I have to say is not better left unsaid.
Cato the Younger

This advice from Cato the Younger is great advice for everyone! Speak only when you know that you have something of value to add to the conversation, and then, say what you need to say carefully, with tact and wisdom, and consider the audience to whom you are speaking.

Most people talk way too much; they apparently feel that they must add their two cents to any and every subject, even if they know nothing about the subject being discussed. They are uncomfortable with silence and feel that they must say something, anything, rather than sitting silently and mentally digesting what has been said.

As an introvert, it drives me crazy to try to discuss something with someone who absolutely will not stop talking. I dislike small talk about unimportant or meaningless subjects that have no bearing on my life. But most people seem to delight in babbling on and on about meaningless subjects, things they know little to nothing about, or other people.

The wise man understands that it is better to be silent, listen, and increase his wisdom and knowledge than to constantly talk. You learn more by listening than you ever will by talking. Don't feel the need to talk just to break the silence or add your two cents to the conversation.

In addition, when you do speak, make sure that what you say is not better off left unsaid. Many people cause themselves trouble by saying things that would have been better left unsaid. Always think before you speak, not only about what you are about to say, but about whether you should voice your opinions on the subject. Always think of the possible consequences of what you are about to say. Think strategically!

Don't allow your tongue to complicate your life! Develop the wisdom to know when to speak and when to be silent, and the self-control to be silent when what you want to say is better left unsaid.

132

You will never have to experience defeat if you
avoid contests whose outcome is outside your control.
Epictetus

This is a very powerful statement by Epictetus! As you know by now, one of the fundamental principles of Stoicism is to focus on what you can control and let go of those things that are outside of your control. If you avoid contests where the outcome is outside of your control, your victory or defeat rests completely on your own words or actions.

Epictetus' statement is more of a truism than advice on avoiding competitive contests. He is not saying that you should never enter a contest or test your skills against others; he is simply stating that if you do enter a contest where the outcome is outside of your circle of control, you may or may not experience failure or defeat. This doesn't mean that experiencing defeat or failure is a bad thing; we all learn more from failure than we do from victory.

However, if your sense of victory is based on things outside of your realm of control, such as other people's opinions or external circumstances, you may feel disappointed or defeated. You will never feel disappointment or defeat if you don't put too much emphasis on whether you win or lose. Base your success on your own criteria—whether you have done your best, maintained your honor and character, and learned from the experience.

The key to avoiding disappointment or the feeling of being defeated is to shift your focus from an external victory to internal mastery. If you do this, you will maintain your feeling of calm, inner peace, and accomplishment, regardless of whether you won or lost the contest or event. Don't put too much emphasis on winning or losing, but on being the best you can be.

Be determined to maintain your focus and inner calm no matter what you are doing or what kind of contest you decide to take part in. Decide for yourself what determines victory or defeat for you. Bruce Lee taught, "Defeat is a state of mind; no one is ever defeated until defeat has been accepted as a reality. You decide whether you are victorious or defeated; nobody else!

133

It is not the word I am concerned with, but the attitude behind it.
Epictetus

To the Stoic, someone's intention and mindset is much more important than the words they use or their superficial appearance. I am sure that you have seen people who can deliver an insult or a slight with a smile on their face, saying what they mean in an indirect and semi-cryptic way. They have perfected the art of insulting someone indirectly, leaving the meaning of what they have said up to interpretation, and leaving themselves an excuse or escape if they are called out on what they have said. They deliver their insults in a roundabout way, but with the same malicious intention.

While we have no control over what other people think, say, or do, we should be wise enough to look beyond the veil and interpret the meaning behind their words or actions. This is not to say we should allow their words to upset or anger us. When you allow someone to anger you, you give them control over you. Develop the mental strength to rise above their petty attempts to push your buttons, but be wise enough to discern their meaning.

Just remind yourself that maintaining your inner peace and character is what is truly important. You don't have to internalize someone's rude attempt to insult you. As Marcus Aurelius taught, "Reject your sense of injury and the injury itself disappears." If you don't value others' opinions or words, they shouldn't disrupt your inner peace or trigger anger in your mind.

That said, you should always listen closely to what others say; they will reveal their true intentions or their true feelings if you listen intuitively. While their words are not that important to you, they will reveal the person's true character, and that gives you important information concerning whether you want to associate with him or her.

Always value someone's true character and underlying intentions more than their external appearances or empty rhetoric. Remember, words can have more than one meaning, and they can be empty if not backed up by virtuous actions. Refuse to allow anyone to disrupt your inner peace!

TEMPERANCE JUSTICE COURAGE WISDOM

134

Virtue is nothing else than right reason.
Seneca

Seneca and the other Stoics believed that all virtuous actions are rooted in rational thought or right reasoning. This is a fundamental Stoic belief and one that guides the actions of the Stoic. As far as Stoic wisdom is concerned, reason is the thought process that distinguishes the wise man from the average person. It is reason that aligns the wise man with nature or the way he should live his life.

If your actions are virtuous, that means your actions are in harmony with rational reasoning. According to the Stoics, right reason involves acting with justice, courage, wisdom, and temperance, which is why I have included the above image on every page of this book.

Your decisions and actions must be guided by rational thought rather than emotional or irrational motivations. When your thoughts, words, and actions are guided by rational thought, you will think, speak, and act with wisdom, courage, justice, and temperance or moderation.

According to the Stoics, virtue has nothing to do with external achievements, status, or your financial situation, but it is simply about making your decisions with wisdom and rational thought. Those who are not living a moral life are not thinking rationally, for if they were, they would not be living as they do.

It takes wisdom and courage to pass on something that at first appears pleasurable or beneficial to you but is not virtuous. Once you begin making your decisions according to rational thought, you find that you naturally make virtuous decisions.

If something is not wise or just, you know it is not the right decision for you to make. If the actions you take are not guided by moderation, then you are out of line with virtue. When you strive to bring all your thoughts, words, and actions in line with right reason, you will feel a sense of righteousness in your spirit. Your rational mind and conscience will guide you.

135

It is inevitable that continuous behavior of any one kind is going to instill new habits and tendencies while steadily confirming old ones.
Epictetus

Science tells us it takes 30-40 days to form a new habit. With that in mind, we can plainly see that Epictetus was correct about instilling new habits in your life or continuing to live with your old habits. As Epictetus stated, if you continue any behavior for long, inevitably, it is going to become one of your habits.

This truism can either work to your advantage or to your disadvantage, depending on your thoughts, words, or actions. When most people think of habits, they only think about their actions, such as waking up early or sleeping late. However, they rarely think about the fact that the thoughts they think and the words they use can also be habit-forming.

Take swearing or cursing, for example. If you use curse words when you are upset, it doesn't take long at all for cursing to become a habit for you, and it is easier to acquire that habit than it is to break it. Think about it. When you have developed the habit of using curse words, they usually accompany a strong feeling of anger or frustration. The combination of strong emotions and the use of specific words can quickly become a deeply instilled habit.

If you pay attention, you will also notice that even if you are working to control your words, those curse words start in your thoughts. Entertaining certain thoughts can also become a habit. Because your subconscious mind remembers the thoughts, words, and actions you consistently take, they will become embedded in your subconscious mind.

To change bad habits, they must be replaced with more positive habits. Aristotle taught that nature abhors a void. This means that if you remove one habit from your life, another habit will naturally take its place. To instill habits that are in line with Stoic teachings, you must first break your negative habits, then consciously replace those habits with virtuous thoughts, words, and actions. Choose your habits carefully!

136

*Since it so happens that the human being is not soul alone,
nor body alone, but a kind of synthesis of the two,
the person in training must take care of both.*
Musonius Rufus

Musonius Rufus was the teacher of Epictetus, and he believed in the holistic nature of human beings. According to Rufus, humans are not simply physical beings, but a combination of, or a synthesis of, both the body and the soul. And thus, we must take care to train both the body and the soul to become virtuous.

I would take that even further and say that human beings consist of spirit, mind, and body, and we must carefully train each of those and keep them in balance. The World Triad is a symbol that is like a yin-yang symbol, except is has three pieces inside the circle. This symbol signifies the harmony between your spirit, mind, and body, which is basically what Rufus was teaching, except he did not include the mind.

Understand that Rufus lived during the first century AD. His teachings focused on practical Stoic philosophy and the importance of both physical training and moral training. From the way he worded his teachings, we can assume that he considered moral teachings to be the training of the soul. But many people now believe human beings are made of spirit, mind, and body.

Moral training has to do with both the spirit or soul, and the mind. To instill the Stoic virtues in your life, you must start with your thoughts. If your thoughts are not right, your words and actions will not be right. Once you have thoroughly trained your mind to the point that your conscious mind and subconscious mind are in harmony, then your thoughts will be more consistently virtuous.

Furthermore, once you bring your thoughts under control, your spirit will become more virtuous, and your physical actions and words will be rational, courageous, wise, and temperate. Everything is connected. Only training one of these means you will be out of balance. If you spend all your time training your body, your mental and spiritual sides will suffer. Think balance!

137

If you could prevent a bad thing but do not,
then you are, in effect, encouraging it.
Cato the Younger

Wow, this teaching by Cato the Younger will really make some people very uncomfortable. Like Cato, Confucius taught this same thought, but in a slightly different way. Confucius stated, "To see what is right and not to do it is cowardice." Taken together, we can plainly see that if you can prevent something bad from happening, but you don't have the courage to step up and act, not only are you encouraging the unacceptable behavior, but you are simply being a coward.

Seneca also addressed having the courage to act when action is required of you, saying, "He who is brave is free." From this we can conclude that a man who is a coward is not free. If you are not free, you are a slave to somebody or something. The coward is a slave to his fear, and his lack of self-confidence and self-esteem. Why else would someone fail to act when they could prevent something bad from happening? No matter what the reasoning is for not doing the right thing, it all boils down to cowardice in one form or another.

But Cato the Younger went even further, saying that if you could prevent a bad thing from happening, but you don't, then in effect, you are encouraging it to happen. We have all seen videos where someone is getting mugged or assaulted on the street and people simply stand around and watch it happen. Some even take video footage of it to get applause on social media.

These people are not only cowards but are complicit in the crime that is happening right in front of them. As you already know, courage is one of the fundamental requirements for living with a Stoic mindset. Without courage, you will find dozens of reasons not to do what should be done.

If you see something bad happening and you can step up and prevent it, then do it! Yes, it is hard to get involved in a dangerous situation; it takes courage. But think about what you would want people to do if it were happening to you? Would you want them to help or just stand by and watch?

138

If you are distressed by anything external, the pain
is not due to the thing itself, but to your estimate of it;
and this you have the power to revoke at any moment.
Marcus Aurelius

This is another hard-hitting Stoic teaching. If you are upset or stressed about something that is happening outside of your control, Marcus Aurelius taught that it is not the external event that is upsetting you, but the way you are perceiving that event. He even went further and said that you have the power to stop being upset or stressed about the event anytime you choose to stop it.

How can you stop being stressed or upset about some external event? The answer lies within your circle of control. You control your mind and how you perceive everything that is outside of your realm of control. If you change how you perceive the event, then you will also get rid of your stress.

The wise pirate character in *Pirates of the Caribbean*, Captain Jack Sparrow, said essentially the same thing, stating, "The problem is not the problem. The problem is your attitude about the problem." Change how you see the problem, and you change your attitude towards it; change your attitude towards the problem and you will see it in a different light. Who knew that Captain Jack Sparrow and Marcus Aurelius shared a common philosophy!

When you are dealing with an external "problem," it is not something that you control. Remind yourself that you only control the things in your realm of control—what you think, say, do, etc. When something is outside of your control, don't allow it to upset you or add stress to your life; think rationally and respond in whatever way you need to respond to it. Not only is that the best plan of action, but it is all you can rationally do.

Of course, you can throw a fit, get angry and upset about it, or allow it to create stress for you, but is that really thinking rationally? No! That is allowing your emotions and an undisciplined mind to cause you to react. When you react, someone or something is controlling you; when you think rationally and respond, you are in control. Stay calm and control the things you can control.

139

What else is freedom but the power to live our life the way we want?
Epictetus

Many people believe they are free in today's world, but they are simply slaves to something other than another person. As I have stated, slavery can mean more than being owned by somebody. It can also mean something external is controlling your actions and preventing you from living the life you want to live. It doesn't matter what that thing is; if you are not totally free from its control, then you are a slave to it.

Epictetus, who was a Roman slave for around 30 years, surely knew something about slavery. He taught that freedom is nothing else but the power to live your life the way you want to live it. Many people have sold themselves into slavery in one way or another. They want so badly to be free but have put shackles on themselves financially or in some other way.

Moreover, the Stoics did not see true freedom as only doing whatever you want to do, but as aligning your will with your rational mind, or with nature, and choosing to act virtuously despite what's happening externally. As you already know, external events and circumstances are beyond your control, but how you choose to perceive those events or circumstances, and respond to them, is entirely within your control.

When looked at from this point of view, true freedom comes from having the self-discipline to master yourself, rather than being controlled by your fears, external circumstances, or uncontrolled desires. To truly be free, you must master your own mind. Being the master of your own mind is something no one can take away from you. External events and circumstances have no power to trouble your mind unless you give them that power.

When you really adopt a Stoic mindset, you have the power to be truly free, regardless of what is happening externally. Think about it. Are you truly free, or are you a slave to your fears, your external circumstances, or your uncontrolled emotions? Isn't it time to free yourself and start living your life your way? You have that power; all you must do is find the will to use it!

140

To accept injury without a spirit of savage resentment—
to show ourselves merciful toward those who wrong us.
Musonius Rufus

One of the hardest things for most people to do is to accept an injury or insult, whether it is physically, emotionally, or socially, without resentment or wanting to get even with that person. In our culture, we are bombarded with movies and entertainment that promote revenge as a natural response to someone who has hurt us in some way.

It doesn't matter if it is a physical attack on you or your loved ones, someone who works to undermine you at work, or some jerk who insults you, if you are not disciplined, you will feel the urge to get even with the person who has offended you. Even if you resist the urge to exact revenge on that person, it can be even harder not to resent them for months or years afterwards.

The storyline in many of the most popular movies today centers on someone who has been injured, or whose family has been injured, and that person devising a plan to exact revenge on the other person. And this type of movie does give you a sense of satisfaction in seeing the guy who was badly mistreated stand up and get even with or defeat his malicious enemy.

However, Musonius Rufus urges us to accept those injustices and insults with a sense of mercy towards those who wronged us. Many sages and teachers have taught this same thought throughout the years, including Jesus, Buddha, and others. While we may mentally understand why we should not hold resentments or unforgiveness in our hearts, it can still be hard to do.

Instead of allowing our anger to control us, causing us to seek revenge or to hold grudges, we should discipline ourselves to maintain our inner peace, because resentment and unforgiveness hurt us more than the other person. By choosing to show mercy to those who hurt us, we refuse to allow external circumstances or other people to control our actions. Respond with a calm mind, wisdom, and class, and refuse to allow the other person's actions to take control of your mind.

141

What is your vocation? To be a good person.
Marcus Aurelius

The Stoics taught that our highest calling in life should not be our profession, our role in society, or our titles, but to work to perfect our own character. It is to be a good person and live with integrity, honor, wisdom, courage, justice, and temperance.

After studying Stoic teachings, you will without a doubt understand this. However, we all get so busy making a living, spending time with our family, maintaining our health and fitness, etcetera, that we tend to forget that our primary responsibility is to perfect our character. Our foremost duty is to cultivate virtue, live with integrity, and simply be a good person who disciplines himself to walk in wisdom and courage.

So, what does it mean to be a good person? As far as the Stoic mindset is concerned, being a good person means living a life filled with moderation, wisdom, courage, and justice, and keeping our focus on the things in life that we can control. If we maintain our focus on these things, we will naturally live as a good person.

Moreover, Marcus Aurelius did not simply say we should be a good person, but that it is our *calling* to be a good person. By connecting being a good person to our calling in life, he reminds us that moral excellence is not just some high ideal we strive for to make ourselves feel good, but a lifelong commitment. It is our most important objective, more important than any external job or career because it comes from within us; it is a vital part of who we are.

Make your personal self-improvement a daily goal. Refuse to allow any day to go by without working to improve yourself—spirit, mind, and body. If you keep your focus on improving yourself and the things that are within your control, you won't have time to get involved in disputes or arguments with others. You won't have time to hold grudges or to allow external circumstances or events to get under your skin. Make it your goal to spend some time each day improving yourself spiritually, mentally, emotionally, and physically.

142

You may be sure that whatever you are seen to protect,
that will become your enemy's focus of attack.
Epictetus

Epictetus is pointing out a truism that many of us forget. If you have a malicious enemy, he will always want to hit you where it hurts the most, and that is to attack what appears to be the most important thing in your life. It doesn't matter if that is your job, your family, or your reputation. If it is important to you, that is where your enemy will seek to maliciously attack you.

In addition, your enemy will want to attack you wherever he sees a weakness. No enemy wants to spend time trying to break through a well-fortified stronghold; he will always seek to attack and take advantage of your weakness. Someone's weaknesses will vary from one person to the next. It is your job to do your best to stay invulnerable to his malicious attempts to harm you or your family.

If you take pride in your reputation or status, your enemy will attack you and try to get you to react in anger. If he can cause you to react in anger, without thinking of the consequences, he doesn't have to work too hard to destroy your reputation; you will do that yourself.

If you place too much emphasis on external things such as your relationships, wealth, or possessions, he will try to attack you there. Your enemy will try to destroy your relationships, cost you money, or even damage your property.

Whatever you appear to protect, or hold dear, that is where your enemy's focus will be. He seeks to hurt you by any means necessary, and he will spend days, months, or even years testing different aspects of your life to find a weakness or flaw that he can exploit.

You must cultivate spiritual and mental toughness to defend yourself against these spiteful people; cultivate your inner invulnerability. Work to shore up your defenses. Don't count on your enemy not attacking, but on your ability and readiness to defend yourself and those you love.

143

Follow where reason leads.
Zeno of Citium

The Stoics taught that we should always live in harmony with wisdom and rational thought. If you do this, your thoughts, words, and actions will be guided by reason instead of allowing your desires, emotions, or societal influences to affect your decisions.

Zeno taught that your ability to discern right from wrong comes through rational thinking. You must be able to discern right from wrong and make your decisions according to your ethics and integrity. Most people simply act on impulse without giving much thought to their actions beforehand. They react instead of responding to external circumstances, events, or other people.

When you react, someone else or something outside yourself is controlling you. When you respond, you are taking the time to think rationally about the situation and how you should respond to it. Think about what happens if a mosquito flies towards your eye. You simply blink without thinking about it; it is an involuntary reflex, a reaction. Your eyelid simply reacts to the external event without you giving it any thought. It is being controlled by something external, in this case, the mosquito.

This is what most people do when they encounter an external situation or event outside of their control; they simply react without taking the time to give the situation any thought. However, if reason is guiding your actions, you will respond instead of reacting. Remember, when you react, something or someone is controlling you; when you respond, you are in control.

Thinking rationally and responding wisely is always a better choice than allowing something external to cause you to react. To act with virtue, you must avoid allowing your emotions or passions to control your words or actions. Let your honor and integrity be your guide. Respond rationally, not emotionally, accepting what you cannot control, controlling what you can, and maintaining your inner peace. As Jimmy Buffett wrote, "Breathe in, breathe out, and move on." Let reason be your guide.

144

We cannot choose our external circumstances,
but we can always choose how we respond to them.
Epictetus

This is one of the fundamental teachings of Stoicism—you must understand what is in your control and what's not. As you already know, you control the thoughts you entertain, your speech, your attitude, and your actions; you have no control over anything external or outside of yourself.

Moreover, you may not be able to control anything external or outside of your realm of control, but you can always decide how you will respond to external events, circumstances, or other people. When you respond calmly and rationally, maintaining your virtue and inner peace, you are on the right track. If you react without rational thought, more times than not, you will cause yourself unnecessary problems or concerns.

Since you have a choice about how you will respond, choose to always respond with your integrity and honor intact. If you are acting in any way that doesn't maintain your integrity, honor, and inner peace, you are not thinking rationally. This should be the deciding factor in all your decisions, regardless of what is happening around you.

Responding with integrity and honor must become a habit in your life. Most people have developed the habit of reacting to external circumstances. Remember, it doesn't take very long to develop a habit. You can develop any habit in 30-40 days. Your subconscious mind doesn't care whether the habit you are fostering is good or bad; it simply follows your lead. And most likely, you have spent decades reacting instead of responding.

It is easy to react to a situation without thinking. That doesn't require any effort whatsoever. But it takes concentrated effort to break that habit and start responding to external situations calmly, and with integrity and honor. Just take it one situation at a time and refuse to allow yourself to respond in any way that doesn't foster your inner peace and integrity. Continue this process until you get to the point where you respond calmly and rationally to every situation.

145

We are disturbed not by things,
but by the views which we take of them.
Epictetus

The teachings of Marcus Aurelius and Epictetus have a lot in common. In fact, many of their teachings are virtually the same, so it is hard not to repeat myself when explaining them. This quote from Epictetus was virtually repeated by Marcus Aurelius in his book, *Meditations*. We are disturbed not by what happens, but by the way we perceive the events and situations we encounter.

Since I explained this teaching in detail earlier, I won't rehash it here. Instead, let's consider how we can change the views we take of external situations; that is where the challenge lies. Your subconscious mind remembers and records everything you say or do; so, it plays a major role in how you perceive external events because of your previous experience.

You can look at the subconscious mind as a computer that you are constantly programming. When you program something into your computer, it remains there unless you take action to remove it. Your subconscious mind works the same way. You have been programming your subconscious mind since you were born.

Your subconscious mind remembers how you respond or react to different situations throughout your whole life, and it believes that you want to continue to react or respond in the same way that you have "programmed" it to respond. That is why many people react to a rude comment either with an insult or by holding on to resentment; they see it as a natural reaction. After all, they have reacted in that way for years, and it has become a habit.

You must take action to reprogram your subconscious mind and reprogram it with a new attitude toward external situations. This is not an easy or fast process. It will take some time; that is why you must slow down and think rationally and then respond calmly. You must do this repeatedly until you start to perceive things differently and respond instead of reacting.

146

Everyone has the gift of speech.
But few have the gift of wisdom.
Cato the Younger

Cato the Younger really said a mouthful with this teaching, and it definitely applies to people today just as much as it did in Cato's day. Everywhere you go, you can hear people babbling on and on about anything and everything under the sun, but it is rare to hear someone speaking words of wisdom. Most people simply like to talk but never stop to consider whether their words are better than the silence they are breaking.

Buddha gave us some brilliant advice about speaking. He taught, "Before you speak, let your words pass through three gates. Is it true? Is it necessary? Is it kind?" You could add Cato's teaching to that and ask yourself, "Is it wise?" The world would be much quieter if everyone followed these teachings.

There is a vast difference between someone who is merely talking and someone who is speaking wisdom. Everyone talks, but few people truly include meaningful insights or sage wisdom in their speech. Most people simply speak without giving what they are saying much thought other than being clever and looking knowledgeable to those around them. Their speech is mostly impulsive and emotional, lacking any deep thought or wisdom.

When someone speaks words of wisdom, it requires deep thought and reflection on the subject at hand. They must also have understanding and personal experience concerning not only the topic being discussed, but people in general. Even brilliant wisdom will be ignored if it is not presented with the right intentions, at the right time, and in the right way.

When it comes to your speech, you would do well to ask yourself if what you are about to say is true? Is it necessary? Is it kind? Is it wise? Is this the right time to share my wisdom or knowledge? Is the other person in the right frame of mind to hear what I have to say? Can I say it in a way that the other person will benefit from my wisdom? Always think about these things before you speak.

147

The first rule is to keep an untroubled spirit. The second is
to look things in the face and know them for what they are.
Marcus Aurelius

No matter what you are doing, you must maintain your inner peace; this is
the only way to keep an untroubled spirit. If your inner peace is disrupted, your
spirit will not be untroubled. When we are stressed or allow the struggles and
challenges of the day to get to us, it is not simply our minds that are troubled,
but our spirits as well.

Moreover, stress affects your body as well. Science shows that around 60-
90% of all illnesses and diseases are either caused or worsened by stress.
Chronic stress has many effects on the body. It can weaken your immune
system, increase inflammation, contribute to heart disease, diabetes,
hypertension, anxiety, depression, and contribute to autoimmune diseases.
Keeping an untroubled spirit is important to much more than your inner peace!

Maintaining an untroubled spirit means that you can maintain your inner
peace and calm, no matter what is happening around you. And to do this, you
must keep your focus on the things that you can control and respond
appropriately to the things that are outside of your control. Reacting to things
outside of your control with anger, frustration, or fear will disrupt your inner
peace every time and make it very difficult to maintain an untroubled spirit.

The second piece of this teaching is to look at things and see them for what
they truly are. This means that you must be objective and rational in how you
perceive the people, things, and circumstances around you. You can't allow
your mental biases, emotions, or expectations to blind you to the truth about
what is happening. Always see things *as they are*, *not as you wish they were*.

If you make it one of your goals to integrate these two teachings into your
everyday life, you will free yourself from the grips of unnecessary stress and
suffering. Your decisions will be wiser, and your life will go smoother.
Remember these two rules anytime you feel yourself getting troubled or
stressed over an external situation or event.

148

If you say you're going to do something,
do it. If you start something, finish it.
Epictetus

Many of us have heard these same words from our parents or grandparents when we were young, and these are good words to live by. If you say you are going to do something, then do it! Saying you are going to do something and then not doing it is basically lying, even if you have good intentions to start with. If you say you are going to do something, you have a duty, not just to someone else, but to yourself, to follow through on your word.

A man of honor will not say one thing and do another. His word is his bond. If he says he is going to do something and then doesn't do it, he has dishonored himself. Of course, there can be extenuating circumstances. If you find you can't follow through on your word because of sickness or an accident, discuss it with the other person, and make good on your word later, if it is at all possible. Always be a man or woman of your word; your honor depends on it!

Few people seem to think about honoring their word in today's world. They give their word as easily as they speak, and then think little to nothing about not following through. The same goes for starting something and then simply walking away from it when it turns out to be too much of a hassle for them. This is not the path of honor and integrity!

If you tell someone that you are going to build a fence for him, don't get started on it, then decide that the project is too hard for you. You gave your word, and you started the project, so you are honor-bound to see it through to the end. Say what you mean and mean what you say! If you give someone your word, it is dishonorable not to live up to it.

Giving your word is not something to be taken lightly, especially if you are a man of honor and integrity. A man of honor will always keep his word. When you give your word to someone, it should be as good as a signed contract. If you say you are going to do something, do it! Be the kind of man who, if you give your word, people know you mean what you say.

149

A person's words can both conceal and reveal their inner soul.
Cato the Younger

I ended the last teaching with the sentence, "Say what you mean and mean what you say." This world would be a much better place if more people adhered to that teaching. However, that is not the world we live in today. Many people have become experts at using their words as weapons, as a way to conceal their true beliefs, or to con others into trusting them when they are anything but trustworthy.

You must keep this truism by Cato the Younger in mind when you are talking to other people. While most people's words give you some insight into who they are and what they believe, many people use words to hide who they truly are. That is exactly what Cato is teaching us here.

You can't always trust the words that people speak; you must become proficient at reading between the lines. Pay attention to how someone says something, as well as what he is saying. Don't simply take everything that someone says as the complete truth. Do your homework when it is important to know whether or not someone is trustworthy. Remember, there is more than one side to every story; and not everyone is honest or trustworthy.

If you maintain a calm and tranquil spirit, your intuition will help guide you in this. When you get a strange feeling that someone is not truthful or is simply putting on an act for you, trust it! Always trust your intuition and then follow through with some research afterwards.

Those with a peaceful, well-meaning spirit reveal their true inner spirit. When you are talking to them, you will have a tranquil, peaceful feeling yourself. Their sincerity will shine through in the words they speak. Those who have an ulterior motive will leave you with an uneasy feeling that you may or may not be able to explain. Explaining it is unnecessary; what is necessary is that you don't ignore that feeling. It is better to walk away and be wrong about that other person than it is to take what he or she is saying as the truth and then regret it later. Be wise and insightful!

150

So, is it possible to benefit from these circumstances? Yes, from every circumstance, even abuse and slander. A boxer derives the greatest advantage from his sparring partner, and my accuser is my sparring partner. He trains me in patience, civility, and even temper.

Epictetus

Epictetus taught we can use every circumstance to our benefit and advantage if we will ask ourselves, "What can I learn from this? How can I use this situation to my advantage or to improve myself?" And he specifically used abuse and slander as examples.

At first, this sounds ridiculous. How could anyone benefit from abuse or slander? It goes back to how you perceive external events or situations. As a martial artist who has been fairly well-known for years, I have had my share of abuse, slander, and libel used against me in an effort to try to ruin my reputation. While it took me a while to realize what Epictetus is teaching here, I now understand exactly what he meant.

At first, I allowed my enemies to get under my skin a bit; then I changed how I perceived the attacks against me. I asked myself, "How can I use these attacks to my benefit?" The answer was that I used their malicious attempts to destroy me to make my writing more concise and to fortify my defenses. I stopped making it easy for them to attack me.

In addition, I carefully edited my articles and writings so that it was very difficult for someone to take them out of context, twist them around, or spin them in a way that they could be used against me. Just as Epictetus taught, I learned patience and civility when responding to personal attacks, and to control my temper when my enemies continued to attack me. In the end, I emerged victorious, honed my writing skills and people skills, and my enemies were proven to be liars and found guilty of defamation in the courts.

Even in the worst situations, you can find some way to benefit from what is going on in your life. Instead of allowing yourself to get stressed, ask yourself, "How can I use what is happening to my benefit or advantage?"

151

God has entrusted me with myself.
Epictetus

At first glance, this seems to be a bit of a strange statement, but when you stop and think about it, Epictetus was exactly right. God has given each of us the personal responsibility for our own development and life. While external events, situations, and other people may present challenges on our path, ultimately, they have no control over our mind or spirit.

We are all given complete control over the thoughts we entertain, the words we speak, and the actions we take. Nobody has the ability to control your will. They can try to influence your choices, but in the end, you always have the final say when it comes to your choices. Your thoughts, beliefs, and moral development are completely under your own control.

What you decide to do with your life is totally up to you, nobody else. And with that power comes responsibility. You are responsible for your own choices and the consequences that come from those choices. While many things happen in your life that you can't control, how you respond to those things is always within your control.

Knowing that your life is in your own hands, you are responsible for cultivating wisdom, virtue, courage, and temperance in your own life. Nobody can do that for you, nor should they. God has given you the free will to choose who you will be and how you will live, and it's nobody else's business.

You have been given a magnificent gift—free will. Now, you must decide how you will use it to transform yourself into the person that you want to be. You can either cultivate a Stoic mindset, or you can decide to go through life being controlled by things outside of your control. You can develop and live your life with honor and integrity, or you can live life as an average person.

The Stoics armed you with a lot of great wisdom to help you change your life and become the best you can be, but they can't force you to internalize that wisdom. This book is packed full of wisdom, but only you can use it to change your life for the better.

152

Do not waste time on nonsense.
Marcus Aurelius

This little gem from Marcus Aurelius definitely applies to our modern culture. There are so many different things that compete for your attention, and many of them are simply a waste of time. Social media is a huge time consumer, and most of what is on social media is nothing more than nonsense. It is not easy to find social media posts that offer any value to your life; therefore, most of your time spent on social media is wasted time.

If you take a more complete look at the days of your life and how little time you have to live your life fully, it will change your attitude towards wasting time. You only have a short time to live on this beautiful planet, and that time goes by much faster than it may appear. Most people's minds find it difficult to contemplate the actual value of their time. So, they are more than willing to waste it in ways that offer no true value.

Time spent on nonsense, or on things that do not improve your life, is truly time spent unwisely. If you are 50 years old, there are only 10,957 days until you reach the age of eighty. At first glance, that seems like a lot of days, but let's look a little deeper.

There are 24 hours in a day. If you spend eight hours a day sleeping, eight hours a day working, and let's say one and a half hours a day for your meals, that only leaves six and a half hours a day in which you are free. If you commute to work, there goes another one to two hours of time, leaving you with maybe five hours a day of free time. And that is the time that you have to prepare your meals, clean your house, maintain your yard, deal with repairs and unexpected issues in your life, spend some time on your hobby, reading, exercising, etc. That is not much time!

Of course, there are weekends when many of us have more free time, but we all know how fast the weekends go by. When you truly examine how little free time you have in your life, you will understand why you should refuse to waste time on nonsense. Stay focused on what really matters!

153

We will come through safely only by allying ourselves with God…
Whatever God wants, we want too; and by inversion, whatever
God does not want, this we do not want either.
Epictetus

Epictetus taught that the safest path in life is to have a good relationship with God and to live your life in sync with what God desires for you. If God wants something, that should be your desire as well. And whatever God does not want, we should not want either. The Bible even gives an example of Jesus praying in this way: "Father, if you are willing, remove this cup from me; nevertheless, not my will, but your will be done."

This is in line with the Stoic philosophy of accepting things as they truly are. Accepting the way things are is much easier if you ally yourself with God and believe that God is overseeing your life. The Bible also teaches this in the book of *Romans*: "And we know that all things work together for good to them that love God, to them who are called according to His purpose."

But how do we know what God wants? By spending time in prayer and meditation and then maintaining control of your mind. What you focus your mind on will increase in your life. The teachings of the *Dhammapada* (the teachings of Buddha) state, "All that we are is the result of what we have thought; it is founded on our thoughts, it is made up of our thoughts…Let him who desires his own good subdue the evil of his thoughts."

There are several teachings in the Bible that echo the teachings of the *Dhammapada*. "For as he thinks in his heart, so is he," and "Do not be conformed to this world, but be transformed by the renewing of your mind." This is a common thread between Stoicism, Christianity, and Buddhism.

The mind is the gateway to all transformation. Marcus Aurelius taught, "The soul becomes dyed with the color of its thoughts." You can't physically see God, but you can speak and listen to God through your thoughts, prayers, and meditation. And the more time you spend with God, the more you will realize what He wants for your life. Give this some thought.

154

You could leave life right now.
Let that determine what you do and say and think.
Marcus Aurelius

Most people don't want to think about their own death, so they simply put those thoughts out of their mind—out of sight, out of mind. The Stoic philosophy values detachment, teaching that what is not within your realm of control should not disturb you or disrupt your inner peace. Thinking about their own death is morbid and gloomy to most people, so why does Marcus Aurelius teach we should consider our own death?

The answer is that since we do not control the fact that we will die, it should not upset us; death is inevitable. Marcus Aurelius taught us to meditate on our own death years before the samurai taught the same thing, and for pretty much the same reason. If you continually consider the fact that you could die at any time, you will take your life more seriously; you won't waste time on nonsense, as I have already covered.

Moreover, if you remind yourself that you could die at any time, that will change how you think, what you say, and what you do. When you have internalized that reality, you look at life differently; you comprehend the value of each moment. This is the practice of *memento mori* or allowing the reminder of your own death to motivate you to live virtuously and to live your life to the fullest.

There is a popular song by country singer Tim McGraw titled "*Live Like You Were Dying*" that has a powerful message that aligns with this Stoic teaching. This song asks the question: "What would you do if you found out you were dying? How would you live?" Take some time, read the lyrics of this song, and meditate on the truth contained in those lyrics.

That is exactly what Marcus Aurelius is urging us to do with this teaching. You don't have to wait for some doctor to tell you that you are dying; you already know you are dying. The only question is, how do you want to live the rest of your life? Think about this.

155

I will keep constant watch over myself and,
most usefully, will put each day up for review.
Seneca

This teaching by Seneca fits perfectly with the last teaching from Marcus Aurelius. As I have discussed, if you remain aware of your own death, you will be more likely to take your life more seriously and be more thoughtful about what you think, say, or do.

Seneca is telling us to take that philosophy a step further and, at the end of each day, take some time and review how you managed the day. Did you live by the philosophy you believe to be true? Are you proud of the thoughts you had during the day? What about the words you spoke and the things you did? Were they in line with the kind of person you want to be and how you want to live your life?

This is something to think about every night before you go to sleep. Review how you conducted yourself throughout the day and then determine that you will improve in the areas with which you are not happy. If you make a habit out of doing this daily, then you will make improvements each day.

Always be determined to improve your thoughts, speech, and actions every day, even if you find you are unsuccessful sometimes. Those minor improvements will add up, and you will be able to look back over your week, month, or year and see how far you have come towards living a life of excellence, instead of just walking through life as most people do.

If you are moving in the right direction, you will make improvements; but if you don't keep this goal fresh in your mind, the challenges and hassles of the day can quickly sidetrack you. It is all too easy to get too busy and forget to keep a constant watch over your thoughts, words, and actions. Keep your focus on the present moment and strive to always be mindful and aware of your overall goal to live according to your own personal philosophy or code. The more mindful you are, the more successful you will be in living with a Stoic mindset.

156

Progress is not achieved by luck or accident,
but by working on yourself daily.
Epictetus

This quote from Epictetus fits perfectly with the previous teaching from Seneca. Your progress in living the life that you want to live, with honor, integrity, and virtue, is not achieved by luck or accident. You must earn it through your own efforts and mindfulness; you must keep your objective on your mind and constantly work to achieve it.

As you strive to become the person you want to be, you will inevitably have off days when you fall short of your goal. We all have days when we are just feeling a little off, everything seems to go wrong, and we feel like we accomplished little as far as moving closer to perfecting our character. The process of perfecting your character is a never-ending goal; each day brings its own challenges for us to overcome.

There is no such thing as a perfect human being, but the more we strive to perfect our character, the closer we move towards the perfection of our character. Your objective should be to make daily progress, not to make perfect progress. As long as you are improving yourself each day, you are moving closer to the perfection of your character and living with a Stoic mindset.

Learning to be mindful and control your thoughts is a major part of this process. When you begin working to perfect your character, you may have a tendency to compare your progress with that of other people. This is a mistake that can rob you of your motivation and inner peace.

Don't compare yourself to anyone else; you are on your own path, not their path. Your calling in life is personal, and only for you; your calling was not meant to be a conference call. There is nobody else exactly like you; treasure your uniqueness. You are meant to be *you* and live *your* life, not to be like anyone else. As the Japanese swordsman Miyamoto Musashi stated, "Today is victory over yourself of yesterday." Make it your daily challenge to be better than *you* were yesterday.

157

No evil is honorable, but death is honorable;
therefore death is not evil.
Zeno of Citium

In this teaching, Zeno was trying to challenge the fear of death by defining it in terms of good and evil, honorable and dishonorable. No evil is honorable, which is something that those of us who live with honor can agree on. To the Stoics, the only true evil is immorality or moral vice, or things that distance us from living a life of virtue.

The question is what makes death honorable. Is the process of dying honorable in and of itself? No, of course not. Death can be honorable or dishonorable depending on how we each face our death and why we are dying. Is the death of a murderer in an electric chair an honorable death? Is the death of someone who was murdered in his sleep an honorable death? Absolutely not! So, what is Zeno trying to say here?

Death is a natural part of life; therefore, it cannot be evil, according to Zeno. It is simply a part of nature, and Zeno believed that living according to nature is a fundamental aspect of Stoicism. But that depends on the actual situation in which death comes for us. Since we do not control the time or day of our death, that should not concern us. What truly matters is how we face death. Will you face death virtuously, with dignity, honor, and courage? If so, your death is honorable.

The Stoics admired people who accepted their death calmly, with courage and dignity. We have no control over death since death is something that is outside our circle of control. What we can control is how we choose to meet death.

Think about how stoically Socrates met his death with honor and courage. His followers, irate over the injustice of Socrates' death sentence, planned to free Socrates and came to the jail to break him out, but Socrates refused to leave with them. He said it was his fate to face his death sentence with honor, and that was exactly what he did as he drank the poison he was given.

158

*At all times, look at the thing itself—the thing behind
the appearance—and unpack it by analysis: cause,
substance, purpose, and the length of time it exists.*
Marcus Aurelius

This is a very useful teaching for the times we are now living in, where so many things are far different from their initial appearance. When Marcus Aurelius urges us to always "look at the thing itself, the thing behind the appearance," he is saying to see things as they truly are. This can be hard to do in today's world.

Baltasar Gracian, one of my favorite philosophers, stated, "Things do not pass for what they are, but for what they seem. Few see inside; many judge by appearances." This is what Marcus Aurelius is teaching us. We must look beyond appearances; to get to the truth, we must look beyond the veil which covers it. This is the difference between perception and reality.

We must evaluate everything rationally and analyze things deeply rather than simply accepting things as they first appear. Detach yourself from first impressions or emotional reactions. Strive to discover the actual truth behind superficial appearances and cleverly concealed facts.

Marcus Aurelius taught that to do this, we must think rationally and analyze things instead of just accepting them the way they first appear. To do that, we should look at what caused it. The law of cause and effect always plays a part in every situation. We must also look at the substance and purpose of the situation. Is it meant to influence you in some way, or is it merely the truth? We must think about the time factor. Is it serious, or will it soon change?

Don't accept things at face value. You must dig deeper to discover the truth behind everything, especially today. Most people have an agenda behind their words and actions. Always take the time to think rationally about what is happening, why it is happening, who it benefits, and how. See the world as it truly is, not as you want it to be or wish it were. Strip away illusions and emotional reactions and dare to look beyond the veil.

159

The fact that someone holds this or that opinion will not
suffice to make it true, any more than we are inclined to
trust a person's word in dealing with weights and measures.
Epictetus

Everyone has an opinion on just about everything, but not everyone's opinions matter. As Epictetus taught, the fact that someone holds an opinion about something doesn't make it true. Most people who freely share their opinions on everything under the sun know little to nothing about what they are talking about. But these people do like to hear themselves talk and try their best to sound educated on every subject imaginable.

I am sure that you have known someone who is a know-it-all. No matter what topic is being talked about, they jump in and try to sound like they know everything about it. They may even sound very convincing, but that doesn't make their words any truer. These people simply like to be the center of attention and can't stand to listen quietly, as that puts them out of the spotlight.

Be very careful about trusting someone's opinion. In fact, I would say not to trust someone's opinion unless you know for a fact that they know something about the subject being discussed. Taking someone's opinion as truth is the way of the foolish man who is too lazy to do his own research. This can be dangerous as well as foolish.

Unless you are talking to an expert, always take the time to do your own research and confirm the opinions of others. Even if you are speaking to someone who has a lot of experience in the subject area, it costs nothing to do your own research just to double check that his knowledge is correct. More knowledge is always better than not enough knowledge.

With today's technology, it doesn't take that much time to research almost any subject. Remember, even licensed doctors disagree concerning the best course of treatment for their patients. Don't trust someone's opinion just because they are supposed to be an expert. Listen to many points of view, do your homework, and then make your decision.

160

> A bad person's character cannot be trusted, it is weak and indecisive,
> easily won over by different thoughts at different times…Just ask
> whether they put their self-interest in externals or in moral choice.
> If it is in externals, you cannot call them friends, any more than
> you can call them trustworthy, consistent, courageous, or free.
> *Epictetus*

At first, this sounds like an obvious statement. Of course, a bad person's character cannot be trusted. But we must look deeper at the people that Epictetus called a "bad person." Epictetus' test of whether someone is a bad person is not necessarily what we might consider a bad person today. He described a bad person as someone who puts their self-interest in externals. He goes on to say that you cannot call these people friends or trustworthy.

Who is someone who puts their self-interest in externals? According to Epictetus, a person who puts their self-interest in externals is someone who bases his happiness, self-worth, status, or identity on external things instead of on their moral character. These people can't be trusted because if their self-interest or financial interest is threatened, they will always put those things ahead of their honor, integrity, promises, or their so-called friendships.

They may seem like friendly, good people on the surface, and may even keep their word, if everything is going their way. But when hard times come, they cannot be trusted because they will always place their priority on what benefits them the most. As Epictetus taught, such a person cannot be completely trusted or called a genuine friend. He is inconsistent because his integrity and character change according to the situation.

A true friend will always prioritize his honor, integrity, and friendship over what may seem best for him personally. His trustworthiness and friendship do not depend on external situations or circumstances; he puts his honor, integrity, and friendship ahead of personal and external concerns. As the old saying goes, there is no honor among thieves. I would add to that, there is no true friendship among people who do not put their integrity and honor first.

161

Just as nature takes every obstacle, every impediment,
and works around it—turns it to its purposes, incorporates
it into itself—so, too, a rational being can turn each
setback into raw material and use it to achieve its goal.
Marcus Aurelius

Think about how nature responds to obstacles. Take a stream, for example. If a boulder is in the path of the stream, the stream doesn't stop at that point; it incorporates the boulder into itself. The water will either flow around it, under it, or over it. The stream doesn't get frustrated and stop flowing; it simply responds to the obstacle and does what it needs to do to continue moving forward.

We should take the same approach to life. Too many people allow challenges, problems, or hardships to cause them to quit or to stop moving towards their goal. Instead of the obstacle becoming a part of their journey, they allow the obstacle to cause them to give up. They don't see the obstacle as a challenge, but as something that they cannot overcome.

Marcus Aurelius taught us we should never allow obstacles or setbacks to stop us, but to use setbacks or obstacles as a steppingstone to achieving our goals. If you do this, every challenge that comes your way becomes a learning opportunity. You simply refuse to give up or to give in. Use the difficulties in your life to practice virtuous character traits such as courage, resilience, and patience.

When you approach life with this mindset, you can turn your frustrations and anger into inspiration and empowerment. Just keep in mind that the obstacle is the way; it is a part of your journey. It can only stop you if you give up and allow it to stop you.

Instead of allowing obstacles to stop you from reaching your goals, use them to become stronger and more focused. Be creative and learn from every obstacle in your path. As Bruce Lee would say, "Be water, my friend." How you respond is more important than what happens to you.

TEMPERANCE · JUSTICE · COURAGE · WISDOM

162

There is only one way to happiness and that is to cease
worrying about things which are beyond the power or our will.
Epictetus

Epictetus didn't beat around the bush with this teaching. Worrying will rob you of your happiness. So, if you want to be happy, you must first stop worrying about things that are outside of your circle of control. While this makes sense to most people and is sound wisdom, it can be harder to accomplish than it appears—it is easier said than done.

Most everyone agrees that worrying about things you can't control is a waste of time; it accomplishes nothing, or at least nothing beneficial for you. We all know this, but most everyone still allows worry to encroach on their mind at some point and time.

Putting an end to worrying about things outside of your control is like any other habit; it takes time and persistence to change it. And since this is a mental habit, it can be harder to overcome and change than many physical habits. You must take control of your thoughts and refuse to allow yourself to worry about anything. It must be a conscious decision.

You do this by being mindful of your thoughts, and anytime thoughts of worry and stress appear in your mind, *refuse* to entertain them. If you are not persistently mindful, you will catch yourself worrying about things before you even realize it. You must consistently bring your thoughts back to the things that you can control.

If you cannot control an event or situation, worrying about it won't change that fact; it only makes everything in your life worse. You must continually remind yourself of this until refusing to worry about external things becomes second nature for you.

Anytime you find yourself worrying about something, ask yourself whether this is something you can control or something outside of your control. If it is outside your circle of control, stop worrying about it. If it is something that you can control, take action and do what needs to be done.

163

Try not to react merely in the moment. Pull back from
the situation. Take a wider view. Compose yourself.
Epictetus

Many of our problems in life come from reacting to an event, situation, or person without taking the time to think about the situation and respond to it appropriately. Most people have trained themselves to react in the moment instead of taking time to think about things before they respond.

When you react without thinking, you are usually allowing your emotions to dictate your actions or words. It is rarely wise to allow your emotions to dictate your actions or your speech. The prisons are full of people who allowed their emotions to cause them to do something that changed their lives forever. Epictetus taught that we should refuse to react emotionally to external events, situations, or other people's words or actions.

Instead, Epictetus is urging us to put our emotions in check, take a deep breath, step back, and think about the situation rationally. Compose yourself, control your emotions, and look at things from a different perspective. By looking at a situation from a different perspective, you will often see the situation is not even worth responding to, much less allowing your emotions to cause you to react negatively to it.

Unless someone is physically attacking you or someone else, there are few situations where you must react to them immediately. Most situations allow us time to compose ourselves and think rationally about how we should respond, if we need to respond at all. But to do this, we must learn to control our emotions.

Make it one of your goals to stop reacting to everything someone says or does, and to maintain your calm demeanor and inner peace in every situation. You will find that not only will your life be more peaceful and tranquil, but that people will also have more respect for you if you can maintain a confident, calm spirit in unpleasant situations. Staying calm when others are losing their cool demonstrates self-confidence and self-control. Stay composed!

164

If your well-being matters to you, be your own savior while you can.
Marcus Aurelius

The Stoics strongly believed in self-reliance and taking responsibility for your own life and happiness. Nobody is going to make you happy or give you inner peace or inner strength; you must be your own savior where these things are concerned. Your happiness and peace of mind depend entirely on yourself, not external circumstances or other people.

So many people today depend on the words or behavior of others to make themselves happy. They search for happiness in external circumstances and material things when they should be going inside themselves to find their happiness. Happiness and inner peace always originate within your own mind and spirit. If you can't find happiness there, you won't find it anywhere else.

True happiness comes from being the master of your own thoughts and choices. When you depend on anything or anyone outside yourself for your happiness or inner peace, you are giving your power away. You are allowing other people to determine your happiness or your discontent, and that is a prescription for a rollercoaster of unhappiness and frustration.

Refuse to allow other people or external situations to dictate your happiness or inner peace. Haven't you already wasted enough time allowing external situations and other people to dictate your mental state? Now is the time to change that! As Marcus Aurelius wrote, you don't have that much time on this earth; you must be your own savior *while you can.*

If your well-being truly matters to you, you must step up and take responsibility for your own happiness and well-being. You have no more time to waste. You don't need another self-help book or some guru to step in and help you live your life to the fullest. Stop waiting for someone else to come along with a magic blueprint. Take responsibility for your own happiness. Focus on what you can control and seize the moment to be your own savior. Nobody cares about your well-being as much as you. Stop putting your faith in other people and be your own savior!

165

Happiness and personal fulfillment are the
natural consequences of doing the right thing.
Epictetus

Think about the times when you have done the right thing, regardless of the consequences. How did you feel after your actions? Did you feel that you should have compromised on what you knew to be right, or did you feel proud of your actions and at peace with how you handled the whole situation?

Now think about a time when, for whatever reason, you compromised your integrity and did something that you felt was not right. How did you feel afterwards? Did you feel at peace knowing that you compromised your integrity or honor, or did you have a nagging feeling in the back of your mind, knowing that you compromised your principles?

We have all experienced a time when our conscience convicted us about something we said or did when we knew it was not the right thing to say or do. This is what Epictetus is trying to get across to us in this piece of wisdom. When you do the right thing, whether it turns out good or bad, you are at peace with your decision. The consequences of what you do matter less than knowing in your heart that you did the best you could to do what was right.

When you do the right thing, regardless of the outcome, you feel at ease with your decision because you know you acted according to your conviction to do what's right. Whether other people agree with your actions doesn't matter; what matters is that you acted with integrity and honor. In fact, even when the outcome of your actions is not positive, you still feel happy and fulfilled because you did your best to do the right thing.

That is why Epictetus taught that happiness and personal fulfillment are the natural consequences of doing the right thing. Doing the right thing makes you feel good about yourself, which in turn makes you happy. Doing something that you know is wrong makes you feel unsettled and bad about yourself and your actions, because you know that you compromised your integrity.

166

We should not blame God for the misfortunes of the wicked,
for they bring them upon themselves by their own actions.
Chrysippus

Many people bring their problems on themselves by their reckless, irrational actions, but always seem to blame everyone and everything but themselves. This is essentially what Chrysippus was teaching in this quote. It doesn't matter if someone is blaming God or the pool boy; the fact remains that many people bring their problems on themselves with their own careless, unwise decisions, actions, and words.

Notice that Chrysippus is speaking of the misfortunes of the wicked in this quote. When the Stoics spoke of "the wicked," they were referring to people who do not live a virtuous life. Remember earlier I discussed a quote from Epictetus about "a bad person," and how Epictetus taught us to recognize a bad person. He wrote that a bad person is someone who puts his self-interest in externals instead of making decisions according to his honor.

Today, we don't really recognize people who put their self-interest in externals as necessarily bad people; we consider criminals to be bad people, and some people don't even agree with that label. But it doesn't matter whether or not you agree with Epictetus, the fact remains that you should not trust someone whose decisions are made solely on what is best for him personally, instead of taking honor and integrity into consideration.

Either way, most people bring their own misfortunes on themselves in one way or another, even if they cannot see how their misfortunes are connected to their own decisions. If we could retrace our steps back to a specific decision or action, we would be able to see the cause and effect that is connected to our actions.

Blaming someone else for your misfortunes doesn't change your circumstances; it is more like burying your head in the sand and refusing to take responsibility for your own life. Blaming others changes nothing. Think rationally and take responsibility for your own life.

Consider how we apply the idea of freedom to animals. There
are tame lions that people cage, raise, feed, and take with them
wherever they go. Yet, who will call such a lion free? The easier
its life, the more slavish it is. No lion endowed with reason and
discretion would choose to be one of these pet specimens.

Epictetus

Epictetus knew a lot about being a slave and what true freedom actually
means. He used a tamed lion as an example. Although a tamed lion, which is
kept in a cage, fed, and taken care of, doesn't have to go out and hunt for its
own food, I don't think anyone would argue the fact that it is not free.

Epictetus associated an easy life with slavery. At first, this sounds kind of
strange, but then he demonstrated that if the lion had reason and discretion, it
would not choose to live its life in a cage, even though it doesn't have to hunt
for its food.

Think about this. Would you rather be free to do whatever you choose to
do, or would you want to be a slave, but never have to worry about where you
will live or what you would eat? I think the answer to that is obvious. No one
would choose to live in slavery.

However, that is exactly how many people live, not as actual slaves, but not
completely free either. If you have a lot of debt, are you truly free to just up
and leave anytime you want, or have you sold your freedom to a job that you
don't like, just to make ends meet every month? Many people have freely put
financial chains on themselves in exchange for material things, many of which
they do not need.

Sure, people are free to quit their job and walk away, but then they lose the
external things that they love so much. So, they choose financial slavery over
complete freedom. You may say that is not truly slavery, but neither is being a
pet, although both put limits on true freedom. Give this some thought the next
time you think about getting a loan for something you don't need.

168

The best answer to anger is silence.
Marcus Aurelius

There is a lot of wisdom in this short quote! When you are angry, be silent. Many people cause themselves unnecessary trouble by speaking emotionally when they are angry or upset. It is rarely a wise move to allow your emotions to dictate your speech.

People say many things that they neither mean nor agree with when they are angry, only to have to go back later, eat crow, and apologize for what they said. People would be much better off taking Marcus Aurelius' advice and remaining silent when they are angry, especially when they are very angry.

However, most people lack enough self-control to remain silent when all they are thinking about is putting the other person in his or her place. They allow their anger to take the reins and not only put the other person in his place, but go even further and say things that they really don't mean.

Later, after they have calmed down, they feel bad about what they said and come back to apologize, but it is too late. Even if the other person says he accepts their apology, those words spoken in anger will always remain in the back of his mind. And you can bet that when the next disagreement comes up, those words will be repeated, demonstrating how little their apology ultimately meant in the long term.

It is much easier and wiser to simply remain silent, at least until you have had time to cool down and think rationally. If the issue still needs to be addressed, then you can at least address it without allowing your emotions to dictate your speech.

Most of us mentally realize this, but anger is such a powerful emotion that we tend to forget it until after the fact. At that point, it is too late. Our emotional reaction has already occurred, and once you say something, it can never be taken back, no matter how badly you may want to. Keep Marcus Aurelius' wisdom in mind anytime you find yourself irate or angry. The best, and safest, answer to anger is silence! Think rationally, not emotionally!

Those who are able to control their passions,
instead of letting their passions control them, are free.
Epictetus

The Stoics taught that true freedom means mastering yourself rather than being mentally controlled by external circumstances or desires. When Epictetus discussed "letting their passion control them," he was talking about your powerful emotions such as anger, jealousy, hatred, fear, or desires for something external.

By allowing your passions or emotions to control your behavior, you become a slave to your passions; you react rather than respond to the external situations and circumstances around you. I have already discussed how allowing your emotions to dictate your speech or actions is a dangerous proposition. If you allow your emotions to run your life, you are not truly in control; your emotions are, thus you are not truly free.

By cultivating self-discipline in your life, you learn to control your emotions, and therefore, you free yourself from the mental slavery of allowing your emotions to control your life. You must take control of your thoughts; be the master of your mind. This is what it means to master yourself, rather than being controlled by your passions.

When you begin to control your mind, your actions will naturally change, and you will regain control over your actions, instead of reacting to every external situation emotionally. It is this inner mastery that sets you free, and that freedom allows you to be happy and fosters your inner peace. Your inner peace and happiness will no longer depend on external events or desires.

Epictetus taught that freedom is not about being able to do whatever you please, but is about having the self-discipline to control your passions and take back control of your mind, your speech, and your actions. Let your values and your code dictate your speech and actions and learn to control your desires and emotions. Once you have mastered your inner self, you will be truly free.

170

Free is the man who lives as he wishes and cannot
be coerced, impeded, or compelled, whose impulses
cannot be thwarted, who always gets what he desires
and never has to experience what he would rather avoid.
Epictetus

Epictetus wrote a lot about being free, which one might expect from a former slave. If you didn't know what the Stoics meant by true freedom, you might see this quote as Epictetus saying that freedom means a life of hedonism, external power, and endless pleasures. But we already know that this is not what freedom meant to the Stoics; they saw freedom as something much deeper than superficial pleasures.

The phrase, "Free is the man who lives as he wishes," could easily be taken out of context. But, as I previously discussed, Epictetus taught that true freedom comes from self-mastery, and self-mastery means taking control of your desires and passions and bringing them in line with your values. So, the free man who lives as he wishes is the man who has mastered his emotions and desires and has brought them in line with his values. Such a man will wish to live a life of honor and integrity.

That is a man who cannot be coerced, impeded, or compelled to compromise on his integrity or honor. He will always get what he desires because his desires are to live with virtue and to continually master his emotions and inner self. And these are completely under his control.

What the truly free man doesn't want is to allow other people or external events and circumstances to control him or dictate his actions. If he is truly free, he has already achieved inner mastery, and therefore, he does not have to experience being controlled by anything outside of his circle of control.

When you align your desires only with the things that are within your realm of control, you will always get what you want because what you want is solely in your own control. Seeking virtue, wisdom, honor, or the perfection of your character cannot be hindered by any external situation or force.

171

Tranquility comes when you stop caring what
they say or think or do—only what you do.
Marcus Aurelius

If you want to cultivate and maintain inner peace and tranquility in your life, you must stop caring what other people think, say, or do. Inner peace comes from staying focused on the things that you can control, and you have no control over other people. You only control yourself and the kind of person you decide to be.

Remember, Marcus Aurelius taught that it is not what happens to you, but how you perceive what happens to you that truly affects you. Think about how many times you have done something and then wondered what someone else thought about your actions. If you dwelled on those thoughts for long, you might assume that the other person was offended or angry with you. Then, you might naturally start allowing those thoughts to disrupt your inner peace.

In this example, nothing physically happened; the whole situation, and the disruption of your inner peace, was because of how you perceived the situation. You allowed your mind to overthink the situation, and then it robbed you of your tranquility. What someone else thinks of you or your actions is none of your business. Everyone has the freedom to think whatever they want to think about anything or anyone. Also, don't assume you know what someone else thinks about you or anything else; most likely, you don't.

Instead of troubling yourself about what other people think, say, or do, keep your focus on the things that you can control—your thoughts, words, and actions. Don't allow yourself to get dragged into other people's drama; it will almost always disrupt your inner peace.

Other people's actions cannot disrupt your inner peace unless you allow them to. When you take the time to see the situation from different angles, your perception will change. You can choose how you want to perceive each situation in your life. By maintaining your focus on the things you can control, you free yourself from stress and anxiety, and foster your own tranquility.

172

In conversation, avoid the extremes of forwardness and reserve.
Cato the Younger

Cato's advice here is very important to your relationship with other people. He urges us to be careful in our conversations, not to be overbearing and obnoxious or too quiet and shy. Both have negative effects on other people and can affect how others perceive you.

When he talks about the extreme of forwardness, he is urging us not to be too direct or familiar when talking to others. This can cause others to see you as arrogant, rude, or self-centered, especially if you are monopolizing the conversation or being overbearing. Nobody really likes a know-it-all, a blowhard, or someone who is constantly interrupting them in mid-sentence.

When Cato refers to the extreme of being too reserved, he is referring to being too quiet, shy, or simply refusing to talk. Many people who are naturally quiet are seen as unfriendly, cold, or indifferent by those around them, when in fact they are simply being themselves. While it is better to listen and gain information than to talk too much, you should seek a comfortable balance between being too quiet and being too forward.

Here, you may be thinking, "I thought we weren't supposed to be concerned about what other people think." This is true, but we also live in a world where our relationships matter and affect our lives. While you shouldn't put too much importance on what others think, you do want to be affable and pleasant. Therefore, you need to consider your own words and actions when you are conversing with others.

Cato is urging us to seek a balance between talking too much and being too quiet. Make sure that when you speak, you communicate effectively and with confidence. When others are speaking, listen actively without zoning out or thinking about what you are going to say next. Know when to speak and when to be quiet. Make sure your speech is appropriate and wise. Good communication means knowing what to say, when to say it, and how to say it in a way that gets your point across without being offensive.

173

Any person capable of angering you becomes your master; he can
anger you only when you permit yourself to be disturbed by him.
Epictetus

Once again, Epictetus is reminding us to keep our focus on the things we
can control, and not to let the things that we can't control affect us. We have
no control over what anyone else says or does. If you allow yourself to become
angry because of someone's words or actions, then you are choosing to give
that person power over you, or as Epictetus put it, to become your master.

A couple of synonyms for the term "master" are controller and conqueror.
When you give anyone else the power to anger you, you are giving them
control over your inner peace. The other person can invade your mind and
control you whenever he pleases, because you are giving him that power.

In addition, the word "master" insinuates a master/slave relationship. When
you read this wisdom from Epictetus with this in mind, you basically become
the slave of anyone you allow to anger you. Unless you strengthen your mind
and refuse to allow anything outside of your control to negatively affect you,
he can control you at will.

If there is someone who continually pushes your buttons and "makes" you
angry whenever he is around you, he has the power to control you, and what's
worse, you are *giving* him that power. Remember, no one can *make* you angry;
you *decide* to be angry. It is all in how you decide to perceive that person's
words or actions. You can decide not to be affected by what he says or does,
or you can decide to be offended. Either way, it is totally up to you.

When you begin to master your mind and emotions, you will start to see the
truth in this wisdom. No matter what someone says or does, you don't have to
internalize it. Many people say or do things simply to get a reaction from you.
When you allow their actions to get to you, you are merely stepping into the
trap they have set for you. These people love drama and enjoy getting a
reaction out of you. Play the game wisely and see their actions for what they
are. Refuse to give anyone else power or control over your mind or emotions!

174

Stay calm and serene regardless of what life throws at you.
Marcus Aurelius

This is another brilliant piece of wisdom from Marcus Aurelius. No matter what is happening, staying calm enables you to deal with it better. When someone loses their self-control or panics, they do not think as clearly as they do when they are calm and collected. Panicking never helps you deal with the challenges at hand; it only hinders your rational thinking process.

A calm and serene mind is able to think rationally and respond to whatever challenge comes its way. The panicked man simply reacts, and more than likely, his actions will not be the wisest. But since he is not in complete control of his mind when he is panicked, he cannot evaluate the situation rationally. Therefore, he will many times make the situation even worse.

Remember, you can't always control what happens to you, but you can always control how you respond to what is happening. When you completely internalize this truism, you will be able to accept things as they are and deal with them appropriately. Inner peace and tranquility come from understanding and internalizing this truth.

This doesn't mean that you should ignore what is happening around you and pretend everything is fine; it is about recognizing that you have no control over what is happening, and then responding to it with wisdom, courage, and honor. There is a big difference between pretending something is not happening and accepting things as they are.

Many people deal with the challenges and problems in their lives by simply choosing to ignore them. This is not an appropriate or healthy response to life's problems. Ignoring a problem never solves it or makes it better.

The Stoic mindset is not about pretending things are not as they are. It is about accepting things as they are, calmly and rationally thinking about how you need to respond, if you need to respond, and then taking whatever action you deem necessary. By maintaining a calm, serene mind, you refuse to allow life's storms to unbalance your mind and emotions. Stay calm and respond!

175

Happiness and freedom begin with a clear understanding of one principle:
Some things are within our control, and some things are not.
Epictetus

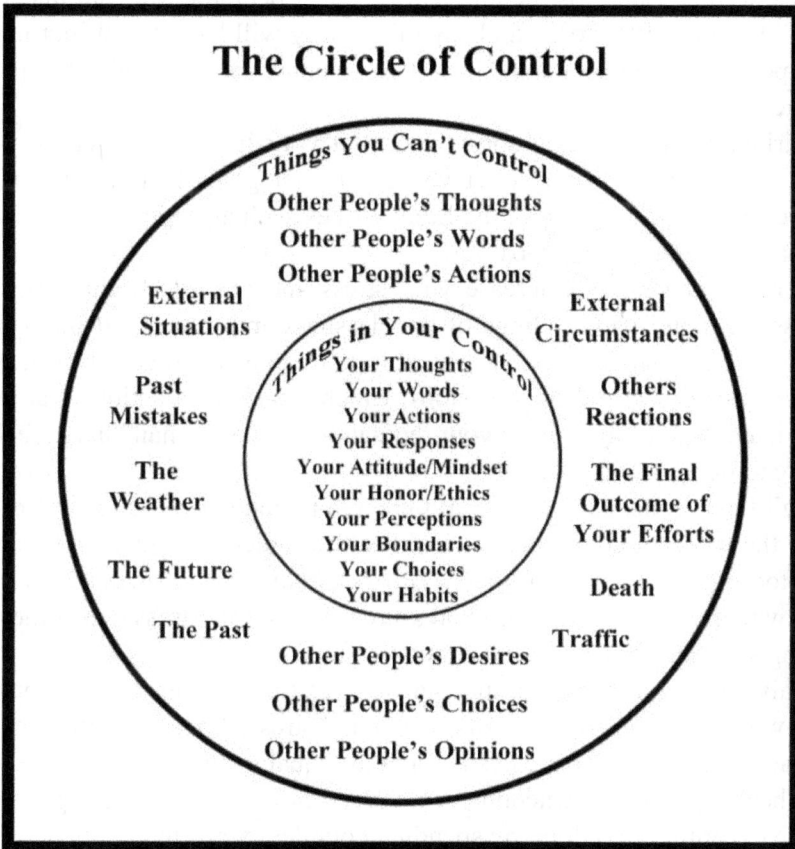

176

How much more harmful are the
consequences of anger than the causes of it.
Marcus Aurelius

This is truer than most people realize. Most people know that unchecked anger can cause them to do and say things they will later regret, but not that many people truly understand the spiritual, mental, and physical consequences of anger.

Spiritually, anger will absolutely disrupt your inner peace, cause you to regret your actions, and distract you from your goals to live with a Stoic mindset. It distracts you from the Stoic virtues such as patience, compassion, and maintaining a calm disposition.

Mentally, anger will increase your stress and anxiety. It can also cause depression, along with feelings of hopelessness and sadness. It plays havoc with your emotions and has destroyed more than a few relationships. Anger frequently causes impulsive decisions, which lead to rash actions that people regret later. And it can damage your reputation and cause many harsh feelings, leading to burned bridges.

If all those consequences weren't enough to convince you to control your anger, the physical consequences and health problems anger causes can't be taken too lightly. Anger increases your risk of having a heart attack or stroke, along with increasing your blood pressure. The chronic stress that comes with prolonged anger weakens your immune system.

It also causes digestive issues and can cause irritable bowel syndrome, along with headaches because of tension and stress. Anger also disrupts your sleep and causes you to have insomnia or low-quality sleep, which causes even more health problems. Uncontrolled anger has caused many people to lose their lives, or their freedom, by spending countless years in prison.

The Stoics considered anger to be one of the most destructive of all emotions. Keep your anger in check and respond to life's challenges with rational thinking and wisdom. Never allow your anger to dictate your actions.

Suffering arises from trying to control what is uncontrollable,
or from neglecting what is within our power.
Epictetus

According to Epictetus, suffering comes in two forms—trying to control the things that you can't control, and neglecting to control the things that you can control. When you are trying to control the things that you have no control over, you are refusing to accept things as they are. And refusing to accept the things that you cannot change is refusing to accept the reality of the situation, which will eventually cause you suffering.

As I have already made clear, you must accept those things that you cannot control. This doesn't mean that you must like the way those things are, merely that you must accept them, then decide how to respond to the situation. You can't successfully respond to a situation until you rationally accept the situation as it is. Once you accept things as they are, then you can devise a plan to work around the situation successfully or find a way to use that situation to your advantage.

This is where you must take action to control the things that are within your control. Many people will simply accept things as they are and then simply put the situation out of their minds. While the specific situation or circumstances may be beyond your control, the wise man will think rationally and find a way to work around the uncontrollable situation.

Giving up and quitting is simply neglecting to control the things within your power of control. Remember, you are not defeated when you lose, but when you quit. Accepting things as they are does not give you an excuse for surrendering to the circumstances.

Making excuses for your inaction is simply neglecting to warrior up and take control of the things that are within your circle of control. It is merely whitewashing the fact that you quit. Don't give up as soon as you encounter an uncontrollable obstacle. Be determined that you will succeed one way or another and then respond as necessary.

178

Speak briefly and to the point.
Cato the Younger

The Stoics taught that your speech should be clear, concise, and purposeful. Say what needs to be said, make your point, then stop talking. Don't go on and on, repeating yourself in a variety of ways. Not only is that boring to the listener, but you are draining your words of their power.

The power of speech contains the energy to change the way others think and can change the things that manifest themselves in your life. People in today's world take their speech for granted; they have forgotten how powerful their words can be if they are used properly.

Make sure your speech serves a specific purpose other than simply speaking to hear yourself talk. The Stoics taught that you should only speak when what you have to say adds something valuable to the person you are speaking to. Avoiding excessive speech can save you from the many problems that come from saying things you should never have said.

The more you talk, the more likely it is that you will become careless and say things that are better left unsaid, or which reveal personal information that should be kept private. Excessive speech can lead to misunderstandings, hard feelings, and can cost you the respect of those around you.

When you speak briefly, succinctly, and to the point, you demonstrate that you have given rational thought to the subject and that you respect the other person's time. Use self-control when it comes to your speech; eliminate unnecessary words and focus on saying only what needs to be said.

Focus on what truly matters when you are speaking to others. If you have nothing useful to add to the conversation, be content to listen to the others speak, and gather useful information. If you have anything to add, make sure that you have given your words rational thought; then speak briefly and to the point, without exaggeration or embellishment. Think before you speak, say what needs to be said, say it at the right time, and in the right way.

179

He is a wise man who does not grieve for the things
which he has not, but rejoices for those which he has.
Epictetus

It is human nature to look at expensive clothes, new cars, fancy homes, or expensive "toys" and dream of being able to afford all those things. Many people take photos of these things and place them on their vision board, hoping to manifest the things they dream of having. Self-help books urge readers to do this to manifest the life they want to have and the material things that they desire.

While many people take part in this exercise, they forget a vital part of the process—being grateful for all the blessings they already have in their lives. You should start each day by being grateful for the many wonderful things you have in your life. When you sit down and really begin to think about all the abundant blessings you have in your life, you realize that you already have a great life.

The problem comes from comparing what you have in your life to what other people have in their lives, especially those who are richer, better looking, or more talented, etc. As Epictetus taught, the wise man rejoices for the blessings he has in his life, instead of grieving or complaining about the things that he doesn't have in his life.

If you can't discipline yourself to stop comparing what you have in your life to what other people have, then compare what you have to the people who are less fortunate than you. When you do this, you will clearly realize how blessed you already are. Do you have decent clothes to wear, food to eat, clean water to drink, or a comfortable home? Then, you are much better off than you may think.

According to the Associated Press, over one billion people live in acute poverty, and around 8.5% of the global population live in extreme poverty. While you may be eyeing that shiny new car or new mansion, they just pray for the necessities in life. Think about this and be grateful for what you have.

180

*We should take wandering outdoor walks, so that the mind might
be nourished and refreshed by the open air and deep breathing.*
Seneca

Even around 2,000 years ago, Seneca realized the importance of taking relaxing outdoor walks to both your mental and physical well-being. Walking in the open air and breathing deeply, especially in nature, can help you clear your mind, reduces your stress, and give you the feeling of inner peace and tranquility.

The Stoics understood the importance of maintaining your physical and mental well-being. Seneca often wrote about being self-disciplined and living a balanced life. By taking walks outdoors, you can de-stress and clear and refresh your mind. This practice also allows you to gain greater clarity in your thoughts, or as Seneca wrote, nourishes and refreshes your mind.

Whenever you find yourself stressed or overthinking some issue you are dealing with, take a break and go for an enjoyable walk. Take your thoughts off the obstacle that is troubling your mind and just relax and take in the beauty and fresh air. After your walk is finished, your mind will be less stressed and better able to focus rationally on the issue at hand.

This is not just a Stoic teaching, but a fact. Science has proven that there are valuable mental health benefits of going for a nice, long walk, breathing deeply, and spending time in nature. If you are able, take a walk through a beautiful pine forest. Science has proven that a walk through the pines can give you a dopamine boost. Dopamine increases your mood, reduces stress, and has a calming effect on your mind.

Pine trees release phytoncides, which reduce cortisol. Cortisol is a hormone that the body produces when it is under stress. Reducing your cortisol level not only enhances your overall mood but also serves to boost your immune system. In addition, the fresh air in a pine forest is rich in oxygen. This increases your energy levels and promotes relaxation and mental clarity. Always make time for a relaxing walk in nature; you will be glad you did.

181

Remember, it is not enough to be hit or insulted, to be harmed, you
must believe that you are being harmed. If someone succeeds
in provoking you, realize that your mind is complicit in the
provocation. Which is why it is essential that we do not
respond impulsively to feelings; take a moment before
reacting, and you will find it easier to maintain control.
Epictetus

Both Epictetus and Marcus Aurelius taught that if someone has insulted
you, you are not harmed unless you allow yourself to believe that the insult
has harmed you. It is your *perception* that is the deciding factor. You can't
control what other people do or say, but you do have control over how you
perceive what they say.

Someone cannot truly insult you or provoke you unless you accept their
attempt to emotionally hurt you. It always depends on your perception. You
have the option of simply laughing at their rude attempt to hurt your feelings
or provoke you. When someone tries to insult you, just consider the source and
move on; don't give them the satisfaction of reacting to their malicious words.

The best way to do this is to simply smile and say, "You have a good day."
Don't allow your emotions to cause you to react impulsively. You have the
choice of either smiling and walking away, or pausing to think about how you
want to respond, if you need to respond at all. As Epictetus taught, if you pause
and think before you respond, you will find it is much easier to maintain your
calm, rational mind.

You don't have to allow rude comments or behavior to offend you. Think
about an archer on an archery range shooting at a balloon attached to the target
face. If his arrow misses the balloon, the balloon is not harmed. Someone's
attempt to offend or insult you can only offend you if you allow their words to
hit the target—your mind. And you control whether or not their arrow hits the
target. No one can offend you unless you *choose* to be offended. Choose not
to be offended, and their efforts to offend you miss their target.

182

You shouldn't give circumstances the power
to rouse anger, for they don't care at all.
Marcus Aurelius

External events or circumstances are not influenced by your anger, your acceptance of them, or your nonacceptance of them. You can get as angry as you want, and it won't affect them at all. As Marcus Aurelius wrote, they don't care about your anger. Circumstances are impersonal; they have no awareness or concern about your anger or your feelings; they simply are what they are.

When you allow external circumstances to rouse your anger, you are not hurting anyone but yourself. The situation is indifferent to you. You can yell, curse, or scream about the situation all you want, but it won't change it in the slightest, *but it will affect you.*

You must learn to control your emotions. Don't react emotionally to external events or circumstances; maintain your calm mind and think rationally. When you react with anger or frustration, you are adding to your stress and reinforcing your mental inclination to allow things outside of your control to anger you. If the situation is outside of your control, what good does it do to get angry about it?

Start practicing emotional discipline. Only get angry on purpose! This means that you only allow yourself to get angry when you decide that anger is the appropriate response to what is going on. Remember, a calm mind is rational; an angry mind is irrational and dangerous. You have the power to choose how you perceive and respond to every circumstance or situation in your life.

Getting angry at an inanimate object or external circumstances is ridiculous; it changes nothing but your mental state. When you stub your toe on a coffee table, and then get angry and kick the table, have you hurt the table or your foot? If you stub your toe, take care of your toe and be more aware of your surroundings; don't get angry at the table; the table couldn't care less. Practice maintaining a calm, rational mind in every situation!

183

Never depend on the admiration of others. There is no strength in it.
Personal merit cannot be derived from an external source...
Grow up! Who cares what other people think about you?
Epictetus

Epictetus is not famous for pulling his punches; he taught the truth bluntly and matter-of-factly. This teaching is especially important for people in today's world, where it appears that almost everyone is willing to do whatever it takes to get the admiration of other people. But, as Epictetus wrote, there is no strength in depending on the admiration of others.

If you give other people the power to build you up, you are also giving them the power to tear you down. If you give others the power to control the things that are inside your circle of control, you are giving away your ability to control those things. By caring about what other people think about what you do, what you say, what you think, how you dress, or how you live, you are giving away your freedom to live your life your way.

Why would anyone in their right mind give away their freedom to control the things within their circle of control? There are already so many things outside your circle of control; you don't need to add to them by surrendering the things that you can control to other people. As Epictetus so eloquently put it—grow up! Stop placing so much importance on what other people think.

Never depend on the admiration of others because people's thoughts change with the wind. They may love you one day and hate you the next. Just look at movie stars or rock stars. Most are popular for only a short time; then they are quickly forgotten. If you depend on the admiration of others, you are setting yourself up for a fall!

True strength comes from living your own life. If you are praised by others for what you have accomplished, great; if you are vilified by others because of how you live, so what? No one has achieved greatness by trying to please everyone else. Greatness is achieved by living your life your way. Items of mass production are cheap; be unique and be yourself.

184

The foundation of every state is the education of its youth.
Diogenes

Diogenes really said a mouthful with this statement! No country can survive and thrive for long if it is not doing a good job of educating its young people. There is no value in having a population that is comprised of ignorant, narcissistic people. If the foundation of a building is faulty, the building will eventually fall; if a country doesn't do a good job of educating its citizens, eventually it will collapse.

An educated citizenry is the cornerstone of a successful country, especially a free republic. If the youth of a country are not well educated, their ignorance will eventually destroy the country. Think about it. The life expectancy in the United States today is about 78 years. In three generations, 60-90 years, the entire population of a country will be composed of people who are now in our education system. If these young people do not get a good education, how will they be educated enough for our country to continue thriving?

An uneducated population is the downfall of a republic. If the population is not intelligent enough to elect virtuous and honorable leaders to run the country, eventually that country will no longer be a free country. The amount of freedom a country can maintain depends on the quality of the individual citizens of that country. An ignorant, narcissistic population that lacks character, integrity, and virtue will soon have to be so overly managed by the government that they will lose their freedom.

Freedom comes with responsibilities, and the education of the young people of the country must be taken seriously. As I write this, we are seeing a dramatic failure in our education system. If this doesn't change soon, our country will be doomed to failure.

If you are a parent, it is vital that you insist on the best education possible for your children. Refuse to allow political correctness or the fads of the day to dictate your children's education. Not only is their future dependent on their education, but the future of their country is as well.

185

Other people's views and troubles can be contagious.
Don't sabotage yourself by unwittingly adopting negative,
unproductive attitudes through your associations with others.
Epictetus

Have you ever been in a good mood, but then had a coworker or friend come over and talk about all his troubles and how bad everything is right now, and your good mood was ruined? This is what Epictetus is talking about in this quote.

Everyone has an energy field that can and does influence others. While you may think this is nothing but metaphysical mumbo-jumbo, I can assure you that it is not. There is absolutely a scientific basis behind the idea that humans emit certain energy fields and that those energy fields can influence the people around them. The way your emotions, physiology, and presence impact others is well-documented.

I do not have the space here to get into all the scientific evidence and the quantum physics behind this science; that is not the subject of this book. But even in Roman times, Epictetus knew that who you associate with can influence your views and how you feel.

For this reason, you should be careful not to allow the views, attitudes, and troubles of other people to intrude on your life. This can happen before you even know what's going on, and it can sabotage not only your mood, but your productivity and your goals.

You can be hard at work on one of your goals and then a friend stops by who dumps a sob story on you and begs you to go to happy hour with him. By the time he is done talking and urging you to do your work later, you start to think that it would be nice to take a break, and off you go.

Be very discerning when it comes to who you associate with; their attitudes, moods, and way of speaking are contagious. Inevitably, you will adopt some of his views, attitudes towards things, and bad habits. Refuse to allow others to sidetrack you! Be very selective with whom you associate.

186

Welcome wholeheartedly whatever comes…not worrying too often,
or with selfish motive, about what other people say or do or think.
Marcus Aurelius

Marcus Aurelius taught that we should not only accept whatever comes our way, but we should actually love it. Man, that one can be very hard to live up to, but nobody said that living with a Stoic mindset was going to be easy. If it were easy, everyone would internalize the wisdom of the Stoics.

When something happens in your life that you have no control over, accept it wholeheartedly. Discipline your mind to accept what is happening without allowing it to stress you out, causing you to worry about what will happen next, or what other people will think, say, or do. Yes, I am aware this is a tall order, but when you stop to think about it, it makes perfect sense.

You can only control the things within your circle of control. If you can control something, then do it. But there are a lot of things in life that you have no control over. When it comes to those things, it does no good to worry about them or to worry about what other people think about them. You can't control external events or what other people think. The best you can do is accept whatever comes your way and respond to it as you see fit.

Moreover, Marcus Aurelius went even further, stating that we should not worry about what other people think, say, or do. That is not to say that we shouldn't be aware of other people's motives and do what we can to ensure that they cannot hurt us or our family. But do so with pure intentions and a rational mind, not with selfish motives.

Make it a habit to accept whatever comes with a calm mind, a pure heart, and good intentions. Control what you can control, and don't worry about the things you can't control. Welcome what comes as a part of life, and deal with it as the situation requires. Life is full of surprises, some of which are pleasurable and others which we had rather not have to deal with, but all of them are simply a part of life. Embrace them and continue to live your life your way, with good intentions, wisdom, honor, integrity, and inner peace.

187

It is unrealistic to expect people to see you as you see yourself.
Epictetus

Epictetus, with his unrestrained wisdom, tells us it is unrealistic to expect other people to see us as we see ourselves. You have a specific way of seeing yourself, both physically, as well as spiritually and mentally. While you may see yourself as a mighty warrior, someone else may see you as an incompetent wimp. Someone who knows you intimately may see you as a man of honor, while someone else may think you have a poor character.

Everyone has a different opinion and sees you differently, but you can bet that nobody sees you like you see yourself. You know yourself better than anyone else; even so, those who know you intimately may see aspects of you which you aren't completely aware of or have never noticed.

This doesn't necessarily have to be a negative thing. A friend or spouse may sometimes see things in you that you don't see in yourself. Where you may have low self-image or poor self-confidence, they may see you as very good-looking and capable. Other people will always see you differently than you see yourself, and that's okay.

What's more, how others see you is really none of your business, unless you are specifically asking someone for advice on improving yourself. What matters is how you see yourself and what you know about yourself. Your self-image has a tremendous impact on your life; so, it pays to be confident and develop a good self-image.

What others see is what you portray to them. If you keep your true self hidden, of course they are not going to see you the way you see yourself. You must develop the self-confidence to always be unapologetically you. There is nobody else exactly like you; you are one of a kind. So, be who you are meant to be! The more you allow yourself to be completely yourself, the closer others will come to seeing you as you see yourself. Don't be scared to allow others to see the true you; that is the only way they can honestly know who you are. Be who you are and let the chips fall where they may!

188

If you seek tranquility, do less. Or more accurately, do what's essential…
To do less is better. Because most of what we say and do is not essential.
If you can eliminate it, you'll have more time, and more tranquility.
Ask yourself at every moment, "Is this necessary?"
Marcus Aurelius

Have you ever taken the time to monitor how much of your time is wasted throughout the day doing unnecessary things? Most people would be shocked to see how much time they waste each day on nonessential things such as scrolling through social media, watching television, or surfing the internet.

Marcus Aurelius urges us to eliminate, or at least minimize, the time that we waste on things that add no value to our lives. Furthermore, this applies not only to the time you waste when you are alone but also to the time you waste on meaningless conversations. It doesn't matter if you are speaking to someone in person, on the phone, or simply texting, ask yourself, "Is this really necessary?"

Take the time to monitor your actions throughout the day and find out just how much of your valuable time is being wasted on things that are not only unnecessary, but that add no value to your life. The more nonessential things you can eliminate, the more time you will have to do the things that are beneficial to your life.

Think about how many of these unnecessary activities disrupt your inner peace and tranquility. When you are scrolling through your social media accounts, do you allow the posts or opinions of people you don't even know to anger, frustrate, or upset you in some way? Is the friend that you talk to often disrupting your inner peace with his negative views? Are you watching news shows that get you stressed about what is happening in the world?

Marcus Aurelius also stated, not only will you have more time if you eliminate your nonessential activities, but you will also have more tranquility and inner peace. The less time you waste, the better your life becomes. As this great philosopher taught, if you seek more tranquility, do less.

The primary virtue is to hold your tongue;
who knows how to keep quiet is close to God.
Cato the Younger

The Stoics valued self-control and wisdom, especially in one's speech. When someone talks constantly, he will inevitably say things that will offend others, anger some people, or expose his ignorance on different subjects. There is nothing I can think of that can cause more issues in your life than being careless with your speech.

The man who understands when to remain quiet is a man of wisdom. Too many people allow impulse to control their tongue. Speaking rashly, or without giving thought to what you want to say, can lead to damaged relationships, unnecessary conflicts, misunderstandings, and ultimately, many regrets, which could have easily been avoided by doing nothing more than remaining silent.

Cato even went as far as to write that the man who knows how to keep quiet is close to God. If you think about this statement, it implies that the ability to remain silent when you should, will bring you closer to God or to divine wisdom. Think about it. If you have a relationship with God, do you hear from God during your times of silence or when you are talking and discussing things with other people?

Most religions and philosophical traditions teach that silence and meditation are the path to self-awareness and a deeper understanding of the world around you, as well as the path to spiritual enlightenment. Each of these requires silent reflection and deep thought to truly discern the more profound aspects of yourself, your world, and your spiritual path.

Maintaining a tight rein over your tongue demonstrates mastery over your emotions, especially negative emotions such as anger, hate, jealousy, fear, and pride. It also exhibits the fact that you are judicious in your speech, which will increase the respect that others have for you. It helps you maintain your inner peace and avoid gossip. As Buddha taught, "Before you speak, let your words pass through three gates. Is it true? Is it necessary? Is it kind?"

190

You must purify your intellect by training your thoughts:
"My mind represents for me my medium, like
wood to a carpenter, or leather to a shoemaker.
The goal in my case is the correct use of thoughts.
Epictetus

Your thoughts are the beginning of your virtues or your vices. To live a virtuous life, as the Stoics advise, you must first learn to purify and control your thoughts. Epictetus compared this process to a carpenter working with wood or a shoemaker working with leather.

Think about how a carpenter takes pieces of wood and turns them into fine furniture or uses the wood to build a home. He first needs to know what his objective is. Then he must plan his project, decide what he needs and how he wants his finished project to look. Then he shapes and cuts the wood exactly as he needs it to be, discarding what is no longer useful to complete his goal.

This is a good metaphor for purifying your mind and training or controlling your thoughts. The first thing you must do is to do some intensive work on your subconscious mind, which is much like a computer. It has been programmed with all your thoughts, words, and actions since you were born. Many of those subconscious thoughts no longer serve you, so they must be removed from your subconscious mind.

Then, you start the process of reprogramming your subconscious mind with thoughts and values that serve you better. But to do that, you must start being mindful of the new thoughts and values that you are programming into your subconscious. This requires you to be strict with your thoughts and words.

To do this, you must break old habits that no longer contribute to the kind of life that you want to live. Then you must replace those old habits with new, more beneficial habits until they become ingrained in your subconscious and conscious mind. Don't allow your mind to run wild. Step up and take your rightful control of your thoughts and reprogram your subconscious mind. Purify your thoughts and infuse them with the power they are meant to have.

191

> Often, injustice lies in what you aren't doing,
> not only in what you are doing.
> *Marcus Aurelius*

Many philosophers, both before and after Marcus Aurelius' time, have taught this same thought—Plato, Aristotle, Seneca, Cicero, Saint Augustine, Immanuel Kant, John Stuart Mill, and even Martin Luther King, Jr. You can commit injustice, not only by the things you say and do, but by the things that you don't do.

At first, this may sound a little strange, but once you think about it, it makes perfect sense. One of the fundamental traits of a man or woman of honor and character is to do the right thing, even when it is difficult or could cost them in some way. It takes courage to live with a Stoic mindset. You must be able to stand up for what is right, even if you are standing alone against the injustice of the majority.

You won't read in any of the Stoics' teachings that you should only do the right thing when it is convenient or to your benefit. Neither will you see any of the Stoics praise acts of cowardice or apathy. Being committed to justice is not always easy, but it is always the right thing to do.

John Stuart Mill put it this way: "A person may cause evil to others not only by his actions but by his inaction." This puts the responsibility of preventing injustice directly on you, if you have the ability to prevent it. Going along to get along simply doesn't cut it. You are either committed to justice, or you aren't. If you are striving to live with a Stoic mindset, then you must have the courage to step up and do the right thing when you can.

If you aren't committed to justice, then you are not living with a Stoic mindset, as justice is one of the fundamental aspects of Stoicism. Don't allow fear to cause you to sit by silently when you should stand up for justice. Don't excuse yourself, thinking that someone else will step up and stop the injustice you are witnessing. What if nobody has the courage to act? You may be the only lifeline that someone has. Be committed to courage and justice!

192

Hold sacred your capacity for understanding.
Marcus Aurelius

Understanding requires wisdom and rational thought instead of rash emotional reactions. The Stoics believed that being able to think rationally and understand the world around them was extremely important. If you allow your emotions to overtake your reasoning, then your judgment will be faulty. Emotions such as hate, fear, anger, or powerful desires can cloud your judgment and cause you to act impulsively instead of taking the time to think rationally about the issue at hand.

While you can't control external circumstances or events, you can control how you perceive and respond to them, and that includes taking the time to think through things to understand what is truly happening and why. When you make a habit of trying to understand what is really going on, or the other person's point of view, it enables you to maintain your self-control and remain calm, even in highly stressful situations.

To truly understand what someone is talking about, or what their issue is, you must think calmly and rationally. The Stoics believed that your power to think about things rationally is one of your most important capabilities. When you don't take the time to think rationally and understand what is truly happening, it weakens you; you will make decisions based on faulty or incomplete information.

You can only understand the truth by taking the time to see things from every angle and logically going deeper into the situation or subject. Whether it is a political issue or the motivation behind someone's words or actions, the truth rarely presents itself on the surface.

In attempting to understand the subject, situation, or the motivation behind someone's words or actions, you are better equipped to respond wisely and appropriately. Reacting or responding without truly understanding what is going on is a trap that many willingly step into in both relationships and business. You have the power of reason, so use it!

193

> The first thing to do—is to stay calm…speak as you see
> most just and fitting, with kindness, modesty, and sincerity.
> *Marcus Aurelius*

One of the first things to do in any situation is to stay calm and think rationally. Refuse to panic no matter how serious the situation may be. Panicking does nothing but make everything worse, and it can be contagious. Simply stay calm and respond in the way that you think is best for the situation.

How do you know what the best way to respond is? Marcus Aurelius taught that you should respond or speak in the way that is most just, and which is appropriate for whatever you are dealing with at the time. This means that you must give the situation some rational thought *before* you respond.

Moreover, he urges us to respond with kindness, modesty, and sincerity. He didn't say to only respond with kindness, modesty, and sincerity if it is best for you or if you feel like it. Since there are no exclusions mentioned, he must have meant that we should initially respond with kindness, modesty, and sincerity in all situations.

You may be thinking, but what about if someone is about to attack you or is screaming and cursing you? If someone appears as if he is about to attack you, responding sincerely and in a kind way may actually change his mind. Portraying a calm, confident demeanor may make him think twice about attacking you. At the very least, it may make the attacker pause for a couple of seconds, which can be an advantage to you in case he does decide to attack.

If someone is screaming and cursing at you, responding in a calm voice, with kindness and sincerity, may very well be enough to calm his out-of-control rage down enough to cause him to pause and see how ridiculous he is acting.

In either case, you have lost nothing by maintaining your calm demeanor and speaking kindly and in a confident voice. In addition, if things escalate, any bystanders will be able to testify that you were calm, cool, and collected, tried your best to diffuse the situation, and didn't want any trouble.

194

The greater the difficulty, the more glory in surmounting it.
Skillful pilots gain their reputation from storms and tempests.
Epictetus

True greatness comes from overcoming great odds. The greater the difficulty, the sweeter the glory of overcoming it. As Confucius taught, there is no honor in blasting a mosquito with a cannon. Using excessive force to overcome a weak opponent or an insignificant problem, while it gets the job done, is not only dishonorable, but inefficient. You have accomplished very little other than stroking your own ego.

There is no glory in defeating an inferior opponent or overcoming a simple problem; if you are competent, you are expected to be able to control inferior opponents or minor problems with ease. Glory comes from triumphing over life's great adversaries or enormous challenges.

Anyone can sail in smooth waters; but it takes great skill to make it safely through rough seas and storms. It is in overcoming great adversity that brings a well-deserved reputation as a skillful sailor. A man of honor welcomes a true test of his skills.

Don't shy away from hard challenges; the harder the challenge, the greater the sense of achievement when you overcome it. See those challenges as tests of your skills, a chance to prove to yourself just how good you truly are.

Tough challenges will also reveal the areas of your life that need improvement. Nobody is perfect; we all have our weak points. But if your skills are never truly challenged, you may never discover the chinks in your armor. You can't improve your weak spots if you don't know what they are.

When you begin seeing challenges or difficulties as tests of your skills, your honor, and your character, your perception of those challenges changes. Instead of seeing them as hassles you must deal with, you start to see them as tests of your resolve or mental and physical skills. You began to see them as opportunities to prove that you can handle anything life throws at you. When you develop this mindset, nothing can intimidate you.

195

In your actions, do not procrastinate. In your conversations, do not confuse.
In your thoughts, do not wander. In your soul, do not be passive or
aggressive. In your life, don't be all about business.
Marcus Aurelius

This passage is a brief summary of living a mindful life with purpose, balance, and clarity. It gives us five outstanding pieces of advice that are helpful for everyone, no matter what stage of life he or she is in. Let's look at each of these individually.

First, in your actions, do not procrastinate. You should be decisive in your actions. Once you decide on the right course of action, act. The more you procrastinate, the greater the chance there is that you will simply never get around to doing what you need to do. When you procrastinate, life has a way of sidetracking you, and your plans get lost in the hustle and bustle of life.

The next piece of advice is in your conversations, do not confuse. There is only one reason to hold a conversation with someone, and that is to communicate and understand each other clearly. Unless you have a specific reason, don't be vague in your speech; be concise and to the point. Say what you mean and mean what you say!

The third gem is to not allow your thoughts to wander. Learn to control your mind. Maintain your focus and have a purpose to your thoughts. If you don't maintain discipline over your thoughts, they can and will cause you issues in your life. Learn to maintain your focus and tune out distractions.

Next, Marcus Aurelius urges you not to be passive or aggressive in your soul. Don't be apathetic to the challenges of others, and don't allow negative emotions such as anger, resentment, or hatred to consume your soul. Maintain your composure and your inner peace.

Finally, realize that life is about living; it isn't all about working, business, or simply paying bills. You only live once, so live your life to the fullest. Work so you can do the things that you want to do; don't live to work. Live in the present moment and be determined to enjoy your life.

196

Good people will do what they find honorable to do, even if it requires
hard work; they will do it even if it causes them injury; they will do
it even if it will bring danger. On the other hand, they will not do
what they find dishonorable, even if it brings wealth, pleasure,
or power. Nothing will deter them from what is honorable,
and nothing will lure them into what is dishonorable.

Seneca

Marcus Aurelius urged us to stop talking about what a good man is and just
be one. In this passage by Seneca, he does a great job of discussing what a
good man is and how he conducts himself. He describes not only what a good
man does, but what he will not do.

A good man will do what he considers to be honorable, even if it is hard to
do, dangerous, or may cause him problems, either financially or physically. A
man who values honor will not set his honor aside for personal gain. As Seneca
put it, he will not perform a dishonorable act, even if it brings him wealth,
pleasure, or power.

Men like this are rare in today's world. In fact, they have always been rare.
We may romanticize the past, but the truth is genuine men of honor have
always been rare, although probably not as rare as they are today.

Think about it. How many people do you know who will put their honor
above power or wealth? Many people seem to have the attitude that they will
do whatever it takes to get rich and powerful and then worry about being
honorable after they have accomplished their objective. These are not
honorable people. They are untrustworthy and will do whatever they need to
do to get what they want. After they have their prize, they then put on a charade
to fool people into thinking they are men of honor.

You are either a man of honor or you're not. If you are willing to set your
honor aside to achieve certain goals, then you are not a man of honor; you're
a fraud. Men of honor put what's right above what is profitable or pleasurable.
If you always strive to do what's right, then you know your honor is intact.

197

Whatever anyone does or says, I must be a good man.
Marcus Aurelius

One thing that you must truly comprehend is that what other people think, say, or do, as long as they are not hurting you or someone else, is none of your business. You have no control whatsoever over what someone else thinks about how you live your life or what you say or do. They are free to think whatever they want.

Furthermore, what they think about you, or anything else, doesn't affect you. You are not responsible for their thoughts. You have enough challenges just keeping your own thoughts in line; don't trouble yourself with what others think.

Everyone has their own opinions. Let them deal with their opinions, and you just continue to strive to live a life of virtue and honor. Never allow what others do or say to throw you off course. Maintain your focus on your ultimate objective—to be a good man, a man of honor and integrity, regardless of what anyone else thinks about it.

That is your primary responsibility in life. What other people do or don't think about your decisions, or how you live your life, should have no influence on you. Even well-meaning people will try to talk you out of living your life your way. While these people mean well, they don't know what God has put in your heart or how you truly desire to live your life.

Always remember, this is *your* life to live, nobody else's. You must listen to your own inner being and allow it to guide you. If you quiet your mind, your spirit will guide you concerning what is right for you, and your code of ethics will guide you as far as what's right or wrong. Don't give authority over your life to anyone else or anything outside yourself.

Learn to quieten your mind and listen to your spirit. The wisdom contained within you is infinitely superior to the opinions of others. Spend time in meditation and listen for guidance that you will find nowhere else. Focus on being a good man, a man of wisdom, courage, honor, and integrity.

198

A good man is invincible, for he does not rush into any
contest in which he is not the strongest...the only contest
the good man enters is that of his own reasoned choice.
How can such a man not be invincible?
Epictetus

In another section of Epictetus' writings, he left no doubt about what he thought about entering contests. He wrote, "You may always be victorious if you will never enter into any contest where the issue does not wholly depend upon yourself." If you only enter contests where you know you can win, then your invincibility solely depends on you; you leave nothing to chance.

Epictetus taught that a good man should not rush into any contest where he is not the strongest or most clever. This means that you must choose your battles carefully. You must give every contest some rational thought and not rush in mindlessly. If you carefully consider every contest, you can be invincible because you refuse to leave your victory to chance.

This would indicate that Epictetus would not gamble on anything that was outside of his circle of control. Anytime you gamble on sports or card games, etcetera you are simply taking a chance to lose your money. You have no control over how a team will play or what random cards may be dealt. The Stoics would consider such actions unwise.

If you want to stay in control of your life and be as invincible as possible, you must carefully deliberate your actions beforehand. While others allow their egos to guide their decisions, the wise man allows his spirit and rational mind to determine what he gets himself into or what he stays away from in life.

When you allow wisdom, common sense, and rational thinking to guide you, you have much better odds of coming out on top in every situation. Of course, you have no control over things outside of your circle of control, but using wisdom in all your decisions will give you an edge. Don't rush into any situation without taking the time to consider it carefully!

If you do not wish to be a hothead, do not feed your habit.
Try as a first step to remain calm and count the days you haven't
been angry…For habit is first weakened and then obliterated.
Epictetus

Many people are addicted to anger. The more you allow yourself to give in to anger, the more anger becomes a habit for you; it becomes your go-to reaction when something does not go the way you want. Someone who is known to have a bad temper is a person who has allowed anger to become not only a habit, but essentially an addiction.

I have already covered how anger can be addictive, so I will not repeat that information. Just know that, like any addiction, an addiction to anger can be broken. As Epictetus stated, if you want to stop being a "hothead," then stop feeding the habit.

You break a habit by first being mindful of your thoughts. Make it a point to remain calm, no matter what is happening around you. Refuse to allow anything to "make" you angry or to cause you to lose your temper. See how many days you can go without getting angry or upset about anything.

And don't get discouraged when you slip up and get angry. Trust me, you will have bad days where you allow something to anger you before you take the time to think about it rationally and determine to stay calm. When that happens, acknowledge it, hit the reset button, and start over again.

You will find that the more you keep your focus in the present moment, the easier it will be to remain calm and control your anger. Anytime you feel anger welling up inside you, pause and ask yourself, "Is getting angry about this situation going to change it or make things worse?"

Getting angry about something rarely makes anything better, but it frequently makes things worse. Stay calm, think rationally, and focus on the solution instead of the words or actions of others. Learn to control your emotions instead of allowing your emotions to control you. The more you control your anger, the less you will have the inclination to become angry.

200

> While it is true that someone can impede our actions,
> they cannot impede our intentions and our attitudes…
> The obstacle on the path becomes the way.
> *Marcus Aurelius*

Throughout your life, you will find that you will encounter many obstacles, no matter what path in life you choose. There will always be people in your life who are less than enlightened, and even malicious and nasty. While these people may be able to impede your actions, cause you hassles, or even become your sworn enemies, they have no control over how you conduct yourself.

You always have control over your intentions, attitude, and mindset, no matter what anyone else says or does. Remember, nobody can "make" you angry or *cause* you to have a bad attitude; you control your emotions and attitude, no one else. If you get angry because of someone's words or actions, just know that you *chose* to get angry; they did not *make* you angry.

Whenever you say that someone "made" you angry, you are playing the victim and being dishonest. You have total control over your will, your attitude, and your mindset. Nobody can *make* you decide to be angry; that is a decision you make on your own. Someone can tempt you to be angry, but they can't *make* you angry. Your happiness, inner peace, and tranquility come from within; nobody can take them from you. You control your mindset, attitude, responses, and intentions.

Work to maintain a Stoic mindset and a good attitude, despite what is happening around you. A bad attitude has never helped solve any problem. Keep your intentions honorable and pure. Not only do you have total control over these things, but maintaining that control helps you overcome any obstacles that you may encounter throughout life.

Obstacles on your life path are a part of your path. Successfully overcoming those obstacles builds character, self-confidence, and self-esteem. Don't see the obstacles in your path as a hassle or a pain; see them as a test of your intelligence and coping skills. Be determined to pass the test with honor!

I will never be ashamed to quote a bad writer with a good saying.
Seneca

This quote by Seneca demonstrates some deep wisdom. You can learn something from everyone. It doesn't matter if they are a poor writer or completely illiterate; if you pay attention, and keep your ego in check, you can learn something from them.

I have had a couple of misguided people who have refused to endorse my books because I included a quote from this guy or that guy who they did not respect for one reason or another. That is merely being simple-minded and speaks more to their ignorance than what they considered to be their "honor."

Of course, everyone has the right to their own opinion, no matter how ridiculous it might be. However, I will side with Seneca on this matter. I use quotes in my books, not because of the fame or esteem of the author of the quote, but because of the wisdom within the quote itself.

After all, my writing is about living with wisdom, character, honor, and integrity. If a quote adds to the overall objective that I am teaching, I will use it and expand on it. I have used quotes from gangsters to presidents, and from all over the world, because the quotes point out essential wisdom that is useful in helping others live a successful and full life.

When someone looks at who the author of a quote is instead of the wisdom the quote contains, he is not thinking rationally; he is allowing his ego to make his decisions for him. It is never a good idea to allow your ego to dictate your decisions. What someone actually means when he disregards a piece of wisdom because of who the author is, is that he believes he is superior to the author. That is being judgmental, which is not in line with true wisdom.

Be wise enough to receive wisdom from whatever source it comes to you. Wisdom can come in many forms and from a variety of sources, some of which you may never expect. If you stay in the present moment and listen to your spirit, you will find that wisdom resides all around you. It's just waiting there for you to take the time to grasp it and use it to improve your life.

Nobody hands out his money to a passerby, but to how many
do each of us hand out our lives! We are tightfisted with
property and money, yet think too little of wasting time,
the one thing which we should all be the toughest misers.
Seneca

Time is the most important thing that we have in our life. It is the one thing
that we cannot get back or buy more of, and the most common thing that people
take for granted. As Seneca taught, we would never simply give our money or
property away randomly, but most people have no problem giving their time
away to anyone and everyone who crosses their path.

This is not to say that we shouldn't be cordial and friendly to others or take
time to talk and maintain our friendships and family relationships; we should.
However, we live in a completely different world than Seneca did. We live in
a world where we are tempted in every way to waste our precious time.

Just think about how much more you could get done if you managed your
time more efficiently. You could read more amazing books, spend more time
in nature or with your loved ones. You wouldn't be stressed trying to get things
done that you have postponed for days or weeks. Your life would be more
tranquil, laid-back, and peaceful.

Most of the things that we waste our precious time on are simply mindless
entertainment, which adds no value to our lives. Simply put, this is a form of
mental escapism. Scrolling on social media, watching reruns on television, and
surfing the internet all offer an easy mental escape from the problems and
challenges of everyday life, but they rarely help you improve your life. They
are just a temporary mental break. But you must remember that putting your
challenges or problems out of your mind does nothing to solve them.

It takes mental discipline to use your time constructively instead of
allowing yourself to zone out and drift into a world of escapism. Start using
your time wisely; become a miser of your time. When you use your time
efficiently, you will have more time to do the things you really enjoy.

203

*This is the mark of perfection of character—to spend each day
as if it were your last, without agitation, laziness, or any pretense.*
Marcus Aurelius

The best way to appreciate and use your time wisely is to live each day as if it were your last. Keep in mind how brief life truly is, and that even what we consider to be a long life is still short in the overall scheme of things. Time passes by much faster than you may think, especially when you are younger. In no time, you find yourself older, and you can't believe that 30, 40, or 50 years have gone by. If you don't believe this, ask anyone in their sixties or seventies and they will enlighten you.

Besides how fast time passes, you truly have no idea when death may come for you. This past Christmas, my younger brother, Russ, was returning home from entertaining kids in his Santa Claus costume for Christmas when a careless driver hit his vehicle head-on, killing him instantly. No one expects to be killed or die unexpectedly, but it happens around the world daily. Keeping this in mind will help you remember to spend each day as if it were your last.

No matter what you think, you don't have time to waste. Do your best not to allow agitation, laziness, depression, or anything else to cause you to waste your precious time. This can be hard to do at times, especially during times of grieving or severe heartbreak.

When you just can't seem to motivate yourself or get your mind straight, you can at least sit in meditation for a while. This will help you get your mind straight and will help you heal so you can get back to living a full life. It's hard to motivate yourself to meditate when you are depressed or grieving, but if you discipline yourself to do so, it will help.

Marcus Aurelius stated that spending each day as if it were your last is the mark of perfection of character, which is something we should all strive for in life. It takes a lot of discipline and wisdom to live each day of your life as if it were your last. Just remember that you never know when you wake up whether today will be your last day. Use your time wisely!

204

Wherever there is a human being,
we have an opportunity for kindness.
Seneca

This statement by Seneca is something that most people forget as they go through their busy lives. Wherever there is a human being, you have the opportunity to be kind. Too often, we see the opposite of this. Many people are so focused on their own problems, desires, and lives that they often don't even think about being kind to others.

Moreover, many times other people make it extremely hard to be kind to them because of their own behavior; some people are rude, thoughtless, and self-centered. It can be extremely hard to even think about being nice or kind to such people, but frequently, these are the people who need your kindness the most.

Always keep in mind that you truly do not know what is going on in someone else's life. Everyone has problems they must deal with throughout life. The woman who doesn't speak may have just lost her husband in an accident and is doing all she can to hold back the tears welling up from her broken heart.

The man who is unfriendly may be completely heartbroken and wants nothing to do with anyone or may be on the edge of wanting to commit suicide. The guy who speeds through traffic and cuts you off may have an emergency that is more important than being a thoughtful driver. You simply do not know what others may be dealing with in their lives, so determine that you will be kind regardless of how others behave.

These are the times where it pays to keep in mind Baltasar Gracian's teaching, "The man of principle does not forget who he is because of what others are." Determine what kind of person you want to be and be that person, no matter what other people think, say, or do. You are not responsible for their actions; but you are responsible for yours. Don't forget who you are because of how other people act. Remember this!

205

There is nothing worse than a wolf befriending sheep. Avoid
false friendships at all costs. If you are good, straightforward, and
well-meaning, it should show in your eyes and not escape notice.
Marcus Aurelius

Fake friends are worse than having no friends at all. As Marcus Aurelius
stated, you should avoid them at all costs. There are many wolves in sheep's
clothing in this world, and have no doubt about it, they have the gift of gab and
know how to weasel their way into people's lives. They have a knack for
getting people to trust them.

They may seem like the greatest friend you can imagine, at least until they
get what they want out of the relationship. Then they suddenly change, or more
accurately, the mask comes off, and you see the wolf behind the facade for the
first time. It can be shocking when you find out that someone you thought was
your trusted friend was never who you thought he was to begin with.

Trusting others is always a tricky proposition. Even someone whom you
have known and intimately trusted for 40 years or more can change and
become untrustworthy or totally blindside you. When it comes to trust, you
need to keep your eyes wide open and never put more trust in someone than
you absolutely must.

There are different levels of trust. There are some things that you can trust
some people with, and other things that you would never consider trusting
someone with. I have learned from experience that it is rarely wise to
completely trust anyone, no matter if they are a family member, a spouse, or
your best friend.

A rule of thumb is never to put so much trust in someone that he can use
what you disclose to him against you later. You cannot control what others will
do or say, but you can always control how much personal information you
disclose to them. Think twice before giving your hand in friendship. And think
a dozen times before disclosing personal information that someone can use
against you. Today's friends can become tomorrow's enemies!

206

In all things, we should make ourselves be as grateful
as possible… Gratitude pays itself back in large measure.
Seneca

There's power in gratitude. Having gratitude for the things in your life will help you maintain your inner peace and live a full life. Be intentionally grateful for all the blessings in your life. As the noble warrior, Tecumseh stated, "When you arise in the morning, give thanks for the morning light, for your life and strength. Give thanks for your food and the joy of living. If you see no reason for giving thanks, the fault lies with yourself."

Tecumseh's last sentence really hits home. If you see no reason for giving thanks, the fault lies with yourself. You have an abundance of things in your life to be grateful for, but most people take those things for granted. Be grateful for even the smallest things in your life. When you see a beautiful flower, smile and give thanks to God for creating it. When you see a beautiful sunset or sunrise, let the beauty and majesty fill your heart with gratitude. As you spend time with your kids or grandkids, be grateful that you were given that time together. Be grateful for everything in your life, all the time.

Seneca goes on to explain that we should all be as grateful as possible, saying that gratitude pays itself back in large measure. Being grateful for all the blessings in your life changes your inner attitude. It puts you in constant communion with God, for it is God who has provided those things that you are grateful for to begin with.

The more grateful you are throughout your day, the happier you become, and the more satisfied and content you will be with your life. Actively look for things to be grateful for. Say thank you to the server, the cashier, the guy who gives you directions. When you walk by a lilac bush and smell the amazingly fresh scent of the lilac flowers or witness a beautiful full moon on a clear night, thank God for the beauty He has provided for you. Be grateful constantly, and you will find that your life will be more mindful, peaceful, and enjoyable. Don't let a day go by without being grateful for everything in your life.

207

The person who does wrong, does wrong to themselves. The
unjust person is unjust to themselves—making themselves evil.
Marcus Aurelius

This is the Stoics' version of karma. If you do wrong, you are essentially
doing wrong to yourself, because what you do in life will come back to you in
one form or another. Not only does this have to do with the law of karma, but
if you are working to live with a Stoic mindset, doing wrong or being unjust
to others means you are off course.

You should strive to improve yourself and the things that are in your circle
of influence daily, while at the same time, accepting those things which you
have no control over with inner peace and a calm mind. If you are doing others
wrong or treating someone unjustly, you are failing in your overall objective.

If you are doing wrong, you are wronging yourself because you are not
living up to your standards; not to mention the fact that you are disrupting your
inner peace. You might wonder what this has to do with your inner peace, but
the answer is clear. Doing what you know is wrong, or treating others unjustly,
your conscience will not allow that to slide. You will have a nagging feeling
inside that will let you know your actions were out of line. This is your
conscience urging you to set things right.

Furthermore, if you ignore your conscience and continue to do wrong and
to treat others unjustly, you will become numb to those actions to where you
will actually start to become an unvirtuous, nasty person, or at the very least,
a person who is untrustworthy and dishonorable. That is completely opposite
of living with a Stoic mindset. Your actions matter!

If you know in your heart that something is wrong or unjust, refuse to do it,
no matter what anyone else thinks about it. Always strive to do the right thing,
no matter what. Be just, be honorable, act with good intentions and integrity,
and always do what you know to be right. Build good karma for yourself. Your
actions come back to you in one way or another. The more good you do in life,
the happier and more content your life will be.

208

> Do not set your mind on things you do not possess as if
> they were yours, but count the blessings you actually possess
> and think how much you would desire them if they were not
> already yours. But watch yourself, that you do not value these
> things to the point of being troubled if you should lose them.
> *Marcus Aurelius*

Instead of focusing on all the things that you don't have in your life, keep your focus on all the things that you *do have* and be grateful for them. One way to do this is to imagine or remember a time when you didn't have what you do now. Remember when you were just getting started in life and how much you desired the things that you now have. Think about how blessed you are to have so many nice things and how much you would love to have them if they weren't already yours.

Remind yourself that not everyone has these things. I think everyone should take a trip to a third-world country to see just how many people live without the everyday things that we take for granted. Since most of us do not see how these impoverished people live, we tend to take for granted how blessed we truly are.

Furthermore, Marcus Aurelius did not end his teaching on blessings and gratitude there. He went on to warn us not to place too much value on the things that we have in our life, saying, "Watch yourself, that you do not value these things to the point of being troubled if you should lose them." This can be a hard teaching to grasp.

It is very hard for most people to imagine losing their home, car, wedding ring, or some other valuable possession and not being troubled because of it. But that is exactly what Marcus Aurelius is urging us to do. He is warning us not to put our trust in external things, but to keep our focus on the things that truly matter—virtue, honor, courage, integrity, justice, and inner peace. Enjoy the material things you have in your life, but don't forget that they are only temporary. It's the internal things that are your true, lasting treasures.

209

What is the product of virtue? Tranquility.
Epictetus

Virtue is the quality of conducting yourself with character, honor, and integrity; it is living in line with your principles, especially the Stoic principles. Epictetus taught that the byproduct of living a life of virtue is tranquility or inner peace. But why is tranquility the product of living a life of virtue?

As far as Stoicism is concerned, living a life of virtue is the basis for a happy life. The four main virtues of Stoicism, as you already know, are wisdom, courage, justice, and temperance. Wisdom is understanding the difference between what is good and what is bad, and choosing what is right. Courage is facing and overcoming your fears. Justice is being fair and conducting yourself with integrity in all your relationships. And temperance is maintaining your self-control and moderation in every situation.

That still doesn't quite explain why the byproduct of virtue is tranquility. The answer is much simpler than you may think. When you adhere to your ethics or code of honor and do the best you can to do what's right in every situation, you are at peace no matter what the outcome of your actions may be. Even if your actions do not produce the results that you were hoping to achieve, your spirit and mind will still be at peace because you did the best that you could to do what's right.

Doing the right thing, no matter what, always strengthens your inner peace. If you start to have negative thoughts because things did not turn out as you wanted, just remind yourself that you can only control those things in your circle of influence. You cannot control external things such as other people's actions or an unexpected turn of events. The best you can do in every situation is to do your best to do what's right.

Therefore, if you are living with virtue, wisdom, courage, justice, and temperance, you will be living in a state of inner peace unless you forget to maintain control over your thoughts. It is only your thoughts that can rob you of your inner peace and tranquility.

210

> We have the power to hold no opinion about a thing
> and to not let it upset our state of mind. For things
> have no natural power to shape our judgments.
> *Marcus Aurelius*

In today's world, it is common to see people arguing over topics that they have no control over, and which truly don't have any bearing on their lives. Many people love to argue or debate things, even when they don't truly know what they are talking about or have no wisdom concerning the topic at hand.

Trying to appear intelligent on a topic with which you are not familiar or ill-informed does little more than expose your ignorance and make you look foolish. There is a popular quote that is attributed to Abraham Lincoln, although there is no evidence that he ever said it, which states, "It is better to remain silent and be thought a fool than to speak and to remove all doubt."

The Bible, in the *Book of Proverbs*, states the same thought, but in a different way: "Even a fool is considered wise when he keeps silent, and discerning when he seals his lips." To put it simply, if you don't know what you are talking about, keep your mouth shut!

This is easy to do if you simply remember Marcus Aurelius' teaching that you have the power to hold *no opinion* about a thing. And you certainly don't have to allow external things to disrupt your inner peace or agitate your mind. Think about what Crocodile Dundee said when he was asked his opinion about all the problems in the city. He responded, "It's none of my business."

You do not have to have an opinion about everything. Life becomes much less stressful and more peaceful when you focus on your own business and your own life. Don't try to impress everyone around you with your opinions on everything going on in the world. Why clutter your mind with opinions on things that don't affect you or your life? Refuse to be pretentious; that is just your ego taking control of your actions. Be content to be yourself and don't concern yourself with impressing others. Just focus on what is yours to do and the things you can control.

211

> Who then is invincible? The one who cannot be
> upset by anything outside their reasoned choice.
> *Epictetus*

Epictetus taught that if you want to be invincible, don't allow anything outside of your reasoned choice to upset you. When he wrote about "anything outside of your reasoned choice," he was referring to anything outside of your own control—external events, other people's thoughts, words, or actions, death, weather, etc.

Your reasoned choice is your power to choose your own thoughts, words, actions, and responses—those things that are within your control. If you can get to the point that nothing outside of your own control can upset you, then you are invincible as far as your heart and mind are concerned.

Of course, it takes time and self-discipline to get to this point because we have all been raised since birth to get upset when something goes wrong in our lives. But think for a second how differently humans would behave if they were raised from birth not to allow anything outside of their control to upset them. People would be mentally stronger and virtually invincible to external things controlling their mind, emotions, or actions.

This brings us to the question of how you develop this mindset. It takes conscious practice. If someone is rude to you or insults you, instead of responding in kind, mentally remind yourself that you have no control over their behavior. What you control is how or if you respond, and whether you allow their actions to affect you.

You must continually remind yourself that you have no control over external events or situations, or over what other people think, say, or do. It is not your business. Let them do what they will do, while you ignore them or respond as you see fit. What you don't want to do is to allow their words or actions to disrupt your inner peace or ruin your day. You can only do this by developing a strong inner spirit and a Stoic mindset. When you have total control over your mind and emotions, you are truly invincible.

212

At every moment, keep a sturdy mind on the task at hand, doing
it with strict and simple dignity, affection, freedom, and justice,
giving yourself a break from all other considerations. You can do
this if you approach each task as if it is your last, giving up every
distraction, emotional subversion of reason, and all drama,
vanity, and complaint over your fair share.
Marcus Aurelius

Marcus Aurelius is urging us to stay focused on the task at hand; don't allow other thoughts, stress, or worries to sidetrack you from whatever you are working on at the moment. He states that you should give yourself a break from all the other distractions in your life. It is amazing how pouring yourself totally into your work will give you a mental break from all the other challenges you may be facing.

Think about it. When you start to feel overwhelmed with stress, bills, your spouse's issues, or all the things on your to-do list, it is refreshing to give yourself a mental break by completely focusing on something else, whether it is yard work or going for a hike. This is what Marcus Aurelius meant by giving yourself a break from all other considerations; he was referring to a mental break.

One way to do this is to approach each task as if it were your last. Focus on doing it as perfectly as possible; don't allow your mind to wander. Forget all other distractions while you are working on that task or activity. Just put all the drama, emotional stress, and worries out of your mind and totally focus on the present moment!

If you remain mindful and keep your focus on the present moment, those other concerns will temporarily disappear. In this present moment, everything is okay; all that other stuff is either in the past or in the future, neither of which affects the present moment. If you make a habit of keeping your mind in the present moment, you will find you have much less stress and more inner peace. Focus on the present moment!

213

A real man does not give way to anger and discontent, and such a man has strength, courage, and endurance, unlike the angry and complaining. The nearer a man comes to a calm mind, the closer he is to strength.

Marcus Aurelius

In this passage, Marcus Aurelius gives us a quick summary of what a real man should be like. He states that anger, discontent, and complaining are not manly character traits. They demonstrate an agitated, undisciplined, and uncontrolled mind and spirit, which are not traits becoming of a real man who has strength, courage, and endurance.

Men of strength, courage, and endurance discipline themselves to control their minds instead of allowing themselves to react mindlessly to every challenge or irritation that they encounter. They control their thoughts and refuse to allow external things to rob them of their composure.

Real men refuse to be controlled by others; they understand that if someone else can "make" you angry, he can control you at will. Men of strength maintain a calm mind and refuse to allow others to manipulate them through their words or actions. They know that they have no control over what other people say or do, so they accept others as they are and respond as necessary; but they refuse to be moved to anger or complaining.

The stronger a man is, the calmer he is. Self-confident men, who know who they are and what they can do, remain unaffected by the words or actions of others. They do not care about what others think about them. A real man has confidence in himself and refuses to forget who he is, no matter how others behave or what is going on around him.

He maintains a calm, unaffected mind at all times and understands that complaining is beneath him because complaining without taking action is nothing more than whining. He remains calm, controls his anger and discontent, and refuses to complain, understanding that getting angry and complaining solves nothing. So, he simply responds to each situation as needed, remaining calm no matter what comes his way.

214

Expecting is the greatest impediment to living.
In anticipation of tomorrow, it loses today.
Seneca

A preoccupation with the future will not only rob you of the present moment, but more often than not, it will lead to disappointment. When you are constantly looking towards the future, waiting for something to happen before you can be happy or feel successful, you are not fully living in the present moment. Instead of living in the now, you are living in your head, always thinking about what is going to happen or what you want to happen.

When you focus too much on what you expect to happen tomorrow, you lose today. By doing this, the present moment becomes a means to an end instead of a precious moment that you will never get back again. This moment should be lived to the fullest and appreciated as the gift it truly is. Living with your mind in the future is not truly living at all.

Too many people believe they will be happy after something happens in the future, when they should be happy now. Your happiness does not depend on something happening or not happening in the future; your happiness depends entirely on you.

When you allow your happiness to depend on something outside of yourself, you have given external events, circumstances, and other people control of your contentment. That will never lead to true happiness. At the most, you will only have temporary moments of happiness, but true happiness, which comes from within, will always escape you.

Expectations tend to lead to disappointment. Life rarely lives up to our expectations. It is better to control the things you can control, accept everything else just as it is, and be determined to be happy regardless of how things turn out. Instead of anticipating what will happen in the future, focus on what you can do today, at this very moment. If you take care of what is yours to do in the present moment, the future will take care of itself. Do your best to minimize your expectations and simply accept everything as it is.

215

> Philosophers warn us not to be satisfied with mere learning,
> but to add practice and then training. For as time passes, we
> forget what we learned and end up doing the opposite,
> and hold opinions the opposite of what we should.
> *Epictetus*

You can read all the philosophical or self-help books you want, but none of them will change your life unless you put into action what you have learned. Merely reading good books or listening to influential teachers won't change your life. More often than not, if you don't immediately start to integrate the things you learn from your studies into your life, you end up forgetting about them and they become little more than temporary entertainment.

If you don't put the principles to work in your life, frequently you will end up doing the exact opposite of what you should be doing. You can read the teachings of the Stoics every single day, but if you don't act on those teachings and integrate them into your daily life, they are meaningless to you.

The teachings of the Stoics are meant to improve your life, not to entertain you. You can read about controlling the things that are within your circle of control and accepting the things that you don't control every day. However, until you act on those teachings, they are worthless as far as changing your life for the better.

Don't just read and agree with the teachings in this book; put them to work in your own life! The Stoic mindset is about living life. It is a way of life that puts you in control, removes your stress and worries, and makes you a better person. But reading the teachings alone won't do any of those things; you must *act* on them.

We all have busy lives today. Even if you have the best intentions to change your life after reading the teachings of the Stoics, if you are not careful, the demands of your busy life will overshadow the teachings you have learned. Gradually, you will forget about these great teachings, remembering them only occasionally. Don't fantasize about the Stoic mindset; walk the walk!

216

Put away the fear of death, and however much thunder
and lightning you have to face, you will find the mind
capable of remaining calm and composed regardless.
Epictetus

Once you have done the mental and spiritual work to get past the fear of death, you will find that it is much easier to remain calm and composed, regardless of what is happening around you or what you may be facing. The fear of death is the fear of the unknown, the fear of losing everything that you hold dear.

To get past the fear of death, you must come to terms with what you believe about death; you must know what your spiritual beliefs are. Moreover, you must go much deeper than that. You must not only know what your spiritual beliefs are, but you must completely internalize those beliefs to where you believe them with all your heart, mind, and spirit. Once you reach this point in your belief, you will be at peace with the fact that one day you will die.

You must come to realize that death is nothing more than a part of life. Accept that death is not something to be afraid of, that everyone who has ever lived has died, and you will experience the same thing that they have experienced.

Marcus Aurelius taught, "All things are woven together, and the common bond is sacred… All things are drawn back to the Logos… All things flow from the Divine Reason, and in time, all return to it." The Stoics believed that all things arise from Logos, and eventually, all things will return to Logos.

If you believe God created all things and that eventually, all things will return to God, what do you have to worry about? To put away the fear of death, you must clarify what you believe about God. Do you see God as a loving father who only wants the best for his children? Do you believe we will all return to the Creator when we leave this world? If so, you should live with calm assurance and courage, and find what the Bible calls, "the peace which passes all understanding."

217

Entrust everything willingly to God, and then make your
way through life—no one's master and no one's slave.
Marcus Aurelius

If you entrust everything in your life to God, and truly trust that God has
your best interest at heart, you can face life without worry or stress. You will
be free to walk your own path, to live your life your way, or as Marcus Aurelius
put it, to be no one's master and no one's slave.

This means that you are focused on your own life and your own business.
You are not trying to control other people or tell them how they must live their
lives. At the same time, you are no one's slave; you don't allow anyone else to
control your life or to tell you what you must think or do. You are free to live
your life your way and allow others the same freedom.

By entrusting everything to God, you are refusing to be ruled by fear or the
need of others' approval. You will take the opinions of others with a grain of
salt. In addition, you won't be interested in trying to control others, thereby
removing the stress of trying to control things over which you have no control.

This way of living is very freeing; you are simply focused on living life as
you should, believing that God is in control of everything outside of your
control. Your only duty is to control the things that God has given you control
over. While, at the same time, you release the need to try to control those things
which are outside of your control.

If you truly entrust everything to God, you will find that you can easily
walk through life calmly with your inner peace intact. Almost nothing will
upset you or disrupt your inner peace or happiness. You will be able to be
happy regardless of what is happening around you because you will trust that
God is in control and has a plan.

The only thing you must focus on doing is your part—being virtuous and
doing the right thing. The outcome will no longer be your concern. You will
rest easy knowing that you did the best you could, with pure intentions. After
you have done your best, trust the outcome to God.

Everything derives from it—that Universal Mind—either as effect
or consequence…focus on the Source that all things spring from.
Marcus Aurelius

Even in ancient Rome, Marcus Aurelius realized that there is one Source
that all things originate from and that we should focus on that Source. The
Stoics called it Logos, which loosely translates to Universal Reason or
Universal Mind. But it doesn't matter if you call it Source, God, the Universal
Mind, or some other name, it remains the Source that all things spring from
and all things return to after their physical death.

If you study ancient wisdom, you find that this is a common theme of many
sages and religions. It doesn't matter if it is Asian philosophy, Middle Eastern
philosophy, Christianity, Viking philosophy, or Native American beliefs, they
all believe in a Source greater than themselves and that we will eventually
return to that Source.

As Marcus Aurelius states, everything derives from this Source, not just
humans, but all animals, plants, trees, fish, creatures of every kind, and even
the rocks. Everything on Earth originates from the same Source.

He urged us to focus on the Source of all things, which is another way of
saying to spend time in prayer and meditation with God. As you read on the
last page, Marcus Aurelius stated we should entrust everything willingly to
God. This means that we should put our trust in God and then do our best to
live a virtuous life.

If you do this, you will be better prepared to handle life's struggles and
challenges. You won't allow the fear of death to haunt your mind or be
overwhelmed by life's hardships and suffering. You will be more likely to
accept the things that you cannot control and strive to live a virtuous life.

Consistently focusing on the Source of all things will help you live the kind
of life that you should live and live by the principles of Stoicism. Not only is
God the Source of every living thing, but He is also the source of virtue,
integrity, courage, wisdom, and justice. Focus on what's important!

219

Each man is the sole lord and judge of his own private actions.
Cato the Younger

Each of us has a private life that nobody knows about but us. We all have our private thoughts and private actions that we don't share with anyone else. And nobody has any control over those thoughts or actions but you; you are the sole lord and judge of your own private thoughts and actions. Only you truly know if your private thoughts and actions are virtuous.

Epictetus stated, "If your choices are beautiful, so too will you be. The soul is dyed the color of its thoughts. So, watch over your thoughts, guard them... even when alone." The genuine man of principle is one who watches over his actions even when he is alone.

If you only strive to be virtuous and to do the right thing when in public or when you are around other people, but do the opposite when nobody is watching, are you truly virtuous? Are you truly living with integrity and honor? Or are you merely putting on a show to impress other people?

Honor and integrity are not character traits that you can put on and take off like your coat. You either take your honor seriously or you don't; you live your life with integrity and virtue all the time, or you are not a man of honor and integrity.

Marcus Aurelius taught, "Be tolerant with others and strict with yourself." You are not meant to control other people's thoughts or behavior, but to control your own. You have no control over others, nor do you really know what is going on in their lives or what they may be dealing with. So, be tolerant of them. Allow them to live their lives as they see fit. You are not their judge or their keeper.

However, when it comes to yourself, you should be strict in both your private and public actions. You should even be strict when it comes to what thoughts you entertain. Strive to be the person that you profess to be. Don't put on a charade to impress others; be genuine and sincere in your beliefs and how you live your life.

220

No one can steal your peace of mind unless you let them.
Epictetus

We often hear people say how this person or that person made them so mad, but that is not accurate. As Epictetus taught, no one can "make" you upset, angry, or disrupt your peace of mind unless *you allow them to do so*. Your inner peace and mindset are completely under your control. Just as you have no control over someone else's thoughts, words, or actions, other people have no control over your thoughts, attitude, or inner peace.

You are solely responsible for maintaining your own peace of mind. You might think, "Yeah, but I have a right to be mad about what he did," or "He needs to be held accountable for his actions." And you would be right in both cases. Of course, you have the right to be angry if you choose, and people do need to be held accountable for their actions. But is getting angry going to change what happened, or is it going to totally disrupt your inner peace? Also, you can hold someone accountable for their actions without allowing his actions to rob you of your peace of mind.

The point is that no one can disrupt your inner peace without your permission; it's a choice that *you* make. You always get to choose how you will allow an external event, circumstance, or someone else's actions to affect you. What others do is their business; how you respond to their actions is yours. What you must decide is whether maintaining your inner peace is more important to you than allowing your emotions to choose your response for you.

Once you have truly comprehended and integrated the Stoic teachings in your life, and are living with a Stoic mindset daily, you will begin to cherish the peace of mind and inner peace that comes from living this lifestyle. You will experience how much better it is to maintain your inner peace instead of allowing anger to permeate your mind and spirit. You will come to love living with a calm, rational mind, and constant inner peace. That is when you know that you have conquered your negative emotions, reactions, and habits, and are choosing inner peace over reacting to external issues or other people's actions.

221

Don't let anything deter you: other people's misbehavior,
your own misperceptions, what people will say, or the
feelings of the body…No longer at the mercy of this or that.
Marcus Aurelius

Once you make a firm decision to live your life with wisdom, justice, moderation, courage, and inner peace, you must strive not to allow anything to sidetrack you. It is all too easy to get sidetracked and lose your cool because of other people's behavior. Many people are rude and will say or do things that can push your self-control to the limit. These people are generally unhappy people who have little to no inner peace or tranquility in their lives.

Why would you allow someone who has no inner peace in his life to rob you of your inner peace? Why would you give someone else control over your emotions or your peace of mind? You might be thinking, "I wouldn't!" But people do it every single day. They put themselves and their inner peace at the mercy of other people's behavior.

Stop allowing other people to control you! You don't have to respond to every rude comment or argument that you are invited to respond to. Don't allow your ego to dictate your emotions or responses. Be so determined to maintain your inner peace that you refuse to allow anything or anyone to deter you. When you get to that point, you will no longer be at the mercy of other people's words or behavior, even of your own misperceptions, how your body feels, or anything else.

You must stay focused on your own objectives. When you lose your focus, it is easy to allow external concerns to cause you to forget about your inner peace and lash out. While that might feel good in the moment, the cost of that temporary good feeling is losing your inner peace, calm mind, and tranquility for hours or days. It is not worth it!

The more you practice maintaining your inner peace, honor, and integrity, no matter what is happening around you, the easier it becomes. Stay calm and rational no matter what is happening or what anyone else says or does.

222

Do not worry if others criticize or laugh at you,
for their opinions are not your concern.
Epictetus

I cannot emphasize enough that you should stop concerning yourself with what other people think of you. People are getting increasingly ruder and discourteous in our current society, but that doesn't mean that you must allow their behavior to bother you or disrupt your inner peace. As Epictetus stated, other people's opinions are not your concern. They are free to think what they want, to criticize anything they want, and to laugh as they see fit. What does it matter to you if they make a buffoon of themselves or laugh at what they don't understand?

There is a popular quote that is attributed to the great actor, Anthony Hopkins, which states, "It's none of my business what people say about me or think about me. I am who I am, and I do what I do. I expect nothing and accept everything. And it makes life so much easier." You should take this quote to heart; this is Stoicism at its core!

It is absolutely none of your business what other people think or say about you or anything else. Your business is to be who you are and to continue to live your life by your own code of conduct. Refuse to allow the opinions of others to affect you. As Hopkins put it, expect nothing and accept everything as it is. Not only will this make your life much easier, but it will also help you maintain your inner peace and maintain your Stoic mindset.

Remember that Epictetus also taught, "It's not things themselves that disturb us, but our opinions about them." And Marcus Aurelius taught, "You always have the option of having no opinion. There is never any need to get worked up or to trouble your soul with things you can't control. These things are not asking to be judged by you. Leave them alone."

Keep these teachings in mind anytime you are tempted to get upset about the opinions of other people. Their opinions don't have to affect you. Just consider their opinions as none of your business and move on.

223

Make the best use of what is in your
power, and take the rest as it happens.
Epictetus

The Stoics tended to repeat their teachings in various ways to get their points across to their students. The above quote is just another way of saying control what is in your realm of control and accept everything else just the way it is. You only have control over specific things in your life, as I have covered many times already.

Epictetus is urging us to do the best we can with those things which we can control. If you are doing this, you won't have much time to stress or worry about all the things that are outside of your control. By seriously focusing on controlling your thoughts, words, and actions, you won't have the time or the interest in controlling external things that are outside of your control.

When you realize that trying to control external things is a pointless waste of time and mental energy, you will start to accept those things as they are and respond as needed. Trying to control things which are outside of your realm of control causes unnecessary stress, frustration, anger, and worry.

Consider the king of a country. The king has absolute power over his own country, and therefore, that is where his focus lies. He is simply concerned with the things over which he has control. It would be ridiculous for him to try to control the people or army in another country where he has no power at all. That would do nothing but cause him major problems he would not have had if he had simply minded his own business.

But that is exactly what many people try to do. Instead of focusing on the things over which they have absolute control, they try to control external events, circumstances, and other people, all of which they have no power over at all. And, by doing so, they cause themselves problems, stress, worries, and frustrations. Focus on the things that you can control and accept everything else as it is. This is the path to inner peace and tranquility.

224

It's time you realized that you have something in you more
powerful and miraculous than the things that affect you.
Marcus Aurelius

Marcus Aurelius' wisdom was truly amazing and beyond his time. You can't read *Meditations* without realizing that Marcus Aurelius had a strong belief in God. Although most people believe that this statement is referring to one's virtue or rational mind being stronger than any external circumstance, once you read his entire book, it is debatable whether he was referring to the rational mind or to God, as he greatly valued both.

For our purposes, I will assume that he was referring to God. When he wrote about God, he taught that God, the universe, nature, and reason are all one; that God is in all things. He often taught and equated God with Logos, the divine principle that governs the universe.

Marcus Aurelius didn't necessarily see God as a personal deity, but as the ordered "Force" behind all things. In his teachings, he suggests that living in harmony with nature is equivalent to living in harmony with God. He wrote, "All things are interwoven with one another, a sacred bond unites them…for there is one universe made up of all things, and one God who pervades all things, and one substance, and one law."

If there is one God who pervades all things, then it is easy to assume that when Marcus Aurelius stated that you have something in you more powerful and miraculous than the things that affect you, he is speaking of God. If God is in all things, then that includes you. And He is more powerful and miraculous than any of the external things that attempt to affect you.

If you will keep in mind that God is in you and is more powerful than anything that you must deal with, then you should fear nothing, and you should allow nothing to disrupt your inner peace. You have something in you that is more powerful than any challenge you must face. If you come to terms with your belief in God, you will find the courage and strength to deal with whatever comes your way, with courage, honor, and peace.

225

Life is short. That's all there is to say. Get what you can from
the present—thoughtfully and justly. Unrestrained moderation.
Marcus Aurelius

The Stoics taught that we should live in the present moment and not focus
on the past or the future. This is part of the Stoic principle of living wisely,
ethically, and fully in the now. As Marcus Aurelius wrote, life is short; it is
impermanent. No matter how long you live, life still goes by quickly.

Knowing this, everyone should live his or her life as fully as possible and
get as much as they can from the present moment. After all, the present
moment is truly the only time you have to live. Remember, the past no longer
exists, and the future is not guaranteed to anyone.

However, living fully in the now is not enough. You must also live
thoughtfully and justly. There is a Stoic principle called Memento mori, which
means to remember death, not to fear it, but to clarify how to live life. By
remembering that life is short and that your life will end at an unknown time
and place, you will be more motivated to live life as you should in the present
moment.

Stoicism is about rational and virtuous living, living your life with wisdom,
justice, moderation, and courage. It takes courage to live your life with
unrestrained moderation, but what is unrestrained moderation? It means letting
moderation guide you in all your ways. Let moderation guide you by being
self-controlled and practicing it fully and freely. Don't force it or fake it;
practice it until it becomes natural for you.

Life is short, so use your time wisely. Don't waste your time regretting the
things you have done in the past or daydreaming about what you may do in the
future. Develop the habit of living in the now, being always mindful of the
importance of the present moment. When Marcus Aurelius taught that you
should get what you can from the present moment, he was urging you to live
your life fully present every minute of every day. Refuse to waste your
precious time. Seize the day and live every minute of your life to the fullest!

226

We should always allow some time to elapse,
for time discloses the truth.
Seneca

We live in a time where people are quick to accept a lie for the truth, without any evidence, and without hearing or understanding both sides of the story. Coming to a snap decision about what is true and false is rarely a wise move, especially when it comes to trusting the media.

Most media outlets have an agenda; they are not in business simply to inform or entertain you. And they certainly can't be trusted to provide you with all the intrinsic details of whatever story they are covering at the time. Many times, they jump to conclusions before they themselves even know the complete truth.

It is always wiser to let some time pass and do your own research to truly understand a specific situation or event. Most people and organizations are less than forthcoming in their actions or the reasons behind their actions. This is particularly true in politics or in organizations with specific agendas.

When it comes to believing what you hear, it is usually best to let some time pass, hear both sides, and look deeper below the surface. That is where the truth usually resides. Being skeptical is a good practice, especially in today's society.

If someone is pushing you to make a quick decision about something, whether it is a purchase or believing something about someone else, it is usually because they are hiding something that they don't want you to find out until after the fact. Anytime someone is rushing you to make a decision, walk away and let some time pass so you can research it and think about it.

Eventually, time will disclose the truth. Don't be too quick to believe any story you see on the news, or anything someone else tells you, without doing your due diligence. Be wise enough to be patient; eventually, the truth will surface. It takes wisdom, insight, and patience to discern what is really going on behind the scenes. Don't jump to conclusions too fast.

227

He has the most who is most content with the least.
Diogenes

According to Diogenes, if you are happy with little, you have everything you need. Many people chase wealth, titles, status, or material things, thinking that such things will make them happy. They forget one of the basic Stoic principles, that happiness does not come from external things, but from living as you should, with virtue, wisdom, moderation, and courage.

Happiness comes from within. What Diogenes was saying is that happiness and freedom come from simplicity. Think about all the people who have expensive cars, big houses, all the nicest things and clothes, but who are stressed, unhappy, and feel like slaves to the rat race. These people have success and lots of material wealth, but they aren't truly content or happy.

Diogenes taught that if you need all these external things to be happy, you're essentially discontented and poor. How can you be truly happy and be a slave to the grind? Happiness is a byproduct of living your life your way, with inner peace and total contentment. It doesn't come from what you own, but from who you are inside.

The less you require to be happy, the more secure your happiness will be. Status, titles, and material things can be lost or taken from you; but nobody can take your happiness away from you, unless you let them.

Alexander the Great revered Diogenes, so much so that he sought Diogenes out for his teachings. When Alexander found Diogenes, he was lying in the sun. Alexander introduced himself and asked if there was anything he could do for him. Diogenes replied, "Yes. Move out of my sunlight."

Alexander the Great was the most powerful man in the world during this time, but he was amused and impressed by Diogenes' boldness and the fact that he didn't attempt to flatter him, nor did he seem impressed with Alexander's reputation or accomplishments. Alexander later stated, "If I were not Alexander, I would be Diogenes." He recognized something he didn't have—inner peace and total self-sufficiency.

228

You carry the living God inside you and are blind to
the fact that you desecrate Him with your dirty words and
dirty thoughts, none of which you would dare repeat if there
were even a mere statue of a god nearby. God himself is there
within, seeing and overhearing everything you do and say.
Epictetus

Both Marcus Aurelius and Epictetus seem to agree that you have a powerful ally who is always with you—God lives within you. But Epictetus goes one step further and makes a point that few of us think about, and even if we do think about it occasionally, we quickly forget about it.

Epictetus points out that you desecrate God with your profanity and negative thoughts. To desecrate God means you insult, outrage, and blaspheme God with your profanity, negativity, and unvirtuous thoughts. He goes on to say that you would never use such words in front of a sacred statue or a place of worship.

Think about it. Even someone with the worst cursing habit would not even consider using his profanity inside a church, as the church is considered a sacred place of worship, a place where God is present. But we all tend to forget that God lives within us, and that He sees and hears everything we do or say.

If you have a habit of cursing or talking negatively, it is very helpful in breaking that habit to remember that God is always with you. If you truly believed that "the living God" lives within you, would you still speak that way? Of course not! But most people forget that God is omniscient and omnipresent. God sees and hears everything; nothing is hidden from God.

If you needed another reason to live by the Stoic principles, Epictetus provides one for you. If you were sitting on a park bench and God was sitting beside you, would you use the same profanity that you would if you were talking to your friend? I think you know the answer. Once you begin living a more virtuous life, you will have little need for profanity. It is simply another old habit that no longer serves your purpose.

229

If it's not right, don't do it. If it's not true, don't say it.
Let your intentions be just and honorable.
Marcus Aurelius

This teaching of Marcus Aurelius is about as straightforward as it gets. If something is not right, don't do it. If something is not true, don't say it. Maintain strict discipline over your words and actions. But he goes one step further and states that we should make sure that our intentions and our thoughts are just and honorable.

Someone can do or say the right thing without being just or honorable intentions. People do it all the time! If you tell the truth, but do it for an underhanded reason, your intentions are not honorable. Some people like to brag about being brutally honest as if that is an admiral quality, and at times, it can be. But if you are being brutally honest when you could have been tactfully honest, your intentions are questionable at best.

The same thing goes for your actions. If you do the right thing just to impress those who are watching, are your intentions to do the right thing because it is right, or are your intentions to do the right thing to manipulate or impress someone else?

An action can be right in one context and wrong in another, depending on the intentions behind the action. Doing the right thing for the wrong reasons is not honorable; telling the truth maliciously or to manipulate others is not honorable. It is the intention behind your actions or your words that makes them honorable or dishonorable.

Yes, your intentions are that important! Even if your actions appear right to the people around you, that doesn't necessarily mean they are just or honorable. Appearances can be deceptive. For your actions to truly be right and honorable, your intentions must be honorable. Bad intentions spoil good actions, just as bad intentions can turn the truth into injustice. Always make sure that your heart and intentions are pure before you speak or act. Be mindful of your thoughts and intentions!

It is part of the cure to wish to be cured.
Seneca

It doesn't matter if we are talking about physical, emotional, or mental healing; if one doesn't have the desire and intention to heal whatever is afflicting him, he will delay or disrupt his healing. To transform anything in your life, the first step is to be willing to change. You can't heal a physical illness, emotional hurt, or improve your ethical habits unless you first want to bring about a change. You must first want to be healed.

No matter what needs to be healed or cured, you must genuinely desire change in order to bring about the necessary healing. Holistic medicine states that healing occurs from the inside out. Things must get right on the inside before they can get right on the outside. The mind plays a crucial role in the healing of the body, the emotions, and in changing your habits.

Your intentions, and will to change and to get well, are the first steps to successfully overcoming whatever you are challenged with. It doesn't matter if it is an addiction, emotional pain, trauma, or some disease, healing begins with your intentions, and your intentions begin with your thoughts. In plain language, you must truly *want to get better* before you can get better.

The moment that you firmly decide to get better is the moment your healing begins. This doesn't mean that it will be quick or easy; it simply means you have started your journey to healing whatever is ailing you. Epictetus taught, "No man is free who is not master of himself." Until you get your mind right, you can't be free; you will continue to be a slave to one thing or another. It could be a disease, emotional pain, hatred, regrets, resentments, or some moral challenge.

Whatever you need to be healed or released from, the cure starts with the will to take responsibility for your own thoughts, emotions, habits, and actions. You must get your mind right! Your thoughts are a powerful source of energy. Once you master your thoughts, you will be able to master your life. You can't be healed until you truly want to be healed!

231

> Don't hope that events will turn out the way you want, welcome
> events in whichever way they happen. This is the path to peace.
> *Epictetus*

Expectations frequently lead to disappointments. Instead of hoping events will turn out the way you want or expecting a specific outcome, Epictetus urges us to welcome events however they turn out. Don't just welcome them however they turn out, but embrace them and be at peace with them.

When you have expectations or hope an event turns out just the way you want it to, and things turn out differently, it leads to disappointment, which can lead to unhappiness and disrupt your inner peace. This allows external events and circumstances to control your emotions, happiness, and inner peace.

Remember, refuse to allow anything, any event, or any circumstance outside of your realm of control to affect you. If you are not in control of the situation, simply accept it as it is, respond, or move on. Don't allow external things to control your emotions or your inner peace.

Let's say you are watching your favorite football team, and they are playing their biggest rival. Of course, you are going to cheer for your team and hope that they win the game. That is what sports are all about. But if you go into the game with high expectations, you are setting yourself up for disappointment if your team loses. And you have no control over who wins or loses the game.

When you watch the game with such high expectations or high emotions, you are not only setting yourself up for disappointment, but you are causing the game to be stressful. Instead of going into the game with such high hopes, why not just sit back and enjoy the contest? Enjoy the rivalry, the great plays, the excitement, and the back and forth of the game.

If you approach the game in this manner, you will enjoy the game no matter how it turns out. Just enjoy the competition. If your team wins, you will enjoy it even more, but if your team loses, you avoid the disappointment and letdown, and don't let it ruin your fun. No expectations—just excitement, enjoyment, and fun!

232

The happiness of your life depends upon the quality of your thoughts.
Therefore, guard accordingly, and take care that you entertain
no notions unsuitable to virtue and reasonable nature.
Marcus Aurelius

Your thoughts have the power to change your attitude and mindset. If you learn to discipline your thoughts, you can get to the place where you are almost always happy, no matter what is happening around you. Being happy is a decision that you make.

Try this little experiment. Sit back, close your eyes, and think about someone you love and a time that you remember that always makes you happy when you think of it. Did it make you smile? Did it bring back good memories? Of course it did!

Now, do the opposite. Close your eyes and think about an event that completely broke your heart or the death of someone who you dearly loved. Did that make you smile, or did it make you sad? Did it bring tears to your eyes? Did it bring up regrets?

This is how much power your thoughts have over your emotions. Marcus Aurelius obviously knew this when he wrote that the happiness of your life depends upon the quality of your thoughts. Your thoughts can bring you happiness, or they can cause you sadness.

The good news is that nobody controls your thoughts but you. You get to decide whether you want to be happy or sad. So, if you want to be happy, you must guard your thoughts and refuse to entertain any thoughts that do not promote happiness, joy, or inner peace. It is up to you. You control your thoughts; therefore, you control your own happiness.

Marcus Aurelius takes it one step further and urges us not to entertain any thoughts that are unsuitable to virtue and reasonable nature. Dwell on thoughts of wisdom, justice, courage, and moderation. Think rationally instead of emotionally. Discipline your mind to refuse to entertain thoughts of anger, envy, or fear. Think happy thoughts and you will live a happy life.

233

Let us prepare our minds as if we had come to the very end of life.
Let us postpone nothing. Let us balance life's books each day.
The one who puts the finishing touches on their
life each day is never short of time.
Seneca

Seneca offers us another technique to help us deal with the certainty of death or the uncertainty of the time of our death. He tells us to prepare our minds as if we have come to the end of our life. Think about it. If you knew for a fact that you were going to die in four weeks, how would you spend your time? What things would you need to take care of? Who do you need to forgive or set things right with? Seneca urges us to deal with these things *now* and not to postpone important conversations or actions until someday in the future.

Legendary rock guitarist, Ace Frehley, turned down an invitation to play with fellow KISS founders, Gene Simmons and Paul Stanley, on the 2025 KISS Kruise because of past disagreements, though he had previously expressed an openness to a future reunion, calling Stanley and Simmons his "rock and roll brothers."

Ace Frehley was still open to the possibility of one day reuniting with KISS, stating, "I don't hate Paul or Gene, you know? We're rock and roll brothers, and Peter, too. So, anything can happen." It seemed that the older the former close friends got, the more open they were towards the possibility of forgiving each other and putting the past behind them. But before someday arrived, the guitar legend, Ace Frehley, passed away unexpectedly. Frehley will never be able to say or hear the things that were left unsaid.

Many people postpone saying or doing important things that desperately need to be said or done, thinking there is plenty of time to take care of those matters someday. The "rock and roll brothers" waited too late to completely put the old quarrels behind them. Don't let this happen to you; the regret will haunt you. Do what needs to be done TODAY! Postpone nothing; you never know when tomorrow will be too late. Sometimes, someday never arrives!

234

Be the same person in public as in private.
Epictetus

Is your character consistent? Are you the same person around your friends as you are in private? What about when you are at work; are you the same person at work as you are at home? Do you have different personas for different people, or do you have the self-confidence and courage to be yourself whether you are in public or in private?

These are important questions for you to consider. True honor and virtue are not things that you can take off and set on the shelf whenever you want to. They must be a part of who you truly are. You either live by your principles all the time or you haven't truly integrated those principles into your life. Live by your principles, whether you are alone or in public.

Some people believe it is okay to "just let their hair down" sometimes. They go out, party too much, act crazy, and then afterwards go back to being their normal selves. This is putting your principles on a shelf in order to fit in with the crowd; but would you truly call that living a virtuous life?

Remember what Baltasar Gracian taught: *"**The man of principle does not forget who he is because of what others are.**"* The man of principle must be the same person in public as he is in private. Don't be honorable sometimes and dishonorable at other times; you must choose one or the other.

Ensure that your inner life and your outer life reflect the same values. This is something that only you can do, as only you and God truly know your innermost thoughts and intentions, and how you behave in private. Practicing self-control is not just for when you are in public; the honorable man is watchful over himself even when he is alone.

Epictetus is urging you to be authentic. Don't pretend to be virtuous and honorable; *be* virtuous and honorable. Don't put on a different mask depending on who you are with; get rid of all your masks and simply be a man of principle. Have the courage to be your authentic self.

235

> Let men see, let them know, a real man,
> who lives as he was meant to live.
> *Marcus Aurelius*

This teaching by Marcus Aurelius fits perfectly with the last quote. Many people, once they change their lives and start living a life of wisdom, honor, and integrity, are shy about exposing their new principles to others. They may think their old friends won't accept them anymore or that they may tease them or try to get them to set their principles aside. It takes courage to let everyone who knows you see that you have changed the way you live your life.

However, that is exactly what you must do if you are going to be your authentic self. As I discussed on the last page, you shouldn't live one way in public and a different way in private. Just be yourself! If others don't like it, that's their problem. You don't control the thoughts or opinions of others. They have the right to their own opinions, and you have the right to completely ignore their opinions.

Just make a firm decision concerning what kind of man you want to be and then *be* that man. Don't be self-conscious about becoming a man of honor and integrity; don't worry about what others may think of your spiritual beliefs or your philosophy. How you live your life is *your* business; stop being concerned about the opinions of others.

As Marcus Aurelius taught, let them see the real you. Let them know a real man who lives as he was meant to live, with Stoic virtues, honor, integrity, wisdom, and courage. Think of the heroes in your favorite movies. Can you imagine them being nervous about being themselves? Of course not! They are who they are, and they couldn't care less about what others think about them.

You should live the same way! Don't hide your virtues and honor away; let the world see a real man who lives his life his way. Live your life with self-confidence and courage. Stand up for what's right, despite what anyone else does or doesn't do. Be a man of honor, courage, and integrity!

236

A companion's crudeness is bound to rub off on the one
he is with, no matter how refined that person may be.
Epictetus

Who you associate with matters more than you know. No matter how strong
you may think you are, you will still pick up some of the habits of the people
you associate with in life. Some of their behavior, attitudes, and character will
rub off on you, even without you noticing it until after the fact. Over time, the
more you are exposed to their behavior, the more numb you get to their
language and manners, until your judgment is numbed and you begin to excuse
behavior that you once found unacceptable.

As Epictetus points out, it doesn't matter how refined you are, if you are
constantly associating with people of low morals, their habits will start to affect
you. Imitating those around us is part of human nature. That is how we learned
as children. You will naturally absorb some of the habits, language, and
emotional responses of the people you spend time with in your life.

It is for this reason that you should be very selective about who you
associate with, especially when it comes to your close friends. You should
choose friends who aspire to live by the same principles that you hold dear.
Choose to be around people who inspire you and make you a better person;
choose friends who challenge you to be more virtuous and honorable.

Of course, sometimes we must deal with people who are less than honorable
or who have poor character. During these times, it is important that you remain
mindful and stay grounded in your principles and integrity. Don't overestimate
your ability to maintain your principles when dealing with people of lower
morals. It takes discipline and resolve to remain true to yourself.

Just remember the old saying that you become like the people you spend
the most time with. Becoming a man of honor and integrity is not something
that you achieve once, and then you can relax on your laurels. You must work
to maintain your honor and your principles. If your principles are important to
you, choose your friends wisely.

237

Steel your emotional response, so that
life shall hurt you as little as possible.
Zeno of Citium

It is one of the principles of Stoicism to respond rationally and reasonably instead of emotionally. This way, external events and circumstances don't cause you to lose your cool or disrupt your inner peace. When Zeno urges us to *steel our emotional response*, he is saying to discipline your thoughts and not allow your emotions to dictate your responses. This is not the same thing as suppressing your feelings, but simply not allowing your feelings to control you.

To do this, you must respond instead of reacting to whatever is happening around you. Remember, not everything or everyone deserves your response; you decide if, when, and how you will respond. Never allow your emotions to decide for you.

If someone is rude or insults you, mentally remind yourself that you have no control over someone else's words or actions. Many times, it is better to simply smile and move on. Don't confuse this with allowing someone to mistreat you. Walking away with your head held high is not the same thing as allowing them to get the best of you or mistreat you. You are merely deciding that they are not worth your time or your response; you are putting your own principles and inner peace ahead of responding to their rudeness.

When you master your mind, you master the way you look at life and the events around you. The more you master your emotions, the easier it will be for you to stay in control of your actions and responses. Remember what Epictetus taught: "It is not events that disturb us, but our judgments about them."

Also remember Marcus Aurelius' teachings, "If you are distressed by anything external, the pain is not due to the thing itself, but to your estimate of it; and this you have the power to revoke at any moment." Refuse to give anyone or anything the power to upset you or hurt you.

238

Preach not to others what they should eat,
but eat as becomes you and be silent.
Epictetus

If there is one thing that the Stoics believed in, it was focusing on what you can control and minding your own business. Here, Epictetus tells us to mind our own business and not to lecture or preach to others about their choices. What other people do is none of your business.

This is true even if you know that your way is better or more honorable. *Knowing that someone else's choices are wrong still doesn't make their choices your business.* They have the right to live their lives and make their own decisions just as much as you do. Whether or not you agree with their choices doesn't matter, because their choices are none of your business.

Instead of lecturing others about how they should live, focus on perfecting your own character. Focus on your own thoughts, words, and actions. Focus on living according to your own values and principles. If you spend your time focusing on the things which are in your circle of control, you won't have time to worry about how others are living their lives.

Epictetus is telling us to do what is ours to do and to be silent when it comes to what others are doing. Spending time perfecting your own honor, integrity, and self-discipline is much more important than trying to control or correct the behavior of others. You have no control over what other people do or how they live anyway. Trying to control their behavior will only frustrate you.

Considering that, lecturing others is nothing more than an unwanted nuisance that will frustrate you and irritate them. Do you like it when other people preach to you about how you should live your life? Of course not! So, why would you ever consider doing that to anyone else? Remember the Golden Rule: "Do unto others as you would have them do unto you!"

Don't tell others how to live their lives; focus on living your life as you should and teach by your example. Let your actions reflect your principles. Let your silent example do the talking for you!

239

> Well-being is realized by small steps, but is truly no small thing.
> *Zeno of Citium*

Developing the Stoic mindset doesn't happen overnight. It happens gradually, or as Zeno taught, it is realized by small steps. It takes time to change habits, and most of us have many habits that are not in line with the Stoic mindset we are trying to develop.

Integrating the Stoic principles into your daily life is a big lifestyle change for most people. These principles are cultivated over time through consistent daily practice. You must constantly remind yourself to consider what things you can control and what things you can't control. And you will have bad days when you fall back into your old habits of trying to control your loved ones, getting angry when someone is rude to you, or getting upset over certain events or circumstances. Recognize your slip-up and get back on the path.

Zeno reminds us that making these changes, even by small steps, is no small thing. That is the way this world works. We don't have a magic wand to simply change ourselves in the blink of an eye. It takes consistent effort to change our mindset, principles, and the way we look at the world around us.

The process may seem slow, but if you are consistent in your efforts to develop the Stoic mindset, you will see the changes in your attitude and inner peace sooner than you might think. Living a life of virtue, honor, and integrity takes effort, but it's worth it.

Once you begin to realize how living a life of virtue, focusing on the things that you can control, and accepting the things that are outside of your control, affects your inner peace, you will see why it is worth the effort. Have no doubts about it; it does take some work and practice to develop the Stoic mindset.

It takes daily practice, persistence, and time to change those old habits, attitudes, and thought processes. But once you see how much more peaceful your life will become, you will want to continue living with a Stoic mindset. Don't give up when you have a bad day; just take it day by day! After a few months, you will be able to look back and see how far you have come.

> Nothing is noble if it is done unwillingly or
> under compulsion. Every noble deed is voluntary.
> *Seneca*

If you are forced to take an action against your will, it cannot be said to be a noble or honorable action. For an action to be noble or honorable, it must be performed freely from the heart and mind, and with the right intentions. True honor, virtue, and nobility come from choice, not coercion.

It doesn't matter if the compulsion comes from fear, external pressure, or even some external reward; if your action does not come freely from the heart, it cannot be honorable or noble. Consider a billionaire who donates millions of dollars to some charity. Is that a noble deed? The truth is that you can't know whether it is truly a charitable, noble action or not without knowing the intentions behind the donation.

Some actions that appear noble on the outside have hidden agendas that have nothing to do with being noble or virtuous. The billionaire may be making that donation out of the goodness of his heart, or he could simply need a large tax write-off. Additionally, it could simply be part of a hidden business agreement. You simply don't know.

The truth is that for an act to be honorable or noble, the intentions behind that act must be honorable and noble. It is not simply the external outcome that matters, but the intention behind the act. Most of the time, you are not privy to someone else's intentions.

One of the fundamental principles of Stoicism is the freedom of your inner will. Your thoughts, mind, and intentions are yours and yours alone. No one can force you to think a certain way; no one can determine your intentions for you. Therefore, only you decide whether your actions are noble and honorable; you are the only person who knows your true intentions.

Virtue, or a lack thereof, comes not from the action itself, but from the intentions behind the act. As Seneca reminds us, no action is noble without the freedom to choose the action without any compulsion or external rewards.

241

On the occasion of every accident that befalls you, remember to
turn to yourself and inquire what power you have for turning it to use.
Epictetus

No matter what happens in your life, look for a way to turn it to your advantage. The Stoics believed that every challenge or setback is an opportunity for knowledge, wisdom, and inner growth. This doesn't have to apply only to accidents; it could be some unexpected event, a loss, a failure, a rude coworker, someone insulting you, etc. Whatever it may be, look past the obvious and try to find a way to get something positive from it.

This may sound strange at first. After all, how could you find something positive in someone insulting you? That's a good question. If someone insults you, it is an excellent opportunity to practice your Stoic mindset by remembering that you have no control over what others think or say. It is also an opportunity to practice your patience and self-control.

If you experience a failure, it is an opportunity to gain knowledge and wisdom. If someone close to you is killed in an accident, it is an opportunity to control your emotions and to evaluate whether you truly believe that God is in control of the external world.

You always have the power to use an external event, issue, or circumstance to your advantage in one way or another. But it takes a Stoic mindset and self-discipline to do it. It may not be what you want to do or what you feel like doing at the time, but it is absolutely better than wallowing in stress, anger, regret, worry, or defeat.

Instead of looking for someone to blame or giving in to despair, determine that you will find a way to turn every situation into something that you can use in one way or another. It might be as simple as practicing self-restraint in how you respond to it. It doesn't matter what it is; every difficulty holds the potential for you to gain wisdom, knowledge, or to practice your Stoic mindset. Remember what Marcus Aurelius taught: "The impediment to action advances action. What stands in the way becomes the way." The choice is yours.

The greatest portion of peace is doing nothing wrong.
Those who lack self-control live disoriented and disturbed lives.
Seneca

If you truly know in your heart that you have done the best you could do and have done nothing wrong, there is no reason not to be living a life full of inner peace and tranquility. When I say that you have done nothing wrong, I am not talking about in your whole life; nobody is perfect. I am referring to the individual situation that you are dealing with currently.

When you strive to live with a Stoic mindset, those situations and events where you know that you have done the best you could and did not intentionally do anything wrong will begin to add up. The more you strive to live with honor, integrity, and wisdom, the more you will find that you respond to situations and events in your life with a calm, rational mindset.

Moreover, the more you respond with a Stoic mindset and good intentions, the more mental and emotional peace you will have in your life. Remember, it is your intentions that matter, not the outcome of your actions; you only control your intentions and responses, not the outcomes of your actions.

Seneca did not simply leave his teaching at doing nothing wrong, but he also described the life of those who lack the self-control to do the right thing or to respond in a Stoic manner. He wrote that they live disoriented and disturbed lives. Living a disoriented life means that you are constantly unsettled, perplexed, and confused about why things are happening as they are.

A lack of self-control leads to a disturbed life, or more accurately, a disturbed spirit. You will consistently allow your anger, temper, words, or reactions to rob you of your inner peace. This is the opposite of being mindful and responding with a Stoic mindset.

Develop the self-control to respond instead of react, and do so with pure intentions and a spirit of striving to do the right thing. You could look at this as coming to a crossroads in each situation. You have the choice of choosing to respond Stoically or of reacting with little to no self-control. Choose wisely!

243

If you find yourself acting to impress others or avoiding action
out of fear of what they might think, you have left the path.
Epictetus

Once you are dedicated to living your life according to Stoic principles, you will find that you no longer have the desire or need to impress others or to worry about what others think about how you live your life. When we were young, most of us tried to impress others or at least were aware of the peer pressure to fit in with our friends.

However, as you start to live with a Stoic mindset, you understand that trying to impress others or worrying about what they may think about your actions, or the way you live, is not worth your time. Remember, you have no control over what others think about you. If you really knew how little most people think about you anyway, you would never worry about impressing them to start with, much less of allowing what they think to dictate your actions.

That said, most people never seem to reach the place in their lives where they stop trying to impress others or stop concerning themselves with what others think of them. Epictetus taught that if you find yourself avoiding certain actions because of what others might think or if you are doing things just to impress others, then you have left the path of Stoicism.

As you know, Stoicism is about striving to control the things that are within your control and accepting the things that are not within your control. You have no control over what others think about you, so why worry about it? Let others think whatever they please; you are not responsible for what they think. Your responsibility is controlling your own thoughts and doing your best to live with wisdom, rational thought, honor, and integrity.

Be mindful of your thoughts and realize that anytime you catch yourself being concerned about what others think about how you live or your actions, you are veering off course. When this happens, take control of your thoughts and bring them back into line with the Stoic mindset. Being constantly mindful of your own thoughts is the key to your freedom.

Do not just say that you have read books. Show that through
them, you have learned to think better, to be a more discriminating
and reflective person. Books are the training weights of the mind.
Epictetus

No matter how many good books you have read or how much you read, if those books don't improve your life in some way, they are nothing more than entertainment. This is not to say that reading novels or fiction is a waste of time. Those who enjoy such books increase their vocabularies, relax their minds, and find enjoyment in reading. It is their chosen form of entertainment.

However, you must realize that most books during Epictetus' time were instructional; there were not a lot of novels or fiction. And even the stories and fables of that time had the purpose of teaching valuable lessons. Epictetus was talking about books that improve your life, such as the writings of the Stoics.

If you are reading self-help or nonfiction books, the entire purpose is to learn to improve yourself or to learn something that can be useful in your life. To Epictetus, those books should teach you to think better, be more self-reflective, and to be more discriminating about how you live your life. Good nonfiction books do just that.

The last sentence in this teaching is an excellent quote: "Books are the training weights of the mind." Think about that for a minute. If you are weight training, the longer you train, the stronger your muscles get. You don't have to tell people you lift weights; they can clearly see the results of your weight training. Your muscles will become firmer, increase in size, become stronger, and you will look better.

This same principle applies to your mind. If you apply what you learn from good books, and integrate it into your life, you won't have to tell people about how much you have changed; it will be obvious. According to Epictetus, reading good books is like weight training for your mind. It should help you see the world differently, be more open, and be a more reflective person.

245

If you accomplish something good with hard work, the labor passes quickly, but the good endures. If you do something shameful in pursuit of pleasure, the pleasure passes quickly, but the shame endures.
Musonius Rufus

This is a powerful contrast between virtuous labor and shameful indulgence. Rufus points out that when you are mentally focused on working towards a goal, time passes quickly, but, in the end, you will be happy because you accomplished something worthwhile. Essentially, the effort or hard work is temporary, but the results will provide you with many benefits such as pride in doing a good job and lasting inner peace from doing what's right. Those results are lasting and become a part of your legacy and character.

On the other hand, if you do something shameful in the pursuit of pleasure, the pleasure you may enjoy is temporary, but the memories of your shameful acts will continue to haunt your conscience. Pursuing temporary pleasures such as unethical gain or lust may give you short-lived pleasure, but the ultimate cost outweighs any pleasure that you may have received from your actions. It will damage your integrity and self-respect, and guilt or regret will linger in your consciousness.

In every situation, think about the consequences. Think long-term instead of the immediate gratification. Stoicism teaches us to prioritize virtue over pleasure and doing what's right over being unethical. Always consider the consequences of your actions, as even brief actions can have long-term consequences that can change the course of your life forever. Wise men think long-term, while fools only think about immediate pleasure.

Always beware of pleasures that can cost you in some way or lead to regrets and disrupt your inner peace. If you strive to always do what's right, you will save yourself the pain of regret, dishonor, and an unsettled mind. This is one reason the Stoics taught so much about rational thinking. Do what's right, at the right time, and in the right way. When you conduct yourself in this way, you will be at peace.

Progress is not achieved by luck or accident,
but by working on yourself daily.
Epictetus

Epictetus was one of the most outspoken and straightforward of the Stoics; he didn't beat around the bush. Here, he doesn't sugarcoat anything. He simply points out the truth that you don't achieve your goals by luck or accident, but by working on them daily.

If you want to develop a Stoic mindset, you must work on yourself daily. Merely thinking about the Stoic principles now and then won't get you anywhere. You must put those principles into practice daily until they become a part of who you are. Personal growth is a deliberate process and takes mindfulness and self-discipline to achieve.

You don't change your life simply because you want to; you change your life through consistently working on your thoughts and actions. Each day you have the opportunity to go through life mindlessly or to be mindful and reflect on your thoughts, words, and actions. Make it your daily practice to live with honor and integrity, and to practice the Stoic virtues.

This is what the Japanese concept of kaizen is all about. Kaizen means constant, never-ending improvement, and that is what it takes to make progress in living with a Stoic mindset. Living with a Stoic mindset is not a goal where you achieve it and then you move on to something else; it is a lifestyle where you must strive daily to improve yourself and become a better person. The path of living by Stoic principles is active, not passive!

It is a mistake to think that you can simply read a book about Stoicism, agree with the principles, and change your life. That is not enough; you must put those principles to work in your life, or they are worthless to you. True growth requires specific intentions and repetition of the Stoic principles. You become the kind of person that you are meant to be, not by luck or hoping to, but by making a choice *to be that person* every single day.

247

> It is not events that disturb people, it is their
> judgements concerning them…So when we are frustrated,
> angry, or unhappy, never hold anyone except ourselves, that is,
> our judgements, accountable. An ignorant person is inclined to blame
> others for his own misfortune. To blame oneself is proof of progress.
> But the wise man never has to blame another or himself.
> *Epictetus*

When you read ancient wisdom that is repeated across time and cultures, you know you are reading universal wisdom. The wisdom of Epictetus in this quote expresses one of the fundamental principles of Stoicism—it is not the event or situation that disturbs you, but your thoughts concerning the event or situation. If you are frustrated, angry, or unhappy, don't blame anyone but yourself, for it is your own thoughts that are making you unhappy, not the event or situation itself.

However, Epictetus had the wisdom to take this one step further and to state that the ignorant person will blame others. Those who lack wisdom always play the victim and blame others for their unhappiness, unable to comprehend that they are responsible for their own happiness.

Epictetus then states that to blame yourself is progress, but the wise man never has to blame others or himself. This same wisdom was taught by the Taoist master, Lao Tzu, in the *Tao Te Ching*. He wrote, "When you blame others, you give up your power to change. When you blame yourself, you still have the power to change."

There is also a Chinese proverb which states, "He who blames others has a long way to go; he who blames himself is halfway there; he who blames no one has arrived." Blaming others makes you a victim. Blaming yourself means you are taking responsibility for your feelings. But never having to blame anyone means you allow nothing external to frustrate you, anger you, or to "make" you unhappy. You learn from observing others, and you accept things as they are, move on, and continue to strive for the perfection of your character.

248

Consider it the greatest of all virtues to restrain your tongue.
Cato the Younger

One of the core Stoic virtues is to restrain your tongue and stay in control of what you say. What you say, how you say it, and when you say it, reflects your self-discipline. When you speak without thinking about what you are going to say, or allow your emotions to dictate your speech, it will often lead to dishonor, regret, and various conflicts. Restraining your speech demonstrates mindfulness, maturity, and strength.

Always remember that words cannot be taken back once they have been spoken. Someone may forgive you for what you said, but you can be assured that they won't *forget* you said it. Silence is better than careless speech. It is better to listen and learn, think about what you are going to say, and then to speak rationally.

All virtues in Stoicism are about mastering yourself, and your tongue is one of the hardest things to master. Restraining your tongue means avoiding thoughtless speech like insults, boasting, gossip, speaking in anger or frustration, reacting instead of responding, and just plain making stupid comments without thinking.

Of all the things under your control, failing to control your speech is the one thing that causes most people more trouble than anything else. The main reasons are a lack of impulse control or speaking when you are angry and upset. People tend to say things that they either don't mean or that should not be said when they are angry or upset.

Be disciplined and restrain your tongue. Refuse to speak without thinking rationally about what you are going to say before you say it. The ability to restrain your tongue, especially when you are upset or angry, is a sign of self-discipline, wisdom, and inner strength. Practice maintaining strict control over your speech daily. Never allow your tongue to outrun your mind. If you do this, you won't have to worry about what you have said or whether what you said will be repeated, because your words will be full of wisdom and truth.

249

The morality of an action is determined by
the motive behind it, not merely by the outcome.
Antipater of Tarsus

Antipater of Tarsus is not as well-known as Marcus Aurelius, Epictetus, or Seneca, but he was a crucial philosopher in the early days of Stoicism during the second century BCE. He was known for being more rigid and traditional than those who came after him and was the head of the Stoic school in Athens after Diogenes.

There are few Antipater of Tarsus' quotes or teachings left. What we know of his teachings comes mostly from later writers such as Diogenes, Cicero, and others who paraphrased or commented on his teachings, but we do have a few of his quotes.

As I have already written, it is the motive, or intention, behind an action that makes it right or wrong, not necessarily the outcome of the action. This is something that Antipater of Tarsus taught over 2,200 years ago. He realized that the only things we have control over are our actions and intentions, not the outcomes of our actions.

You don't control the outcome of your actions, but you can always control your intentions. Therefore, it is your intentions that determine whether your actions are right or wrong. You may have good intentions and be trying your best to do what's right, but that doesn't mean that the outcome of your actions will turn out how you want.

Furthermore, a negative outcome does not reflect on the morality of your actions or intentions. You can have the best intentions and do everything exactly right, but the outcome of your actions may still turn out negatively. The best you can do is to think about things rationally, decide what you think the best course of action is, and act with honorable intentions. If you always do this, you will never have a reason to regret your actions, even if they don't turn out how you want them to. While others may judge your actions by their outcome, you will be at peace because you know your intentions were just.

250

We are not given a good life or a bad life. We are
given life, and it's up to us to make it good or bad.
Epictetus

At first, this may appear to be a false statement to many people. They will give examples of how they grew up poor, abused, without a dad, etcetera, while others are born into a rich family, get to go to the best schools, and have everything handed to them in life.

However, when you think about how Epictetus was born into slavery in Rome during a time when slaves were routinely treated brutally, you must give this teaching more thought. Epictetus eventually gained his freedom and became not only a highly respected Stoic teacher, but his writings, known as the *Discourses* and the *Enchiridion*, have remained foundational texts in Stoicism for over 2,000 years.

The fact is, it is up to you to make out of your life what you will. This doesn't mean that life is fair; life has never been fair and never will be fair. But that doesn't mean that you can't rise from your meager beginnings to live the kind of life that you want to live.

There are multiple examples of people who were born into poverty, and even into slavery, and lived amazing lives and even became motivational figures for decades after their death. Think of Frederick Douglass, Booker T. Washington, George Washington Carver, and Sojourner Truth, all born into slavery. What about Andrew Carnegie, Abraham Lincoln, Michael Oher, and the many others who were born into poverty and made something special out of their lives.

When you examine Epictetus' teaching more closely, you realize he was exactly right; your life is what you make it. While life is not fair, it doesn't need to be for you to make a good life for yourself. Think about what Theodore Roosevelt said: "Do what you can, with what you have, where you are." If you have the motivation to make something out of your life, you can do it. Your life is in your hands, so make it a good one!

251

The greatest remedy for anger is delay.
Seneca

It can take a lot of self-control to maintain a calm demeanor and your inner peace when you allow yourself to get very angry. But Seneca gives you the perfect remedy for anger—delaying your response. This is the power of self-control!

Anger can come on quickly if you are not mindful enough to control your thoughts and think rationally. It invites you to react impulsively without thinking. However, if you delay your urge to react, and let the initial emotional storm pass, you give yourself a chance to take control of your rational mind. This gives you time to think about the situation rationally and avoid saying or doing something that you will later regret.

Seneca wrote an entire essay on anger and described it as a "temporary madness." By delaying your response, instead of reacting quickly, you give yourself time to overcome this temporary madness and think rationally again. Delaying your response is like hitting a pause button on your speech and actions until you regain command of your rational thought process.

For example, if someone is rude to you or insults you, you might very well be tempted to get upset, allow your emotions to dictate your actions, and respond in kind. But if you delay your urge to react, it gives you time to question your anger and think rationally. Ask yourself, "Is what this person said or did worth disrupting my inner peace? Will responding to his rudeness make the situation better or worse?"

If you react to someone's rude behavior, they have just temporarily taken control of you. This is not the way of the Stoic! Your duty is to control the things within your circle of control, not to give that control away to any stranger who is rude or obnoxious. When you *allow* someone to "make you angry," you are *allowing* them to take control of your emotions. If you do this, he can control you anytime he decides to, like a puppet on a string. Refuse to allow anyone to take control of your mind and disrupt your inner peace!

252

Attach yourself to what is spiritually superior,
regardless of what other people think or do. Hold to
your true aspirations, no matter what is going on around you.
Epictetus

If you consistently focus on what is spiritually superior, you won't have to be concerned about allowing someone else's words or actions to control your emotions. This brings us to the question of what it means to be spiritually superior? Knowing what we do about Epictetus, it certainly doesn't mean comparing yourself to others and feeling superior to them spiritually. It has nothing to do with status or power.

If you attach yourself to what is spiritually superior, you are mastering and transcending your ego and passions, living with integrity and compassion, and acting with wisdom and humility. You are staying more attuned to God and transcending your attachment to material things, fear, greed, and anger.

The best way to keep your mind on what is spiritually superior is to consistently remind yourself that God lives within you. Since God knows your innermost thoughts, you will strive to keep your thoughts pure and just. Knowing that God sees everything you do and hears everything you say will help you strive to master both your speech and actions, and bring them in line with the principles of Stoicism.

When you do this, it won't matter what other people think, say, or do, or what is going on around you; if you stay focused on what is spiritually superior, other people won't be able to push your buttons. The secret is having enough emotional self-control to remember this during trying times.

Develop the habit of reminding yourself of your true objectives and desires to live by Stoic principles anytime you are faced with someone's rude behavior or events that are out of your control. It is all too easy to forget your true aspirations if you don't remain mindful of who and what you want to be. Let others think and say whatever they want and keep your focus on what is spiritually and morally superior. Don't allow anyone to sidetrack you!

253

The mind that is anxious about future events is miserable.
Seneca

To be anxious about the future is to allow yourself to wallow in stress and worry, and of course, this will not foster your inner peace, tranquility, or a calm mind. It is a form of self-inflicted suffering caused by an uncontrolled mind. When you begin to worry about something that may or may not happen in the future, you are no longer living in the present moment; therefore, you are not fully living your best life.

Have you ever stopped and considered that most of the things that you fear never come to pass; they exist only in your imagination? You cannot see the future, nor predict how it will unfold. When you worry about something bad happening in the future, not only are you suffering unnecessarily, but you are energizing something that you don't want to manifest in your life.

The law of attraction states that we attract into our lives what we think about and give energy to with our thoughts. So, allowing yourself to become emotionally fearful and worrying about what could happen attracts negative things into your life. In short, you are possibly manifesting the very things that you don't want to happen.

Remember Seneca's teaching that I already covered: "We suffer more in imagination than in reality." Worrying about the future simply adds suffering and stress to your mind and disrupts your inner peace. We all have enough stress in life without adding to it. Worrying about tomorrow is robbing you of today.

The Stoic principles give us the perfect remedy for worrying about the future—control the things that you can control! The only time you have any control over is the present moment. So, focus on what you can control now and let go of the rest. Train your mind to prepare for the future without allowing it to worry you or imagining the worst. Preparing for the future is not the same thing as worrying about the future. It is simply being wise. Learn from the past, prepare for the future, but live in the now!

254

Do not mistake your assumptions for the truth.
Epictetus

There is a tremendous difference between assumptions, perceptions, judgments, and the truth. It is popular today to hear people talking about "my truth." The fact is that there is no such thing as your truth or my truth; there is only *the* truth; everything else is merely assumptions or perceptions. It is a big mistake to assume your perception of what's going on is the actual truth.

Epictetus knew this 2,000 years ago, but our modern culture seems to have forgotten this cold, hard fact. That is why he taught, "What disturbs men's minds is not events but their judgments on events." It is our assumptions and perceptions that we take of the situation or event that cause our stress or anger. When you accept your assumptions as facts, you set yourself up for poor decisions, stress, and conflicts.

There are many examples of this in today's culture. Most people today have a cell phone. Consider the following situation. You text or call someone and leave an important message, but they do not get back to you. You assume he must be upset with you, or he is ignoring you, but maybe he couldn't get back to you right away or forgot to charge his phone. Never come to conclusions or make decisions based on unfounded assumptions.

The truth is, you have no idea about what's going on; you are simply making assumptions. Those assumptions may or may not be true, but if you assume they are true with no evidence, you are making a mistake. An assumption is simply a theory, belief, or hypothesis; it is not the truth. Your assumptions are just your theories or guesses about what is going on.

To avoid making this mistake, it is helpful to ask yourself, "Is this true or is it just my perception?" Often your first assumption is influenced by your emotions or bias. You must train yourself to be more objective. Assume less and observe more. Don't allow your mental chatter to cause you to assume the worst. Develop the habit of believing the best about someone unless you have a reason to believe otherwise. Act on truth and facts, not assumptions.

255

The whole future lies in uncertainty. Live immediately.
Seneca

If Seneca had lived in modern times, he would have been a popular self-help author. Once again, he is urging us not to worry about the future, but to live in the present moment. We do not know what the future holds in store for us; all we can do is live in the now.

So many people are obsessed with what might happen in the future instead of focusing their energy on what is happening right now. No matter how much you may want to control and plan for your future, there are no guarantees. Worrying about what might happen is a waste of time. If you have a reason to be concerned about something, then take action to prepare for it, but don't worry about it. There is a big difference between being concerned and preparing, and in stressing out and worrying about things.

Waiting to live your life until sometime in the future is a mistake that many people make. They postpone enjoying their life until everything in their life is perfect, but they never stop to consider that everything may never be perfect. Don't postpone the things that you want to do in life; now is the time to live your life to the fullest, not sometime in the future.

Seneca believed that most people simply exist, but they don't truly live. While they are making plans or worrying about what the future may hold for them, life passes them by. Don't procrastinate! Live with purpose and live in the present moment. Don't put off being happy or doing the things you want to do until something changes. What if those changes never come?

Live each day completely; be happy NOW! Don't waste time because you have no idea how much time you may have on this earth. Learn to be okay with not knowing what the future holds for you. Just be happy where you are, with what you have, in the present moment.

Too many people put off truly living until they are too old, sick, or physically unable to do the things they want to do in life. Refuse to be one of those people. Start living your life immediately and live it to the fullest!

256

The best indication of a man's character is
how he treats people who can't do him any good.
Seneca

Your true character is revealed in how you conduct yourself when you have nothing to gain from your actions. If you treat the president of the company differently than the janitor, then you are doing it for some type of personal gain. Acting one way towards someone who can benefit you and another way towards someone who can't do anything for you is not being sincere.

You should treat people kindly and with respect simply because it is the right thing to do, not for personal gain. When you do it for personal gain, that is flattering someone to manipulate him in some way. It is playing politics. Character is not a strategy; it's who you truly are.

Your true honor is shown when no one is watching and there is nothing at stake but your own integrity and honor. An honorable person conducts himself with honor and respect, not for praise or personal gain, but because of his personal code and his principles.

Seneca stressed the importance of personal integrity, especially when you are not being observed by others. In his Letters to Lucilius he states, "I will govern myself as though I were under public scrutiny." He went on to write, "What is the point of having a good reputation if I am guilty within?"

When your reputation does not line up with who you truly are, something is wrong; you are not on the right path. This same wisdom can be found in the writings of Confucius. He wrote, "The superior man must be watchful over himself even when he is alone."

If you remember from some of the teachings I have already covered, the Stoics believed that God is always with you. Since God is always with you, you are never truly alone; He sees not only your actions, but also the intentions behind your actions. If you keep this in mind, it will help you stay on the right path and maintain your honor and integrity. Maintain your integrity and honor whether alone or in public!

257

We should not, like sheep, follow the herd of creatures in front
of us, making our way when others go, not where we ought to go.
Seneca

To be virtuous and follow the Stoic principles, you must learn to think for yourself, not follow the crowd. Those who live with honor and integrity have always been in the minority. If you follow the crowd, you are merely living by imitating others, not by examining your inner self and doing what you feel to be right. That is acting like a sheep, mindlessly following the herd.

Those who follow the crowd only do what others do; they are constantly concerned about what others think, say, and do. These people act blindly, never stopping to ask whether they are doing the right thing or if their actions are in line with Stoic principles.

Conformity without reflection is not living with a Stoic mindset. The Stoic mindset is about controlling what you have control over and doing your best to be virtuous and to do what's right. When you simply follow what others are doing, you are conforming to their actions instead of searching your mind and spirit, and determining what is right for you.

Refuse to follow social norms or popular opinion without questioning whether they are right. Make reason and rational thought your guide, not popular opinion. Remember that just because everyone else is doing it, that doesn't mean it is right.

To do this, you must have the self-confidence and courage to walk alone. Many times, doing the right thing means you have to go your own way and leave the crowd to make their own decisions. Customs and trends change, but living with honor and integrity is a constant if you are living with a Stoic mindset.

Whenever you are tempted to follow the crowd, ask yourself, "Is this what I think is right, or am I just going along with everyone else?" Instead of following the crowd, follow your conscience; it will guide you in the right direction. Always do what you think is right and do it with pure intentions.

You become what you give your attention to.
Epictetus

The Stoics believed that your character is shaped by what you focus on; what you give your attention to is what you become. This is why they put so much emphasis on controlling your thoughts, thinking rationally, and remaining focused on virtuous traits.

This same thought can be seen in ancient China and India. Confucius stated, "The will to be virtuous begins with self-awareness and reflection." Buddha taught, "All that we are is the result of what we have thought. The mind is everything. What we think, we become." And the Bhagavad Gita taught, "Wherever the mind wanders, due to its flickering and unsteady nature, one must bring it back under the control of the Self," meaning that the mind shapes you and you must control it in order to control your destiny.

We see the same thought in today's culture. It is frequently called the Law of Attraction or manifesting what you want in life. Basically, Epictetus is saying that your mind is molded by the thoughts that you dwell on. If you give your attention to being virtuous, you will become virtuous; if you give your attention to anger, fear, or worry, those emotions will increase in your life.

Your thoughts contain power that we are only starting to understand. You can think of your mind as a garden and your thoughts as the seeds you plant. Just as it is with any garden, what grows there depends on the seeds you plant. Moreover, you can't simply plant the seeds that you want to grow in your garden; you must continually be watchful to remove any weeds which start to grow there as well. The weeds are negative thoughts, toxic influences, and useless distractions that sidetrack you.

Don't take this process lightly! You decide what you will become by being mindful and thinking thoughts that move you towards the person you want to be. This is not a passive exercise, but one that you must give daily attention to, because in the end, it determines who you become. What are you giving your attention to? What seeds are you planting in your garden?

259

Let us say what we feel and feel what
we say; let speech harmonize with life.
Seneca

In this teaching, Seneca is urging us to be morally consistent, to make sure that what we feel, what we say, and what we do are in harmony with each other. Basically, don't simply talk the talk, but walk the walk. Be sincere in what you say and stay away from actions such as flattery, saying what you think others want to hear, and lying.

Flattery and lying are all empty forms of speech. You don't truly believe what you are saying, but you are simply speaking to manipulate someone else for a personal purpose. This is dishonest. Say what you mean and mean what you say! Your speech should reflect your character; what you say truly matters.

When Seneca taught to let your speech harmonize with your life, he was saying to live in such a way that your words and your actions are in harmony with each other. Don't say one thing but do or mean another. If you are going to advocate living with virtue, wisdom, honor, and integrity, then you should actually live those traits yourself. Don't teach others to live one way while you live another. Teach by example!

Living with a Stoic mindset means that you must strive to make your life as authentic as possible. You must work to become more virtuous, wise, courageous, and honorable each day. Don't be shy when it comes to letting others see how you live your life. Say what you believe is right and true; don't simply say what you think someone else wants to hear because you are afraid of what they may think about you. Remember, what they think about you is none of your business.

Does your speech reflect your values? Do you keep your honor, integrity, and wisdom to yourself out of fear of what others may think? You must have confidence in what you believe. Don't worry about what others may think; just be the person that you want to be. What others think about how you live your life is not your business; your business is to live your life your way.

The mind, when distracted, absorbs nothing deeply.
Seneca

This speaks directly to retaining what you read or learn and is a powerful argument against multitasking. If you are reading a good self-help book or a quote book full of wisdom, while, at the same time, watching television, checking text messages or emails, or people watching on the beach, you most likely won't retain much of what you read. You must give it your full attention to absorb the wisdom you are reading.

When your mind is constantly shifting focus from one thing to another, it is hard to focus enough to retain or understand what you really want to focus on. If you are reading a book, but you are not giving it your full attention, you will not get much from the book.

To retain or absorb whatever you are reading or working on, you must give it your full attention. And it is not just physical things that can shift your focus. Uncontrolled thoughts will make it all but impossible to recollect the wisdom of a good book, much less to help you use that wisdom to transform your life. If you can't control your thoughts and keep them focused on what you are reading, you might as well just put your book down until you can.

Allowing mind chatter, different noises, or the people around you to constantly sidetrack your mind, is robbing yourself of the wisdom or skills you are trying to obtain. Trying to learn like this is like glancing at the truth, but never actually grasping it. You must learn to calm your mind and control it to where you can concentrate on the task at hand when you need to. Attention and concentration are forms of self-discipline and self-control.

Developing and integrating the Stoic virtues into your daily life requires your attention. You can't grasp a philosophy with a distracted mind. This is why the Stoics valued focused reflection, contemplation, and self-examination. Today's culture is plagued by divided attention and multitasking, which hurt productivity and weaken the mind. It is not how much you study that matters; it's how much knowledge and wisdom you understand and retain.

261

> Nothing is more hostile to a firm grasp
> on knowledge than self-deception.
> *Zeno of Citium*

Self-deception is something that many people have issues with during their lives. Self-deception is lying to yourself and then believing those lies to be true. It is believing *what you want to be true* instead of what *is* true. Wanting something to be true is not the same thing as it being true.

People fall into this trap because believing what they want to be true is more comforting and easier than accepting something that they wish wasn't true but is. You may be thinking that it really doesn't matter whether someone believes something about themselves that isn't true, but doing so prevents true spiritual understanding and slows self-improvement.

Ignoring uncomfortable truths or rationalizing destructive behavior is nothing but twisting facts to protect your ego. The danger is that it not only prevents true understanding, but these people begin to believe their own lies. You can't live an authentic life when your life is based on self-deception or an illusion. You must be willing to see things as they are, not as you wish they were or want them to be.

It is easy to see how it can be very damaging to a firm grasp of knowledge and reality, as self-deception is the opposite of seeing *what is* so you can understand and improve it. Self-deception will hinder you on your path to living by the Stoic virtues. It can easily sidetrack you, cloud your thinking, and cause you to refuse to accept your shortcomings and change your flaws.

The Stoics believed that right thinking leads to right behavior, and wrong thinking leads to wrong behavior. You must refuse to deceive yourself if you want to accurately reflect on your virtues or honor. If your mind is clouded by self-deception, then you are not living in harmony with virtue, honor, or integrity. Even modern psychology states that when one distorts facts to reduce mental discomfort, it causes issues in one's life. This is called cognitive dissonance. Free yourself of all illusions and self-deceptions!

Nothing is more honorable than a grateful heart.
Seneca

Gratitude is definitely a part of the Stoic mindset. Marcus Aurelius, Epictetus, Seneca, and Musonius Rufus all wrote about gratitude. Marcus Aurelius taught, "When you arise in the morning, think of what a precious privilege it is to be alive—to breathe, to think, to enjoy, to love." Rufus taught, "He who is not grateful for little things will not be grateful for bigger things."

Gratitude is a profound moral virtue; it reveals your inner sincerity and character. You should be grateful even for the smallest things that anyone does for you. In this life, nobody owes you anything. If someone does a favor for you or gives you something, be honorable enough to show sincere gratitude for what he or she has done. It is dishonorable not to be grateful for whatever others do for you.

Not only is a grateful heart honorable, but it is a sign of wisdom. Instead of complaining about the way things are, be grateful for all the good things in your life. Remember that no matter how little you have or what is happening in your life, you could always have less, and things could always be worse.

Gratefulness is another virtue that is taught throughout the world. Buddha taught, "A person of integrity is grateful and thankful. This gratitude, this thankfulness, is advocated by all wise people." Lao Tzu wrote in the *Tao Te Ching*, "Be content with what you have; rejoice in the way things are. When you realize there is nothing lacking, the whole world belongs to you."

Gratitude keeps the ego in check and is a sign of wisdom, nobility, and honor. It costs you nothing to be sincerely grateful for everything in your life, and, as a bonus, living with a grateful heart changes your overall attitude. When you feel gratitude for everything in your life, it gives you a calm, peaceful mindset, and a heart full of love and tranquility.

There is literally nothing in your life that you can't find some reason to be grateful for. It all depends on your perspective. Living with a grateful heart will change your mindset and your perspective in every situation.

263

We should, every night, call ourselves to an account.
Seneca

This is another teaching that is common throughout the world, especially in Asia. *The Hagakure*, a book of samurai wisdom compiled by Yamamoto Tsunetomo, states, "Even if you are not a warrior, practice cleansing your heart every night." The samurai took life seriously because they never knew when death might overtake them.

They made a practice of examining and "cleansing" their hearts each night. Even though your life is not in the hands of some feudal lord, tomorrow is not promised to you anymore than it was promised to the Japanese samurai.

So, what does it mean to "call ourselves to account" every night? It means that at the end of each day you should reflect on your actions, words, thoughts, and intentions and take an inventory of what you did right or what areas you need to improve.

The above quote is just the first part of Seneca's teaching on this subject. He went on to explain further, giving us examples of how we should call ourselves to account, urging us to ask ourselves, "What weakness did I overcome today? What passions did I oppose? What temptation did I resist? What virtue did I acquire?"

These are great questions to help you mentally review your thoughts and actions of the day. Each night before bed, take a few moments to do a daily self-reflection and self-examination. Identify your areas of growth and the areas where you fell short of how you want to live. Where did you excel in your goal to live by Stoic principles? Where did you fall short? What areas do you need to improve?

This practice will strengthen your character if you make a point of doing this each night. Remember the principle of kaizen—constant, never-ending improvement. That is what this practice is all about. Self-examination is crucial to living a virtuous life and integrating the Stoic virtues into your everyday life. Always strive to be a better man than you were yesterday!

264

He who spares the guilty harms the innocent.
Seneca

There is a Persian proverb that states this same philosophy: "To spare the ravening leopard is an act of injustice to the sheep." While we may wish to live in peace with all people and animals, that is not the world we live in. Just as there are predators in the wild that will ravage your sheep or cattle, there are evil people in this world who will continue to hurt innocent people unless they are stopped.

When a predator in the wild is devastating a rancher's cattle, the rancher has two choices. He can do nothing because he wants to spare the wolf, or he can shoot the wolf to protect his cattle. Unfortunately, he cannot spare both. Sparing the wolf would be sacrificing the life of his cattle and his livelihood.

Seneca makes the same point concerning human predators. If you spare the guilty murderer, you are doing an injustice to the innocent victim and his loved ones. This is not only an injustice to the victim, but puts other innocent people at risk of being victims as well. Predators will continue to prey on the weak and elderly until courageous warriors stand up and stop them.

To allow criminals to continue to hurt innocent people is to allow injustice and fear to permeate the community. As you already know by now, justice is one of the fundamental principles of Stoicism. While you may feel a certain empathy for all people, it is unjust to allow your compassionate heart to allow the guilty to go unpunished for his crimes. The innocent victim deserves more compassion than the vicious criminal, and sparing the guilty is being more compassionate to the criminal than the victim. This is unjust!

Martial arts master and the founder of Shotokan Karate, Gichin Funakoshi, stated it this way: "When faced with a matter of justice, one must stand firmly on the side of justice, even at the cost of one's life." The Stoics felt just as strongly about justice. You can't be just if you are willing to play favorites when it comes to justice. Either you are just, or you are unjust; there is no middle ground. Remember, he who spares the guilty harms the innocent.

265

Everything is interwoven, and the web is holy; none of its
parts are unconnected. They are composed harmoniously, and
together they compose the world. One world, made up of all things.
One divinity, present in them all. One substance and one law…and one truth.
Marcus Aurelius

It never ceases to amaze me how this same philosophy was taught throughout the world in ancient times. Lao Tzu taught, "The great Tao flows everywhere, both to the left and to the right. All things depend on it for life, and it does not turn away from them. It accomplishes its task but does not claim credit. It clothes and feeds all things but does not lord it over them…There is something undifferentiated and yet complete, which existed before heaven and earth. Silent, formless, and alone, it does not change, goes around and does not get weary. It can be called mother of the world. I do not know its name; I call it Tao."

The Bible states, "For in Him all things were created: things in heaven and on earth, visible and invisible…all things have been created through Him and for Him. He is before all things, and in Him all things hold together." Even Native Americans taught that the Great Spirit created everything, and His spirit is within all things.

Likewise, Marcus Aurelius has the wisdom to understand that there is one Divinity, present in all things, one substance and one truth. Furthermore, science has now proven that everything on our planet is made from the same energy, even though we cannot see it.

If we could see the reality of a common wooden table, we would see that it is not truly solid; it is made up of matter like atoms and molecules, and this matter contains energy which holds its particles together. Matter can be converted into energy, and energy can produce matter. While everything appears to be solid, it is actually vibrating energy, thus, everything is made of energy, and everything is connected by this energy. It doesn't matter if you call it "God," "Tao," "The Great Spirit," or "One Divinity," it is God.

266

If you must be affected by other people's misfortunes, show them pity
instead of contempt. Drop this readiness to hate and take offense.
Epictetus

When someone makes a mistake or suffers some kind of misfortune, many
people react to it with anger, frustration, and scorn, but this is not the way of
Stoicism. Stoicism teaches us we should respond, not react, and that we should
respond with a caring, empathetic heart instead of harsh judgments or anger.
As Epictetus taught, show them empathy and pity instead of contempt.

In addition, Epictetus wrote, "If you *must* be affected by other people's
misfortunes…" You do not *have to be affected* by other people's misfortunes,
mistakes, or their actions; it is a *choice* you make. You cannot control how
other people live their lives or the decisions that they make, which lead to
various consequences. But if you *choose* to be affected, don't be hateful or take
offense; be empathetic and kind.

God did not put you on this earth to judge the thoughts, words, or actions
of others; He is the judge, not you. Let your Stoic virtues guide your words
and actions. You always have the choice of whether to be kind and loving, or
contemptuous and judgmental. We all make mistakes and bad choices at some
point in our lives. Choose to be compassionate and understanding.

Also, you can be empathetic and feel sorry for what someone is going
through without allowing their misfortunes to affect your own happiness or
inner peace. Help others as much as possible, but remember that your primary
duty is to live with wisdom, honor, and integrity, and to control the things that
are within your realm of control.

We all must live with the consequences of our actions; that is just another
reason you should strive to do what's right and live according to the Stoic
principles. While we have no control over the consequences of our actions, we
can assume that good actions will produce better consequences than
thoughtless actions, which are unvirtuous. Live your life with pure intentions
and always do your best to be kind and understanding with others.

> To expect bad people not to injure others is crazy.
> It's to ask the impossible. And to let them behave like that
> to other people, but expect them to exempt you is arrogant.
> *Marcus Aurelius*

In this teaching, Marcus Aurelius gives us the cold, hard truth that many people in our modern world need to learn. If you expect bad people to respect the law and not to rob, cheat, steal, or injure others, then you better get ready to be disappointed. That is what they do; they may or may not change sometime in the future, but that has nothing to do with their behavior in the here and now.

Furthermore, if you allow them to behave like that to other people, but expect them not to behave like that with you, you are sorely mistaken, or as Marcus Aurelius put it, you are being arrogant. Criminals choose their victims according to what they want and whether you appear to be an easy target. They don't exempt you simply because you think that something like that will never happen to you.

This wisdom also insinuates that we should not allow bad people to injure others. That doesn't mean you must go out and confront them yourself, but you must not allow them to get away with their criminal actions. If you let someone get away with a crime once, you are doing nothing more than encouraging him to commit more crimes.

Seneca wrote, "He who spares the wicked injures the good." This means that if you spare the guilty criminal, you are doing the innocent victim an injustice, as well as all the future victims of this criminal. This is obviously not the way of the Stoic, as justice is one of the fundamental principles of Stoicism.

To expect criminals not to commit crimes is crazy, but to allow them to get away with their crimes unpunished is an act of injustice to the entire community. Allowing them to get away with one crime simply puts the rest of the community at risk of being victimized. Be kind and loving, but not so much so that you are willing to put others at risk for the sake of criminals.

I do what is mine to do; the rest doesn't disturb me.
Marcus Aurelius

When you get to the point that you have this Stoic mindset in your life, you will be well on your way to living by the Stoic principles. Marcus Aurelius is stating that he is only concerned with the things that he can control, those things such as his thoughts, intentions, words, actions, and attitude, and that he accepts everything else just as it is without allowing it to disturb his inner peace.

Your duty is only to control the things which are within your control. If you do this with the right intentions and always try to do what's right, then you are fulfilling your role in society and your duty to yourself. That is the first step in developing the Stoic mindset.

The next step is even more challenging—not to allow the things which are outside of your realm of control to disturb your inner peace. This includes other people's opinions, words, choices, actions, or the outcomes of your own choices and actions. It also includes all external events and situations that you can't control, like the weather, the future, the past, politics, etc.

Inner peace and tranquility come from focusing on your duty and letting go of external circumstances and events. Refuse to allow external circumstances and events to disrupt your inner peace; witness them, but don't allow them to permeate your mind or your spirit. See them as if you are watching them from a distance and they have no power to control you.

This is easy to forget during the heat of the moment or when something truly disturbing happens. You must constantly remind yourself of this wisdom until it becomes an integral part of who you are. This teaching of Marcus Aurelius is a great quote to memorize and remind yourself of daily. When you start to feel irritated, angry, or frustrated by someone's words or actions, or some external event or situation, remind yourself of this wisdom. Do this until the Stoic mindset becomes completely natural to you. Take care of your duty and refuse to allow anything else to disturb you.

269

Let no act be done without a purpose.
Marcus Aurelius

The Stoics taught that we should be intentional and mindful of our actions. To be intentional and mindful of our actions, we must think rationally and act deliberately, being conscious of our purpose. All your actions should align with virtue and reason; they should have some purpose behind them.

If you are not acting deliberately and with a specific purpose, you are acting by thoughtless impulse, habit, or to please others. As Miyamoto Musashi, Japan's greatest swordsman, stated, "Do nothing which is of no use." When you consider this philosophy, the first thing you must do before you act is to determine what your purpose is. Why are you doing what you are doing?

If you don't know what your purpose is, then you can't act with a deliberate reason, and if you don't act with a deliberate reason, then you can't act intentionally or mindfully; you are simply wasting time. Every action should be decisive, practical, and necessary. Don't waste time or effort; every action is an opportunity to act with self-control, wisdom, honor, justice, courage, and integrity.

If you are not acting with a purpose, you can't be living in the present moment, and if you are not living in the present moment, you are not being mindful. That is simply functioning on autopilot and acting without any focused thought. It doesn't matter what you are doing, it can be done mindfully and with a specific purpose. As Marcus Aurelius taught in another passage of *Meditations*, "In everything, do nothing without a purpose. Otherwise, you'll be acting aimlessly, and your life will be disordered."

If your life is disordered, it is chaotic, disorderly, and disturbed; this does not lead to inner peace, tranquility, or a calm mind. Get your life organized, and you will get more done in less time. Write a to-do list in the order that you want to get things done and stick to it. Even if you are doing nothing but relaxing, do it with purpose; relax fully, mentally, spiritually, emotionally, and physically. Let no act be done without a purpose!

270

Where you arrive does not matter so much as
what sort of person you are when you arrive there.
Seneca

Where you go and when you arrive don't matter as much as the kind of person you are. This demonstrates the importance of Stoic principles over external circumstances or events. Seneca is not necessarily talking about traveling as much as the external achievements you gather as you go through life, things like wealth, status, or reaching your goals. All of these are far less important than who you become internally in your spirit, mind, and character.

To put it bluntly, the kind of person you become is more important than the place you end up in life, or the titles, status, or wealth that you acquire. If you are living with a Stoic mindset, you will develop virtue, wisdom, courage, honor, integrity, a sense of justice, and conduct yourself with moderation. These are the genuine sources of living a good life.

Many people are confused about what a good life entails. They put more emphasis on material things, money, titles, and status. These material things don't matter as much as the internal character traits you develop as you live your life. Material things are things that you temporarily own; the internal character traits that you develop become a part of who you truly are.

It is the same concept as facing a challenge. It is not really the challenge that matters, but how you respond to it. Do you face it with good intentions, rational thought, courage, patience, a correct attitude, and a wise response, or do you face it with anger, frustration, and allow it to disrupt your inner peace? This choice is always yours to make!

Ultimately, Seneca is urging us to shift our focus from external objectives, many which are only temporary or totally outside of our realm of control, to internal objectives of developing our inner strength, inner peace, character, honor, and integrity, all of which you have total control over. Work to become who you want to become in life, but just make sure when you get where you want to be, that you are a person of honor, wisdom, and integrity.

271

Do not be overheard complaining…not even to yourself.
Marcus Aurelius

Most people never stop to consider that not only is complaining a waste of time, but it is bad for their physical and mental health. Science has proven that complaining increases your cortisol levels, otherwise known as your stress hormone. The more you complain, the higher your level of cortisol. Essentially, when you complain, you are doing nothing more than stressing yourself out for no reason.

Higher levels of cortisol in your body can lead to several health problems, including depression, sleep issues (which can lead to even more health problems and more depression), higher blood pressure, digestive issues, and even an increased risk of heart disease.

Scientific studies have proven that complaining also makes you more likely to think negative thoughts, which obviously are not conducive to maintaining your inner peace or your Stoic mindset. The more you complain, the more you train your mind to think negatively.

The remedy for complaining is gratefulness. Be grateful for all the blessings in your life instead of focusing on the negative things in your life. You have total control over whether you take the time to be thankful for all the blessings that God has provided you; but you have no control over the things you are complaining about.

If you want to stop the habit of complaining about the irritations or inconveniences in your life, then start replacing thoughts of frustration and irritation with thoughts of thankfulness and gratefulness. There is much more to be grateful for than there is to complain about in your life. You simply need to shift your focus.

Remember what President Theodore Roosevelt said, "Complaining without offering a solution is just whining." Instead of complaining about the things that bother you, stoically accept them, and find a solution for them or simply just move on. Make it a point to remove all complaining from your life.

272

It is not what we say or think that defines us, but what we do.
Seneca

While what we think and say are important, and we should work to make sure our thoughts are positive and upright, and that we speak carefully and wisely, ultimately, that is not what defines us; it is what we do that defines who we are.

Many people think certain unvirtuous thoughts but refuse to act on them because they don't want to be that kind of person. Others speak without giving much thought to what they are saying, and say things that are ridiculous, hurtful, mean, or rude. They can always go back and apologize and try to set things right for their thoughtless, careless words, even though those words can never be unspoken and can still cause them many problems.

Ultimately, what defines you is what you do—your actions. Many people threaten to do bad things or to hurt other people out of anger or frustration, but they never follow through on those threats. Therefore, they can't really be called violent or malicious people, but people who are not in control of their thoughts or words.

On the other hand, if they act on those threats, they will be defined as a malicious, violent person. Their thoughts lead to their words; although their words may cause them to lose respect, they don't completely define them. Words are not set in stone; actions are.

Consider this example. Two workers are frustrated about what they were asked to do. They both stated that they would not do the work. One quit and went home; the other, though he griped and was not happy about it, regained control over himself and did the work that needed to be done. While they both said the same words, in the end, they were defined in a very different way. One was defined as a quitter, while the other was defined as a dependable worker.

It is your actions that define you, not your words. Controlling your speech is important, but doing the right thing is vital. Develop a Stoic mindset and learn to control your thoughts, words, and, most importantly, your actions!

273

It is not possible to change your behavior
and still be the same person you were before.
Epictetus

Your behavior and your character are deeply linked. When you change how
you behave, you change yourself as a person. Your actions not only reflect
your character, but they shape and build your character. Changing your
character requires building new habits mentally, emotionally, spiritually, and
physically.

To develop the Stoic mindset and become virtuous, you must change your
behavior. First, start deprogramming and reprogramming your mind. You must
remove the old beliefs that no longer serve you and replace them with the
teachings from the Stoics that you have learned. Once you get your mind right,
your behavior will naturally begin to change.

Changing your behavior also includes changing the way you speak. We
develop certain habits in our speech, just as we do in our actions. You may be
in the habit of speaking negative affirmations to yourself without even being
aware of it or of constantly complaining about things outside of your control.
Or you could be in the habit of speaking without thinking or saying things
simply to please others instead of being honest and speaking from your heart.
These are habits that must be changed as well.

However, I would say the most important behavior to change is the way
you respond to other people's actions or external events and circumstances.
Once you integrate the Stoic principles into your life, you will begin to respond
differently to other people's rude or unexpected behavior. You will also stop
allowing all those external things, over which you have no control, to disrupt
your inner peace, which will lead to your being calmer and being able to
respond more rationally to whatever is happening.

Once these behaviors start to change, whether or not you notice it, you will
start to become a different person than you were before. Your life will begin to
change, and you will become the person you want to be.

We should conduct ourselves not as if we ought to live
for the body, but as if we could not live without it.
Musonius Rufus

There are two separate parts to this teaching of Musonius Rufus. First, he says we should conduct ourselves not as if we ought to live for the body. If you are living for your body, you are fulfilling all your bodily desires; you are living a hedonistic, pleasure-seeking lifestyle. We constantly put things like our comfort, pleasure, or indulgence first place in our life. Rufus urges us not to live in this way, but to make virtue and wisdom a higher priority than our physical desires.

The second part of this teaching is that we should live as if we could not live without our body, which is completely true. You could sit in your living room and read every Stoic book, every self-help book, and every wisdom-based book, but if you don't take care of your body, what good are they going to do for you?

What good is taking care of your thoughts and spiritual virtues if you don't take care of your health? Your body is the vehicle that allows you to practice virtue and fulfill your duties, responsibilities, and to attain your goals. Ignoring your health and neglecting your body is simply being shortsighted. You can't help others or achieve your higher purposes if you are always sick and tired.

What Musonius Rufus taught is that your body is a tool, and you must maintain it with proper balance. If you spend too much time striving for the pleasures of the body, the health of the body will suffer. This interferes with the development of the Stoic principles and mindset. You must seek moderation and balance.

Of course, you should enjoy all the amazing things life has to offer, but don't make them your sole purpose for living. Enjoy them in moderation while you also take care of the needs of your body. Without your body, you couldn't enjoy the pleasures you enjoy. Developing a Stoic mindset is important, but you must also take care of your health!

275

> True nobility is not about being better than someone
> else; it is about being better than you used to be.
> *Seneca*

When a piece of wisdom is taught over the centuries and throughout different world cultures, it qualifies as universal wisdom—wisdom that holds true throughout the world, in every country or culture. This is another one of those wise teachings that is universally accepted wisdom, and another piece of wisdom that the samurai taught as well.

If you have been paying attention, you may have noticed that there are several Stoic teachings that were also taught by the samurai, who most likely learned them from teachers such as Lao Tzu, Sun Tzu, or Confucius. The famous swordsman, Miyamoto Musashi, taught, "Today is victory over yourself of yesterday; tomorrow is your victory over lesser men."

Of course, Musashi was teaching warrior philosophy, not Stoic philosophy. In Stoic philosophy, Seneca said it slightly differently: "True nobility is not about being better than someone else; it is about being better than you used to be." But becoming better than you used to be will also give you an advantage in dealing with those who do not work to improve themselves.

Develop the mindset that today, you will improve yourself so much that you can declare victory over yourself of yesterday because you have become a better person. This doesn't mean that you have become perfect or a completely different person; self-improvement generally comes in small steps. However, if you make small improvements every day, those minor improvements add up very quickly. By the end of a few months or a year, you will not even be the same person you were.

The trick is in being consistent. Develop the philosophy of Kaizen—constant, never-ending improvement. Work to improve yourself spiritually, mentally, emotionally, and physically every day. Don't compare yourself to what others are doing; you are not in competition with anyone else. Compare yourself to who you were yesterday and be determined to be a better person.

276

To begin is half the work.
Marcus Aurelius

When you have a project to do, it always seems like the hardest part is getting yourself in the right frame of mind to get started with it. Once you decide to get started and start organizing what you will need, how you will approach it, and figure out a roadmap, it seems like half the work is done.

You can liken this to getting a boulder to the top of the hill and putting it in position to roll it down to the bottom. The hard part is getting motivated enough to get up and get the boulder up the hill, to do the busy work. But once you have it up the hill, half the work is done. When you start it rolling, the rest of the work flows easily and seems to get done much quicker than you expected.

Taking the first step is where the battle is. Often, our minds can feel overwhelmed by the size or complexity of the job. The hardest part is controlling your mind. You must stop looking at how complex or big the job may be and break it down into smaller pieces that don't appear so overwhelming. Once you do that, the job seems more manageable, and you have overcome the resistance of procrastination.

Then you can see the possibilities, and your mind begins to work on ideas to help you complete your task. Once you begin, there is a mental momentum that takes over, building your confidence and clarity as it expands. Overthinking leads to procrastination and paralysis in our actions; controlling your mind and taking positive action leads to purpose and overcomes procrastination.

Don't let the fear of how big or complex the job may be cause you to procrastinate or feel overwhelmed. Think of the Stoic principles and focus on what you can control; then think rationally, organize your job into smaller pieces, and work with purposeful action. Every job, no matter how big or complicated, gets completed one step at a time. Get your mind straight and simply begin the job; the rest will come one step at a time.

Nothing ought to be unexpected by us. Our minds should be
sent forward in advance to meet all problems, and we should
consider not what is inclined to happen, but what can happen.
Seneca

I have mentioned in passing several times in this book that being prepared
for what may happen is not the same thing as worrying about what might
happen. There is a fine line between the two. Worrying is a mental exercise
based on the fear of what could happen; being concerned is considering what
could happen, but instead of worrying about those things, doing the best that
you can to prepare for what may come your way.

The difference between the two is fear and action. When you worry about
something happening in the future, your mind is being controlled by fear. You
sit and worry, but you don't take any action; you just wallow in your fear of
the future.

When you are concerned about what could happen, you are thinking
rationally about all the conceivable possibilities and then doing what you can
to be as prepared as possible to deal with those issues should they happen.
There is no fear involved in this preparation, only determination that you will
be as prepared as possible for whatever may come your way.

If you believe anything is possible, it is hard to catch you off guard, and
your mind becomes more resilient. By rehearsing potential scenarios in your
mind, you train yourself to be prepared for them, rather than surprised by them.
This activity is called visualization.

Visualization is a mental exercise where you visualize something
happening in the future, and here's the vital part, you visualize yourself
successfully managing whatever challenge it may be. Always visualize
yourself being successful! You want your visualization to be positive and
helpful, not negative. A negative visualization will produce fear; a positive
visualization will produce confidence. Look at the things that could go wrong
and mentally decide in advance how you would handle those challenges.

278

Time is a sort of river of passing events, and strong is its current;
no sooner is a thing brought to sight than it is swept by and
another takes its place, and this too will be swept away.
Marcus Aurelius

Just like a river, time never stands still; it continues to flow 24 hours a day and is ever changing. The river has a strong current, which sweeps things away; time, while its current may not be as strong, steadily flows at the same pace, never stopping to allow you to catch up.

While the current of time seems to flow slowly, it is very deceptive. It goes by much faster than it appears, changing every event, situation, thought, emotion, and proving that everything in this world is transient and will eventually be carried away by the river of time.

Time is one of the most deceptive things on our planet. As people go through each day, doing their jobs, taking care of their family, eating, sleeping, and getting up to do it all again, day by day, time continues to flow through their personal hourglasses.

We all have our own invisible personal hourglass which contains the days of our lives or the time that we have available to us to live our lives on this earth. None of us can see our own hourglass, but we each have one, nonetheless. And since we cannot see how much sand (time) is left in our hourglass, we do not know when our time will run out.

Therefore, the wise person refuses to waste time; it is the most precious thing you have; but for most people, it is one of the most ignored things in their life. They never seem to think about it until something happens that forces them to think about how much time they have wasted or how little time they have left to be with their friends or family.

Be grateful for every minute of every day! Time is the most valuable thing that you have, so use it wisely. Don't waste time thinking that you will live your life later and do the things you really want to do after this or that happens. You never know when your hourglass will run out of time.

279

A man must stand upright, not be kept upright by others.
Marcus Aurelius

There are some things that others can help you with and some things that you are responsible for yourself. When it comes to living with virtue, honor, integrity, courage, wisdom, and moderation, you are the only one who has control of that. Thus, you must stand upright on your own two feet; nobody is going to keep you balanced when it comes to your character.

Living by your code of honor is something that you must uphold on your own. If you are merely conducting yourself with honor in public to receive praise, approval, or for some external reason, then you are not truly an honorable or virtuous man; you're a dishonest fraud.

As the Celtic hero, Rob Roy MacGregor, stated, "Honor is something a man gives to himself." True honor comes from within, not from praise, recognition, or approval of others. The only approval you need to be concerned with as far as your honor goes is that of your own conscience—the quiet inner voice inside which guides you.

Social approval is meaningless when it comes to the subject of honor; most of the public are ignorant of the true meaning of honor and are not qualified to judge anyone's true honor. Honor is the foundation not only of your reputation, but of all the other virtues. It is something no one can take away from you, and no one can give you. No man can force you to live with honor, and no man can keep you from living with honor.

You must hold yourself accountable for your own virtues and principles. While books like this, and others, can guide you concerning living with Stoic principles, honor, integrity, and other character traits, ultimately, it is you who must take action to integrate them into your daily life.

A man of honor is not interested in what others think about how he lives his life. He acts with honor, integrity, and virtue, even when no one's watching. His honor is not an act to impress others, but a way of life based on living by higher standards than most men aspire to. He keeps himself upright!

280

Never esteem anything as of advantage to you that will
make you break your word or lose your self-respect.
Marcus Aurelius

Anything that makes you break your word, lower your standards, or lose your self-respect will never turn out to be an advantage for you in the long run. It may appear to be an advantage at first, but that is merely an illusion; it is being shortsighted and unwise.

Your word is your honor. When you break your word, you lose your honor, and when you lose your honor, you lose your self-respect. Self-esteem and self-respect are fragile concepts that can be easily lost if not carefully maintained.

Once you decide to live by a code of honor and to live by the Stoic principles, lowering your standards and breaking those principles will damage your self-respect and self-esteem. That means that anything that tempts you to lower your standards, set your honor aside, or go against what you know is right, will not be a true advantage for you, no matter how it may appear.

While it could be a temporary advantage in a specific situation, you must think rationally and look at the long-term effects of setting your honor and principles aside. You will have many chances throughout life to compromise your principles or honor, but none of them will be a true advantage to you. They are nothing more than a mirage that promises you riches, status, or some other external reward; but in the end, the mirage disappears and all you are left with is the damage done to your character and self-respect.

Don't esteem anything as being more important than your honor or principles, no matter who you are with or what you are doing. Once again, I will remind you what the great sage, Baltasar Gracian, wrote, "The man of principle does not forget who he is because of what others are." Remember who you are, what you stand for, and what is truly important to you, and you'll never lose your self-respect. Keep your word and maintain your honor and your self-respect. Your word is your honor!

281

How rotten and spurious is the man who says:
"I have decided to be straightforward with you."
Marcus Aurelius

If you are an honorable, honest man, there is never any reason for you to make a comment like, "I have decided to be straightforward with you," or "I am going to be honest with you." That is simply false sincerity. People who announce that they have decided to be honest with you are basically saying that they aren't always honest, but that they have decided to be honest with you this time.

A man who is not always honest is not an honest man. That is what Marcus Aurelius is trying to teach us in this quote from *Meditations*, and he calls men who say these things "rotten" and "spurious." This means they are bogus, fake, and unauthentic, and Marcus Aurelius knew it.

He is calling out the hypocrisy and insincerity behind such words. Think about it. If a man must tell you something like, "I have decided to be honest with you," that should be a red flag for you. Being honest is not a choice you make occasionally; it is a virtue by which you live your life. When someone says something like that, it is just another way of saying, "I am usually deceitful and manipulative, but today, I am going to do you a favor and be straightforward with you." Would you trust someone like that?

Honesty should be a part of your code, your natural state. You should not have to announce it as if it is something special. Genuine honor and integrity are silent, not something to brag about. A truly honest person is just honest, period; he doesn't have to convince you he is honest.

Practice being straightforward and honest until it is a habit, a part of your being, not an occasional performance to impress others. Let your actions speak for themselves. Don't claim to be a man of honor; be a man of honor! Take your code of honor and integrity seriously; make it your way of life. And if anyone doubts your honor or contradicts the point, just move on and allow them to believe what they will and continue to live in their ignorance.

282

A sword never kills anybody; it is a tool in the killer's hand.
Seneca

This fact stated by Seneca is nothing more than common sense. I have swords in several rooms of my home for both décor and self-defense, but guess what? Not one of them has ever killed anyone while I was out of the house, or in the house as far as that goes. They are not dangerous in and of themselves; they are nothing more than a tool. They can be used as beautiful décor, or they can be used as a blade of self-defense.

Seneca had the sense to understand this simple concept 2,000 years ago, but there are still millions of people in today's culture who, for some odd reason, can't seem to comprehend this simply fact. These people still don't understand that it is not the tool that does evil, but the man who uses the tool.

You could confiscate every single firearm and knife in the world, but the murder rate would not change. Men and women have been killing other human beings since the beginning of time, when Cane killed Abel with a *rock*! If someone wants to murder another human, there are an unlimited number of tools he can use to achieve his objective.

You simply cannot remove enough things from this planet to stop bad people from hurting other people; it's impossible! If you remove all the firearms, they will use blades. If you remove all the blades, they will use screwdrivers, pipes, sticks, rocks, etc. Get the point?

Bad people do bad things, period. If they can't get what they want one way, they will figure out another way to accomplish their criminal goals. In addition, bad people don't care if we outlaw guns, knives, pipes, or any other weapon; it doesn't mean anymore to them than if we outlaw carrots, toothpaste, or baby toys. Why? Because bad people *do not obey the law*, period!

Not only is this a statement of fact from Seneca, but it is also an endorsement of common sense. Anyone with any common sense should be able to understand that inanimate objects don't *do* anything; it is the human who uses the object who is responsible for the action.

283

By silence, I hear other men's imperfections and conceal my own.
Zeno of Citium

Zeno is expressing the advantages of remaining silent and listening to others talk, instead of babbling along with them. When you allow others to talk, they will eventually expose their own imperfections and secrets. People tend to have a strong desire to share their secrets, even though it is not a wise practice. Silently allow them to share while you listen and learn.

By actively listening and allowing others to talk, you will learn valuable information about them and their character. Moreover, by remaining silent, you avoid revealing personal information and conceal your own imperfections, which are no one else's business. Wise men always listen more than they talk.

Baltasar Gracian stated, "Fools always speak before they think. They disclose not only what they have done, but also what they are going to do. Their thoughts run before their deeds. They are the reverse of wise men, who keep silent about the future while acting expeditiously on the present."

A foolish man will always reveal his imperfections and unvirtuous deeds if you allow him to talk long enough. He will reveal exactly what kind of man he truly is; his character, or lack of character, will shine brightly through his own thoughtless speech. He will even brag about his unvirtuous, dishonorable deeds as if they are something to be proud of.

The wise man, on the other hand, is careful with his speech and keeps his imperfections to himself, where he continues to work to improve upon them daily in the privacy of his own sanctuary. He refuses to speak without thinking about what he wants to say and why. In this way, he maintains his privacy and does not say things that could have undesirable consequences for him.

Develop the discipline to control your desire to share your secrets or personal information with others. Be content to listen and learn, instead of feeling that you must share simply because those around you are sharing their personal information. What they share is their business; what you share is yours. Make silence your constant travel companion and friend.

284

Be wary of the man who urges an action
in which he himself incurs no risk.
Seneca

As you go through life, you will find that people love to give you unsolicited advice on what you should do or how you should live. They will urge you to put your boss in his place or to invest your money in a certain investment. But what you rarely see them do is follow their own advice. It costs them nothing to urge you to take a risky action, while they sit safely on the sidelines, incurring no risk at all.

Most of the time, unsolicited, free advice in which the other person is urging you to take a risky action, while he incurs no risk, is bad advice. Many people find it entertaining to encourage others to take a risky action when they have no skin in the game. Some colleagues will freely boast about how they would put the boss in his place if they were you, while refusing to take any action themselves. They sit safely by, encouraging you to take an action that will benefit them, while you take all the risks.

Always be wary of anyone who is urging you to take an action which could cost you in some way, while they incur no risk at all. If things go badly, you are the one who will have to deal with the consequences, not them. They will sit by quietly while you get the axe, not saying a word in your defense, even though it was their idea.

Be very careful and selective when it comes to whom you take advice from and whom you trust. Only listen to the advice of wise men of honor and character. They will advise you carefully and consider all the potential risks and consequences of the action you are considering, as they will have your best interest in mind.

Take advice only from people you trust and who have a lot of wisdom and knowledge about the subject at hand. Then, follow up with your own research. Always remember, you are the only one who will have to deal with the consequences of your actions. Unsolicited free advice is usually too expensive!

285

Be like the cliff against which the waves continually break,
but it stands firm and tames the fury of the water around it.
Marcus Aurelius

I have given you everything you need to develop a Stoic mindset and start living the Stoic lifestyle. However, it won't benefit your life unless you put all this wisdom and these principles to work in your life and stand firm on the principles in which you believe.

There will be daily challenges to your lifestyle. People will tempt you to react in a way that is contrary to your Stoic principles by being rude, obnoxious, hateful, underhanded, deceitful, and selfish, but stand firm on your principles anyway. Constantly remind yourself that you have no control over what other people think, say, or do; they decide how they will behave, and you decide how you will respond or if you will respond to their actions.

Marcus Aurelius gives you good advice to use when you find yourself having to deal with someone who is pushing your buttons. Be like the cliff which the waves continually break, but it stands firm and tames the fury of the water around it.

Don't let the behavior or opinions of others get to you! Stand firm on your principles and let others think and say what they will. Their beliefs, words, and behavior can't affect you unless you allow them to. If you stand strong on the Stoic principles in this book, you will find that it will become increasingly harder for anyone to push your buttons and make you react.

You will develop and maintain a calm mind despite the constant waves of negativity, other people's opinions, or rude behavior. Those will all crash into your wall of inner peace like the ocean waves hitting the massive cliff. No matter how many times the waves crash into the cliff, the cliff is not affected; it remains strong, calm, and beautiful. The Stoic mindset gives you the ability to tame the fury of life's difficulties, and to do so with a calm mind and inner strength, while maintaining your inner peace and tranquility. Stand strong on the Stoic principles that you have learned; they will make you mentally strong.

"Whenever we think that someone has spoken frankly about their personal affairs, somehow or other, we are impelled to share our secrets with them too, and think this is being honest…because it seems unfair that we should hear news from our neighbor, and not share with them some news of our own; and secondly, because we imagine that we will not make a forthright impression if we keep our personal affairs confidential.

Additionally, we believe that it is safe to confide in someone who has already entrusted us with private information, on the assumption that they would never betray our secrets lest we betray theirs, which is just how incautious people are entrapped by soldiers. A soldier in civilian dress sits down beside you and begins to criticize the emperor. Then you, encouraged to trust them by the fact that they initiated the conversation, open up on this score too. The next thing you know, you are being hauled off to prison in chains.

"Yes, but it is unfair to receive the confidences of your neighbor and not share anything of your own with him."

Did I invite your confidence, sir? Did you open up to me solely on condition that you would get to hear my secrets? Just because you are so stupid as to suppose that everyone you meet is a friend, why expect me to do likewise? You were right to trust me with your secrets, whereas you cannot well be trusted with mine; should I then be indiscreet?

If you see someone fond of externals, someone who values them over their own moral integrity, you can be sure that he is vulnerable to thousands of people who can frustrate or coerce him. Remember that sharing intimate details calls for people of faithfulness and sound principles; and how easy is it to find people of that description today?"

Epictetus

I hope that the teachings of the Stoics and my commentary on each one have been helpful to you on your journey. If you integrate these teachings into your daily life, it will absolutely change your life for the better. You will find that you will start to see things in a different light; your perception of the world around you will start to change. You will have more control over your emotions and mindset as you begin to adopt the Stoic mindset.

The more you work to perfect the principles of Stoicism, the more you will respond calmly to whatever is happening in your life. You will no longer react to external things that you can't control; instead, you will respond calmly and rationally, with wisdom and courage. Wisdom, justice, courage, and moderation will guide you in your quest for the perfection of your character.

As you work towards the perfection of your character, honor, and integrity, you will find that you have more inner peace and tranquility in your life. You will have more control over your thoughts, bringing them in line with the Stoic virtues that you want to develop. Your emotions will no longer guide your words or your actions; you will be in control of your emotions.

You will gradually take control of every area of your life, staying focused on the things that are within your circle of control, while refusing to allow the things that you can't control to disrupt your inner peace. Once you realize and internalize the truth that you have no control over what anyone else thinks, says, or does, you will let go of the desire to try to control others. Instead, you will begin to accept everything outside of your circle of control as it is, and will do so without it affecting your happiness or inner peace.

When you truly realize that you are in complete control of your own happiness and that nobody can *make* you unhappy, angry, sad, or upset, your overall attitude and mindset will change. You will find that you are living a life full of freedom that is more relaxed, controlled, rational, happy, and peaceful.

It is my hope that *The Stoic Mindset: Ancient Wisdom for Today's World* will be a guide for you to integrate the Stoic teachings into your life, and that you will experience more spiritual, mental, and emotional peace and happiness while you live your life your way.

Bohdi Sanders

The Serenity Prayer

GOD,
grant me the
Serenity
to accept the things
I cannot CHANGE;
Courage
to CHANGE
the things I can;
and
Wisdom
to know the DIFFERENCE.

Do It Anyway

People are often unreasonable, illogical, and self-centered;
Forgive them anyway.

If you are kind, people may accuse you of selfish, ulterior motives;
Be kind anyway.

If you are successful, you will win some false friends and some true enemies;
Succeed anyway.

If you are honest and frank, people may cheat you;
Be honest and frank anyway.

What you spend years building, someone may destroy overnight;
Build anyway.

If you find serenity and happiness, they may be jealous;
Be happy anyway.

The good you do today, people will often forget tomorrow;
Do good anyway.

Give the world the best you have, and it may never be enough;
Give the world the best you've got anyway.

You see, in the final analysis, it is all between you and God;
It was never between you and them anyway.

Mother Teresa

THE 35 GOLDEN PRINCIPLES OF THE STOIC MINDSET
Bohdi Sanders, Ph.D.

1. Always keep an untroubled spirit and maintain your inner peace.
2. Take control of everything that is within your circle of control.
3. Accept the things outside of your circle of control as they are.
4. You don't control what others think, say, or do, and it is not your business.
5. True freedom is living your life your way; be your own savior!
6. Replace all complaining with a spirit of appreciation and gratitude.
7. When you are angry, be silent, remain calm, and think rationally.
8. No one can make you angry or upset without your permission.
9. If it's not right, don't do it; if it's not true, don't say it.
10. Always remind yourself that God lives within you and is omniscient.
11. The more you value external things, the less control you have.
12. Your perspective determines how you feel about situations and events.
13. Be selective when it comes to who you associate with.
14. Trust yourself! Don't be influenced by the opinions of others.
15. Your word is your honor—say what you mean and mean what you say.
16. Strive for understanding and always search for the truth.
17. Do not mistake appearances or assumptions for the truth; look deeper.
18. Find peace in your spiritual beliefs; know what you believe and why.
19. Your happiness comes from within and depends on your thoughts.
20. Be watchful over your thoughts, speech, and actions with others or alone.
21. You have the power to hold no opinion about any topic; refuse to argue.
22. Always ensure your intentions are pure, just, and honorable.
23. Meditate on your death and prepare to meet it with courage and honor.
24. Master Yourself! No man is free who is not master of himself.
25. Be content with, and grateful for, what you have in your life.
26. You always have the choice about how you respond to every situation.
27. Refuse to waste time; strive to spend each day as if it were your last.
28. Be kind, understanding, and tolerant with others and strict with yourself.
29. Always ask yourself, "Is this something that is or is not in my control?"
30. Refuse to worry about anything for any reason; always think rationally.
31. The obstacle on your path is a part of your path; don't let it stop you.
32. Whatever anyone thinks, does, or says, always do what you know is right.
33. Refuse to compare yourself to others; be happy being uniquely you.
34. Life is unpredictable; refuse to postpone living your life your way.
35. Your character determines your destiny; always live with honor.
36. Always remember that what we do now echoes in eternity.

IF

If you can keep your head when all about you
Are losing theirs and blaming it on you;
If you can trust yourself when all men doubt you,
But make allowance for their doubting too;
If you can wait and not be tired by waiting,
Or, being lied about, don't deal in lies,
Or, being hated, don't give way to hating,
And yet don't look too good, nor talk too wise;

If you can dream - and not make dreams your master;
If you can think - and not make thoughts your aim;
If you can meet with triumph and disaster
And treat those two impostors just the same;
If you can bear to hear the truth you've spoken
Twisted by knaves to make a trap for fools,
Or watch the things you gave your life to broken,
And stoop and build 'em up with worn-out tools;

If you can make one heap of all your winnings
And risk it on one turn of pitch-and-toss,
And lose, and start again at your beginnings
And never breathe a word about your loss;
If you can force your heart and nerve and sinew
To serve your turn long after they are gone,
And so hold on when there is nothing in you
Except the Will which says to them: "Hold on!"

If you can talk with crowds and keep your virtue,
Or walk with kings - nor lose the common touch;
If neither foes nor loving friends can hurt you;
If all men count with you, but none too much;
If you can fill the unforgiving minute
With sixty seconds' worth of distance run -
Yours is the Earth and everything that's in it,
And - which is more - you'll be a Man, my son!

Rudyard Kipling

Appendix B: The Stoics

Antipater of Tarsus—Antipater of Tarsus lived around 210 to 129 BCE and was a prominent Stoic philosopher. He became the head of the Stoic school in Athens after Diogenes of Babylon.

Cato the Younger—Cato the Younger lived from 95 to 46 BCE and was a Roman statesman, Stoic philosopher, and a prominent figure in the late Roman Republic. He was known for his incorruptibility, strict moral integrity, and unwavering commitment to the Stoic ideals of virtue and duty. He became a symbol of Stoic resilience and political integrity.

Cleanthes—Cleanthes lived somewhere between 330 and 230 BCE. He was the second head of the Stoic school in Athens, succeeding Zeno of Citium. He developed the Stoic concept of Logos—the divine reason that permeates and governs all things. And he viewed the universe as a single, living, rational organism.

Chrysippus—Chrysippus lived from 280 to 207 BCE in Athens. After studying under Cleanthes, he became the third head of the Stoic school in Athens. He wrote over 700 manuscripts, but almost all of them have been lost. Most of what we know from his writings came from Cicero, Diogenes, and Seneca.

Diogenes of Babylon—Diogenes of Babylon lived around 230 to 150 BCE. He was a prominent Stoic philosopher and played a key role in spreading Stoic philosophy to Rome and the wider Hellenistic world. He succeeded Chrysippus as the head of the Stoic school in Athens and emphasized living in accordance with nature, virtue as the highest good, and rationality as the defining human trait.

Epictetus—Epictetus lived from 50 to 135 CE. He was born a slave, but despite his status, he studied philosophy under the Stoic teacher Musonius Rufus in Rome. He eventually gained his freedom and became one of the most well-known of the Stoic philosophers. Interesting enough, Epictetus wrote nothing down. His teachings were recorded by his student, Arrian, who compiled *The Discourses* (a collection of his lectures) and *The Enchiridion* (a concise guide to Stoic living).

Hecato of Rhodes—Hecato lived from 100 BCE to somewhere around the second century BCE. He was a significant Stoic thinker in the middle Stoic period. Although most of his writings are now lost, later Stoics like Seneca often quoted him, which suggests that his influence was substantial.

Marcus Aurelius - Marcus Aurelius lived from 121 to 180 CE. He was the last of the so-called Five Good Emperors of Rome. Originally, his writings in *Meditations* were not meant for publication; they were basically a philosophical diary. Although he only lived to the age of 59-years-old, his writings in *Meditations* have become one of the most widely read and beloved works of ancient philosophy. He is considered the model of the philosopher-king and is one of the most widely read of the Stoics.

Musonius Rufus - Musonius Rufus lived around 30 to 100 CE and was an influential Stoic philosopher during the Roman Empire. He was often called the "Roman Socrates" because of his practical approach to philosophy. He focused on practical ethics, emphasizing how to live a virtuous life, but he did not actually write books himself; his teachings were preserved by his students.

Posidonius—Posidonius lived from 135 to 51 BCE and was a Greek Stoic philosopher, scientist, historian, geographer, and statesman. He was a key figure in the middle Stoic tradition. Posidonius was known for his integration of science and philosophy, his theory of emotions, and universal sympathy.

Seneca—Seneca lived from 4 BCE to 65 CE in Rome. He was a Stoic philosopher, a Roman statesman, and served as a tutor and advisor to Emperor Nero. He was one of the key figures in Roman Stoicism and focused on practical ethics and how to live a good life. His writings include *Letters to Lucilius*, *Essays*, and *Tragedies*. Seneca's writings influenced thinkers such as Montaigne and Descartes. After being accused of plotting against Nero, Seneca was forced to commit suicide, where he met his fate with his characteristic Stoically calm mind.

Zeno of Citium—Zeno of Citium lived from 334 to 262 BCE and is known for founding Stoicism somewhere around 300 BCE. He taught at the Stoa Poikile, which means painted porch, a colonnade decorated with frescoes. This is where the name Stoicism originated. He wrote several works, but none of them survives today.

INDEX

enemies
enemy, 11, 55, 65, 95, 150, 200, 205, 291
enlightenment, 14, 122, 189
envy, 30, 60, 232
Epictetus, iv, v, vi, xii, 1, 2, 6, 7, 9, 13, 14, 17, 18, 19, 24, 26, 29, 30, 34, 38, 40, 45, 49, 51, 54, 61, 63, 66, 69, 73, 76, 83, 85, 92, 95, 97, 99, 102, 105, 109, 113, 118, 121, 125, 128, 132, 133, 135, 136, 139, 142, 144, 145, 148, 150, 151, 153, 156, 159, 160, 162, 163, 165, 166, 167, 169, 170, 173, 175, 177, 179, 181, 183, 185, 187, 190, 194, 198, 199, 209, 211, 215, 216, 219, 220, 222, 223, 228, 230, 231, 234, 236, 237, 238, 241, 243, 244, 246, 247, 249, 250, 252, 254, 258, 262, 266, 273, 284, 294
ethics, v, 143, 209, 295
evil men, 96
Excellence, 314
expectation
expectations, 82, 98
expectations, 101, 128, 147, 214, 231
external circumstances, 4, 10, 38, 92, 107, 132, 139, 140, 141, 143, 144, 164, 169, 182, 192, 268, 270
external events, iv, 4, 6, 17, 25, 37, 38, 40, 44, 52, 54, 84, 86, 113, 139, 144, 145, 150, 151, 163, 169, 170, 182, 186, 211, 214, 223, 231, 237, 268, 273
external things, 5, 6, 17, 37, 38, 40, 44, 45, 53, 66, 91, 92, 104, 107, 113, 115, 118, 126, 142, 160, 162, 167, 208, 209, 210, 211, 213, 223, 224, 227, 231, 273, 288, 292
fame, xii, 10, 20, 97, 118, 201
family, iv, xiv, 5, 8, 13, 29, 30, 32, 60, 63, 68, 70, 76, 79, 80, 81, 96, 127, 140, 141, 142, 186, 202, 205, 250, 278
fear, xiii, 4, 13, 30, 33, 39, 43, 54, 56, 59, 63, 70, 74, 86, 90, 95, 97, 105, 120, 122, 123, 125, 137, 147, 157, 169, 189, 191, 192, 216, 217, 218, 224, 225, 232, 240, 243, 252, 253, 258, 259, 264, 276, 277
fearful, 17, 76, 90, 105, 253
fears, 38, 59, 63, 70, 74, 90, 105, 123, 139, 209
finances, 29, 47, 97
flattery, 108, 259
fortitude, 32, 98, 105
foundations of Stoicism, 67
Friedrich Nietzsche, 3, 42
friend
friends, x, 1, 30, 160, 161, 185, 187, 188, 205, 228, 283, 284
friends, 8, 13, 39, 55, 61, 63, 79, 160, 205, 233, 234, 235, 236, 243, 278, 291, 293, 312
friendships, 75, 160, 202, 205

WANT MORE?

Now you can get
daily teachings to
help you stay motivated!

Follow Dr. Bohdi Sanders' teachings on *The Stoic Mindset* every single day!
Dr. Sanders shares free teachings daily on many of his sites:

https://thewisdomwarrior.com

https://www.facebook.com/BohdiSandersFB

https://tinyurl.com/TheStoicMindset

https://www.facebook.com/The.Warrior.Lifestyle

https://www.facebook.com/TheGentlemanWarrior

https://www.youtube.com/c/BohdiSanders

https://www.facebook.com/The.Art.of.Inner.Peace

https://www.facebook.com/groups/TheWarriorSage

https://www.facebook.com/groups/warriorphilosophy

https://www.instagram.com/bohdisanders

https://www.linkedin.com/in/bohdisanders1

https://x.com/BohdiSanders

https://www.pinterest.com/BohdiSan

Please take a couple of minutes and review *The Stoic Mindset!*

Reader reviews are very important to authors in today's fast-paced world, and I value your opinion. Reviews are the lifeblood of an author. Posting a quick review on Amazon, Facebook, and other social media really helps independent authors.

If you have enjoyed *The Stoic Mindset: Ancient Wisdom for Today's World*, please consider taking just a couple of minutes and reviewing it on Amazon, on your social media pages, and elsewhere. Also, please tell your friends about *The Stoic Mindset: Ancient Wisdom for Today's World,* and let's help others develop and maintain their inner peace as well! Thank you!

Please review it on *The Stoic Mindset* book page on Amazon at:

https://www.amazon.com/dp/1937884333

Thank You Very Much!

Bohdi Sanders

312

Other Titles by Kaizen Quest

• *Modern Bushido: Living a Life of Excellence* by Bohdi Sanders

• *The Art of Inner Peace* by Bohdi Sanders

• *Musashi's Dokkodo: The Way of the Lone Warrior* by Bohdi Sanders

• *BUSHIDO: The Way of the Warrior* by Bohdi Sanders

• *LEGACY: Through the Eyes of the Warrior* by Sifu Al Dacascos

• *Men of the Code: Living as a Superior Man* by Bohdi Sanders

• *WARRIOR: The Way of Warriorhood* by Bohdi Sanders

• *Defensive Living: The Other Side of Self-Defense* by Bohdi Sanders

• *Wisdom of the Elders: The Ultimate Quote Book* by Bohdi Sanders

• *DEFIANCE: The Dark Side of the Martial Arts* by Bohdi Sanders

• *The Warrior Lifestyle: Making Your Life Extraordinary* by Bohdi Sanders

• *Warrior Wisdom: Wisdom for the Modern Warrior* by Bohdi Sanders

• *Secrets of the Soul: Uncovering Your Hidden Beliefs* by Bohdi Sanders

• *Martial Arts Wisdom: Quotes, Maxims, Stories* by Bohdi Sanders

• *Secrets of the Martial Arts Masters Volume 1* by Bohdi Sanders, (Ed.)

• *Secrets of the Martial Arts Masters Volume 2* by Bohdi Sanders, (Ed.)

• *Strategic Wisdom: Mastering the Game of Life* by Bohdi Sanders

About the Author

Dr. Bohdi Sanders is a multi-award-winning and bestselling author. His work has won several national and international book awards and has thousands of readers throughout the world live a better, more rewarding life full of character, honor, integrity, and inner peace.

Bohdi has two wonderful sons, two amazing grandsons, and one absolutely beautiful granddaughter, who he loves to spend time with as much as possible.

Dr. Sanders' books have received high praise, and he has won several national and international book awards, including:

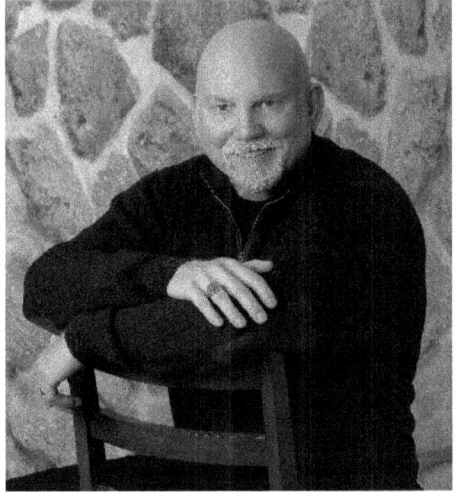

- #1 Bestseller Amazon.com: Musashi's Dokkodo 2023
- NIEA Awards 1st Place Winner: *The Art of Inner Peace* 2022
- BIBA Awards 1st Place Winner: *The Art of Inner Peace* 2022
- Ultimate Warriors Hall of Fame Inductee 2022
- #1 Bestseller Amazon.com: *Secrets of the MA Masters* 2018
- Elite Black Belt Hall of Fame Inductee 2017
- Lifetime Achievement Award, Elite Black Belt Hall of Fame 2017
- #1 Bestseller Amazon.com: Men of the Code 2015
- #1 Bestseller Amazon.com: *Modern Bushido* 2013
- The Indie Excellence Book Awards: 1st Place Winner 2013
- USA Book News Best Books of 2013: 1st Place Winner 2013
- USA Martial Arts Hall of Fame Inductee 2011
- United States Martial Arts Hall of Fame Inductee 2011
- The Indie Excellence Book Awards: 1st Place Winner 2010
- USA Book News Best Books of 2010: 1st Place Winner 2010

Dr. Sanders resides in beautiful Colorado, just outside of Rocky Mountain National Park, and can be reached by email at:
WarriorWisdom@comcast.net

www.ingramcontent.com/pod-product-compliance
Lightning Source LLC
Chambersburg PA
CBHW071406090426
42737CB00011B/1372